Empire of Culture

SUNY series, Studies in the Long Nineteenth Century
—————
Pamela K. Gilbert, editor

Empire of Culture

Neo-Victorian Narratives in the Global Creative Economy

WAIYEE LOH

Cover art: Yōshū (Hashimoto) Chikanobu. Western Clothing from the series *An Array of Auspicious Customs of Eastern Japan* (*Azuma fūzoku, fukuzukushi-Yōfuku*), 1889, and *A Contest of Elegant Ladies among the Cherry Blossoms* (*Kaika kifujin kisoi*), 1887. The Metropolitan Museum of Art. Gifts of Lincoln Kirstein, 1959.

Published by State University of New York Press, Albany

© 2024 State University of New York

All rights reserved

Printed in the United States of America

No part of this book may be used or reproduced in any manner whatsoever without written permission. No part of this book may be stored in a retrieval system or transmitted in any form or by any means including electronic, electrostatic, magnetic tape, mechanical, photocopying, recording, or otherwise without the prior permission in writing of the publisher.

For information, contact State University of New York Press, Albany, NY
www.sunypress.edu

Library of Congress Cataloging-in-Publication Data

Name: Loh, Waiyee 1985– author.
Title: Empire of culture : neo-Victorian narratives in the global creative economy / Waiyee Loh.
Description: Albany : State University of New York Press, [2024]. | Series: SUNY series, studies in the long nineteenth century | Includes bibliographical references and index.
Identifiers: LCCN 2023050591 | ISBN 9781438498270 (hardcover : alk. paper) | ISBN 9781438498294 (ebook)
Subjects: LCSH: English literature—19th century—History and criticism. | Great Britain—Colonies—History. | Civilization—British influences. | British—Foreign countries.
Classification: LCC PR468.C64 L64 2024 | DDC 820.935893—dc23/eng/20240207
LC record available at https://lccn.loc.gov/2023050591

10 9 8 7 6 5 4 3 2 1

Contents

List of Illustrations — vii

Timeline of Major Historical Events — ix

Acknowledgments — xiii

Note on Japanese Names and Translations — xv

Introduction — 1

Part I

Chapter One: Who Owns the Victorians? — 23

Chapter Two: All in the Anglo-American Family — 49

Part II

Chapter Three: Japanese Tourists in Victorian Britain — 75

Chapter Four: Empire of Cool — 97

Part III

Chapter Five: Becoming "Victorian" — 127

Conclusion	163
Notes	175
Works Cited	183
Index	201

Illustrations

Figure I.1	The librarians at Viceroy's House disagree over which books should go to India or to Pakistan.	2
Figure I.2	The iconic statue of Sir Thomas Stamford Raffles at Boat Quay.	18
Figure 2.1	Establishing shot of the church in Lincoln where Christabel LaMotte is buried.	55
Figure 2.2	Establishing shot of Seal Court, Christabel LaMotte's ancestral home.	55
Figure 2.3	Kenilworth Castle brochure.	56
Figure 2.4	The main page of the official website of Leighton Hall, which stood in for Seal Court in *Possession*.	57
Figure 3.1	The front cover of the Harrods catalog.	82
Figure 3.2	"The Definitive Twenty-First Century Edition!! How to Make Perfect Tea."	87
Figure 4.1	Bell gazes upon Lady Ethel with admiration.	100
Figure 4.2	Sebastian "invents" the curry bun or *karee pan*.	103
Figure 5.1	Chris and her friends celebrating Halloween at the St. Regis Hotel, Singapore.	127
Figure 5.2	Chris and Lisa cosplaying Sebastian and Ciel (disguised as a girl) from *Kuroshitsuji*.	129
Figure 5.3	Farah and her friends wearing Lolita fashion.	130

Figure 5.4 Jennifer wearing Lolita fashion.   130

Figure C.1 Hideko looking out towards the sea on the ferry
            to Shimonoseki, Japan.   168

Figure C.2 Hideko in male attire looking out towards the sea
            on the ship to Shanghai, China.   168

Figure C.3 The main entrance to the English half of Kōzuki's
            mansion. The Japanese half lurks around the corner
            on the far right of the screen.   172

Timeline of Major Historical Events

1819
Raffles establishes a British trading port in Singapore.

1839
First Opium War begins.

1842
First Opium War ends.
Britain and China sign the Treaty of Nanking.

1853
Commodore Perry arrives in Japan.

1854
Japan and the US sign the Treaty of Kanagawa.

1858
Japan and the US sign the Harris Treaty.
Japan and Britain sign the Elgin Treaty.

1859
Opening of Yokohama and other treaty ports in Japan.

1868
Meiji Restoration in Japan.

1876
Korea and Japan sign the Treaty of Kanghwa.

1894
First Sino-Japanese War begins.
Britain and Japan revise unequal treaties.

1895
First Sino-Japanese War ends.
Assassination of Korean Queen Min.
China cedes Taiwan to Japan.

1899
End of the treaty port system in Japan.

1904
Russo-Japanese War begins.

1905
Russo-Japanese War ends.
Korea becomes a Protectorate of Japan.

1910
Japanese annexation of Korea.

1914
First World War begins.

1918
First World War ends.

1919
March First independence movement in Korea.

1929
Great Depression.

1931
Manchurian Incident.
Japanese occupation of Manchuria begins.

1932
Formation of Manchukuo.

1937
Marco Polo Bridge Incident.
Second Sino-Japanese War begins.

1939
Second World War begins in Europe.

1941
Japan attacks Pearl Harbor.
Japan invades Southeast Asia.

1942
British forces surrender in Singapore.
Japanese occupation of Singapore and Malaya begins.

1945
Atomic bombings of Hiroshima and Nagasaki.
Surrender of Japan and the end of the Japanese Empire.

Acknowledgments

In Sheridan Le Fanu's 1872 short story "Green Tea," scholar turned green tea addict Mr. Jennings proclaims that "everyone who sets about writing in earnest does his work . . . *on* something—tea, or coffee, or tobacco" (22). This book was happily not written *on* anything, except for the guidance and support that many people have given me in the past ten years that I have been working on this project. Firstly, I would like to thank my PhD advisors Ross Forman and Michael Gardiner, whose mentorship over the years has been invaluable. Without them, I would not be the teacher and researcher that I am today.

This book would also not have been possible without the support of the Department of Japanese Studies at the National University of Singapore, whose generous provision of a visiting fellowship from August to December 2019 allowed me to conduct the research that now forms the basis of chapter five. During my time in Singapore, I also benefitted from the kind assistance of the librarians and archivists at the Raffles Institution Archives and Museum, the Lee Kong Chian Reference Library, and the National Archives of Singapore. I would also like to thank the Singapore Examinations and Assessment Board for providing access to the database of prescribed texts for the *O* and *A* level English literature exams. I am grateful to the Wodehouse Society (US) and the Wodehouse Collection at Vanderbilt University for their generous help in locating the elusive *Plum Lines Supplement* magazine, and to *South Atlantic Quarterly* for taking the time and effort to scan and email articles from back issues of the journal that were not available in digital form. As a first-time author, I have also benefitted immensely from the detailed guidance provided by Rebecca Colesworthy and the editors at SUNY Press.

I would also like to express my gratitude to friends and colleagues from the University of Warwick. Although we now live and work in different places around the world, this book continues to bear traces of the wonderful times we had together. Lastly, I dedicate this book to Chris, who made so many sacrifices so that I could bring this project to completion in the lovely city of Yokohama, Japan.

An earlier version of chapter three was originally published as "Japanese Tourists in Victorian Britain: Japanese Women and the British Heritage Industry" in *Textual Practice*, vol. 34, no. 1, 2020, pp. 87–106. The original article may be viewed on the journal's website: https://www.tandfonline.com. Parts of chapter four originally appeared in "Superflat and the Postmodern Gothic: Images of Western Modernity in *Kuroshitsuji*" in *Mechademia*, vol. 7, 2012, pp. 111–27.

Note on Japanese Names and Translations

Japanese names in this book are written in the conventional Japanese order of family name first, with the exception of contemporary Japanese scholars who publish in English. All English translations of Japanese text from the Harrods catalog, the *Emma Victorian Guide*, *Lady Victorian*, and *Kuroshitsuji* are my own. English translations of Korean and Japanese dialogue in *The Handmaiden* are taken from the English subtitles of the Curzon Artificial Eye DVD (2017 edition).

Introduction

In 2017, to mark the seventieth anniversary of the Partition of India, BBC Films released *Viceroy's House*, a film about the last viceroy of India, Lord Louis Mountbatten, and his well-intentioned but hapless efforts to ensure a peaceful transition from British rule to independence. As the Indian characters struggle to decide whether to pledge allegiance to India or to Pakistan, Lord Mountbatten (played by *Downton Abbey* star Hugh Bonneville) informs the domestic staff at his residence that the Partition Council has decided to apportion eighty percent of the national assets to India and twenty percent to Pakistan. He then announces that "[w]e will be following that same formula in this great house." The film cuts to a montage sequence depicting the staff at Viceroy's House dividing items ranging from silver cutlery to musical instruments into separate portions for India and Pakistan. The sound of an official checking off items on a list carries over several shots: "Soup spoons, fifteen cases for India, three cases for Pakistan. Teaspoons, forty cases for India, ten cases for Pakistan. Butter knives, twenty cases for India, five cases for Pakistan. Tuba, India. French horn, Pakistan. . . ." The ludicrousness of dividing the viceroy's property in this pedantic manner culminates in a scene in the library, where two female librarians are arguing over which books should go to India or to Pakistan. The scene begins with a close-up of two sets of bookshelves, the one on the left labelled "India" and the other on the right labelled "Pakistan." The camera slowly zooms out to show the librarian on the right proclaiming that "*Wuthering Heights* must come to Pakistan," and the librarian on the left replying, "Then *Jane Eyre* stays here and all of the Jane Austen" (figure I.1). The camera zooms out further to reveal the two librarians standing in the center of the frame surrounded by stacks of books, with a male assistant on the right carrying books to and fro. Although the librarian on the left claims that "break[ing]

1

Figure I.1. The librarians at Viceroy's House disagree over which books should go to India or to Pakistan. *Source: Viceroy's House.* Directed by Gurinder Chadha, Pathé, Reliance Entertainment, BBC Films, Ingenious Media, and British Film Institute, 2017.

[up] the encyclopedias . . . would be a crime," she eventually accepts that India will have volumes A-R while Pakistan gets volumes S-Z.

This scene in the library suggests that, like the other objects in Viceroy's House, the canon of English literature is an inheritance that the British colonialists are giving to the newborn nations of India and Pakistan. However, unlike the tableware and the musical instruments, the gift of English literature cannot be neatly divided into portions for India and Pakistan. As the librarians quarrel over the encyclopedias, the camera cuts to Lady Mountbatten and her daughter Pamela entering the library and witnessing this exchange, which prompts Pamela to turn to her mother with the exclamation, "This is absurd!" The shot-reverse shot of the librarians arguing and Lady Mountbatten and Pamela watching them encourages the viewer to share the latter's assessment of the situation. *Viceroy's House* implies that it is indeed "absurd" for India and Pakistan to claim that *Wuthering Heights* or *Jane Eyre* belongs to either country, because the cultural legacy of *Wuthering Heights* and *Jane Eyre* will remain with both countries, regardless of how the librarians divide the books in the collection. English literature, the film implies, is a cultural inheritance that belongs to everyone.

Yet the library scene in *Viceroy's House* opens up possibilities for a completely opposite reading. By encouraging the viewer to identify with Lady Mountbatten and her daughter, the film seems to be telling British viewers in particular that this tussle between India and Pakistan is "absurd," not because *Wuthering Heights* and *Jane Eyre* are part of a common inheritance, but because these classic works of English literature ultimately belong to "us" and not to "them." The opening close-up shot of the library bookshelves brings to mind Thomas Babington Macaulay's infamous assertion in 1835 that "a single shelf of a good European library [is] worth the whole native literature of India and Arabia" ("Minute on Education in India" par. 10). The British colonial administration brought British literary works to India, not to make the canon of English literature "Indian" (or "Pakistani"), but to make the Indians "English in tastes, in opinions, in morals and in intellect," as Macaulay put it (par. 34). Wherever English literature traveled to, Macaulay implied, it would always remain firmly "English." The echoes of Macaulay's anglicization program in the film's library scene suggest that, despite all the failures of the British imperial project in India, the British still have something left at "the remains of the day"—to borrow the title of Kazuo Ishiguro's novel about the end of the British Empire—and this something is the enduring power of English literature.

Empire of Culture: Neo-Victorian Narratives in the Global Creative Economy explores these questions of cultural heritage, ownership, and what remains after the heyday of British imperialism has long passed. How does the globalization of British cultural forms and practices, and especially English literature, in the long nineteenth century shape the global marketization of historic buildings, films and television dramas, women's magazines, fashion, and other forms of "culture" in the late twentieth and early twenty-first centuries? How did this earlier wave of globalization encourage Britain's imperial subjects, then and now, to think that British culture is global in the sense that it constitutes a benchmark of civilizational development for the entire world? Furthermore, how does this myth of British universality affect cultural commodity production and consumption in countries that, unlike India and Pakistan, were not formally colonized in the long nineteenth century? Correspondingly, what happens when this idealization of British culture takes root in former colonies that, also unlike India and Pakistan, have since come to perceive British rule as a benevolent process of modernization?

Whereas *Viceroy's House* is a period film set in 1947, *Empire of Culture* turns to representations of Victorian Britain in an array of contemporary cultural texts and practices, both literary and popular. This book focuses on texts and practices from Britain, as well as from the United States, Japan, and Singapore: three locations where British imperialism took on different forms in the long nineteenth century. By bringing together neo-Victorian cultural materials ranging from A. S. Byatt's novel *Possession* and its Hollywood film adaptation to Japanese Lolita fashion and the *Lady Victorian* manga series, this book explores how Britain's past entanglements with its colonies, spheres of influence, and fellow imperial powers have come to shape the interconnectedness of global cultural commodity production, export, and consumption today. Why do young Japanese and Singaporean women consume British high-culture commodities such as heritage tourist attractions, period dramas, and luxury brands with long histories? Why do the Japanese state and cultural industries focus on marketing manga, anime, cosplay, and other Japanese popular culture products to international audiences under the banner of "Cool Japan"? Examining trans-imperial interactions then and now through the lens of the neo-Victorian allows us to recognize that the imperial past inheres in how post-imperial subjects—both in and outside of Britain—commodify this amorphous thing called "culture." Like all forms of historical fiction, neo-Victorian narratives from Britain, the US, Japan, and Singapore look back on the past from their perspective in the present. In doing so, they remind their readers and viewers that the expansion of British imperialism in the long nineteenth century not only introduced new systems of government and new modes of extraction and enterprise; it also brought people around the world into contact with British "culture"—its forms of textual representation and social practices—against a backdrop of highly unequal power dynamics. In particular, the neo-Victorian narratives discussed in this book reveal that the widespread dissemination of English literature in the long nineteenth century, along with British forms of dress, dining, and etiquette, has encouraged many to think of British high culture as a universal standard of civilizational accomplishment to which everyone should aspire. As highly commercial cultural products of the late twentieth and early twenty-first centuries, the neo-Victorian narratives discussed in this book further reveal that this presumed universality of British culture has significantly shaped the formation of three cultural empires in particular in today's global *creative economy*: one founded on British high culture and heritage, one on the global reach of multinational media corporations based in the US, and the third on Japanese popular culture. International tourists and consumers today gravitate towards British high-culture products that speak to the enduring assumption that Englishness constitutes a global touchstone of cultural excellence. While supporting the growth of the British heritage industry, however, this fantasy of Englishness also brings this new incarnation of British imperialism into competition and collaboration with the other two cultural empires, as they too respond to the legacy of British universalism in the context of a post-Fordist global economy. Since the 1980s, Britain, the US, Japan, and other industrialized nations have turned increasingly towards information, media, services, and other intangible goods as lucrative forms of economic production. Reading historical fiction, watching period dramas, going sight-seeing, and other kinds of leisure might seem like mere entertainment, yet these activities have become central to contemporary economic life and are in fact, as this book argues, profoundly informed by the trans-imperial networks and structures of power engendered by an earlier wave of globalization.

The global economy in the late twentieth and early twenty-first centuries is one that foregrounds the commodification of culture. Robert Hewison coined the term *heritage industry* in 1987 to describe how the Conservative government under Margaret Thatcher was actively marketizing historic monuments and museums in Britain as a means of regenerating local economies hit by the shift from manufacturing to services. Neo-Victorian texts and practices from Britain, the US, Japan, and Singapore reveal that the historical transmission of British culture under the aegis of British imperialism dovetails with these more recent post-Fordist developments, thereby contributing to the rise of the British heritage industry since the 1980s. The British heritage industry draws on the enduring idealization of British culture to attract international tourists, shoppers, readers, and viewers to its high-cultural attractions, brands, and media products. On the one hand, the British heritage industry invites American, Japanese, and Singaporean consumers to partake in its form of high culture, as a shared Anglo-Saxon heritage or as a source of self-improvement and social distinction for non-white subjects. On the other hand, cultural producers and consumers in the US, Japan, and Singapore are actively engaging with this new wave of British cultural globalization. Cultural industries, state bodies, and individual consumers in these three locations work with the British heritage industry for their mutual benefit, while competing with it or claiming to provide an alternative to its high-cultural offerings. *Culture* is a notoriously amorphous and contested term, whose definition ranges from "a general process of intellectual, spiritual, and aesthetic development," to "the works and practices of intellectual and especially artistic activity," and to "a particular way of life, whether of a people, a period, or a group" (Williams, *Keywords* 90). John Storey's *Introductory Guide to Cultural Theory and Popular Culture* broadens this already expansive definition to include any text or practice that produces meaning, even if it is not "intellectual" or "artistic" (2). In the field of cultural policy studies, policymakers and scholars often define *culture* in specific terms to denote the music, film, and television industries; the fine and performing arts; museums and historic monuments; sports; urban planning; and even the Internet.[1] For the purposes of this book, I foreground what we might call *high culture*; namely, textual representations and social practices that claim to be the best that humankind has developed, and which thereby enable their readers, viewers, and participants to *distinguish* themselves as a superior social class, as Pierre Bourdieu has famously argued in *Distinction*.

To put it another way, the British heritage industry presents a particular image of Britain to the world, one that positions Britain as a producer of high culture that is universally admired. As culture increasingly becomes a commodity that is bought and sold internationally, more and more nation-states are engaging in the practice of *nation branding* to compete for overseas markets, not to mention foreign investment, skilled labor, soft power, and other benefits associated with international cultural prestige. As Keith Dinnie has argued in his seminal introduction to the subject, nation branding is the cultivation of a highly selective cultural identity or image, which would enable the nation-state to differentiate itself from others and thereby stand out from the global competition (*Nation Branding* 15, 17–18, 46). This book focuses on British attempts at nation branding, as well as American and Japanese responses to those attempts; but unlike much of the literature on marketing the nation, this book recognizes that nation branding is not always fully conscious and intentional. Nation branding in the global economy often draws upon deeper layers of meanings and associations that are shaped by the nation's past interactions with other nations. Nation branding thus does not occur in a historical vacuum but is mediated through the history of imperialism—including but not limited to British imperialism—in the long nineteenth century. The British heritage industry's promotion of an "old England" full of history and tradition acts in conjunction with an ideology of British universalism that derives from the country's imperialist past. Likewise, the competition and collaboration amongst the British heritage industry, the American media industries, and the Japanese pop culture industries is refracted through American and Japanese engagements not only with the British nation-brand, but also with the imperialist past that has connected Britain with the US and Japan. With their emphasis on Britain in the nineteenth century, neo-Victorian narratives, especially those that are partly or entirely aimed at audiences outside of Britain, play out these abstract processes of historical mediation. This book therefore examines the film and novel *Possession*, which speak mainly to an Anglo-American audience; Japanese neo-Victorian manga and magazines that mostly cater to young Japanese women; as well as Lolita fashion in the former British and Japanese colony of Singapore.

In mediating between past and present, these neo-Victorian texts and practices have the capacity to illuminate the trans-imperial and transhistorical dynamics that inflect the commodification of culture in the global economy today. As texts and practices designed for popular consumption, many of the neo-Victorian cultural materials discussed in this book (re)produce stock images of Victorian Britain, thereby lending themselves to the accusation that heritage films and other neo-Victorian narratives present the past as a "flat, depthless pastiche" that has no relation to historical reality (Higson, qtd. in Jeffers 46). Nevertheless, the Victorian British setting of these narratives raises the question not only of how the present appropriates images of the past for its own purposes, but also of how the past shapes the present, including the ways in which we perceive that past. While the neo-Victorian narratives discussed in this book are certainly guilty of rehashing all the familiar stereotypes of the Victorian, from maids and butlers to tea and top hats, they also provide a lens for contemplating how the historical transmission of British cultural forms and practices has given these stereotypes their particular valence. As Victorian Britain floats free of its geographical and temporal specificity, the stock images that make up Victorian Britain coalesce into a fantasy of British cultural universality and superiority. At the same time, these tropes of the Victorian also provide a foil for new forms of "universal" popular culture, as well as a site for cultural localization and playful performativity. In this way, neo-Victorian narratives comment on the global creative economy in which they themselves are situated, revealing how the cultural industries that produce and circulate these neo-Victorian narratives are in effect positioning themselves in response to the historical globalization of British culture and its accompanying myth of universality. On a related note, other scholars have looked at how specific canonical works of Victorian literature have traveled abroad and been adapted into neo-Victorian fiction.[2] This book, on the other hand, takes a broader perspective to consider how *the assumption that British culture itself is canonical* has traveled outside of Britain and become entrenched in the long nineteenth century and after. This assumption that British culture constitutes a global standard of cultural excellence is not quite reducible to the gains and losses in the canonical status of individual literary works. While specific literary works have come and gone, British culture retains its privileged status as a universal ideal, thus continuing to inhere in the present, not least in global flows of cultural commodity production, distribution, and consumption.

Neo-Victorian texts and practices from Britain, the US, Japan, and Singapore offer an insight into this history of cultural globalization and its legacies in the late twentieth and early twenty-first centuries.

~

The nineteenth century often brings to mind the emergence of the nation-state and the rise of nationalism. However, as Jürgen Osterhammel demonstrates in *The Transformation of the World*, the nineteenth century was also characterized by multiplying and intensifying transnational networks of trade, travel, and colonization, especially between the middle of the century and the First World War (710–11). In recent years, scholars of Victorian studies have increasingly directed their attention to these transnational networks, especially in cases where these networks take the form of intertwined and competing empires.[3] Moving between the nineteenth century and the present, *Empire of Culture* integrates this global turn in Victorian studies with two recent strands of research in neo-Victorian studies: 1) reading neo-Victorian texts as meditations on Britain's transnational interactions in the nineteenth century, and 2) approaching neo-Victorian texts as cultural commodities that are produced and consumed globally. In *Neo-Victorianism and the Memory of Empire*, Elizabeth Ho argues that the Victorian "has become a powerful shorthand for empire in the contemporary global imagination," so much so that "the return to the Victorian in the present offers a highly visible, highly aestheticized code for confronting empire again and anew" (5). Like the neo-Victorian narratives that Ho discusses, the texts and practices under examination in this book use Victorian Britain as a setting to engage with the history of the British Empire, although they do so less self-consciously. Empire in the case of these texts and practices, moreover, refers to a highly informal and indirect process of cultural influence, more than to the ruling of territories or even to the enforcement of free trade via unequal treaties (which in fact came to an end in Japan relatively quickly with Britain agreeing to revise its trade treaty in the 1890s).[4] In focusing on the cultural dimension of empire, this book is indebted to Frantz Fanon's *Black Skin, White Masks* and the tradition of postcolonial scholarship on decolonizing the mind, while contributing to ongoing efforts to globalize both Victorian and neo-Victorian studies. *Empire of Culture* takes as its premise Antonija Primorac and Monika Pietzrak-Franger's call for a "global" neo-Victorian studies (1).[5] It pushes beyond the boundaries of Britain, the formal British

Empire, and the English language to argue that cultural flows from Britain to the US, Japan, and Singapore in the long nineteenth century have a lasting impact on cultural commodity production, export, and consumption in these four locations today.

In foregrounding the production and circulation of cultural goods ranging from novels, films, and manga to luxury brands and heritage tourist attractions, this book adds a new dimension to scholarship on the globalization of Englishness and English literature in the long nineteenth century. Ian Baucom has argued that, while British imperialism sought to disseminate Englishness as a form of control, this paradoxically resulted in Englishness becoming fragmented and susceptible to redefinition in the spaces of the empire (4–6). This production of Englishness in the colonial encounter, as Simon Gikandi asserts, continues to shape identities both in Britain and its former colonies (13). In Gikandi's words, we are still "[l]iving in the shadow of Englishness" (20). For Gikandi, Baucom, and other scholars in the field, Englishness is an amorphous set of idealized images that is open to reinvention and appropriation by diverse political agendas, and which has little or nothing to do with England as an actual place.

While *Empire of Culture* borrows this useful understanding of Englishness, it is less interested in the construction and contestation of "English" identity. It is also not primarily concerned with rejecting abstract ideas of Englishness in favor of a more concrete identity based on England as a physical location and nation (although this is an important project, as Michael Gardiner demonstrates in *The Return of England in English Literature*). Rather, *Empire of Culture* considers how Englishness often evokes the idea that British culture is universal, and how this equation of Englishness with universality gives rise to relations of competition and collaboration between the British, American, and Japanese cultural empires in the late twentieth and early twenty-first centuries. For Gardiner, the adjective *English* in English literature refers not to a particular place or people, but to a function of projecting Englishness across the territorial boundaries of England to Scotland, Wales, Ireland, and beyond. This globalizing impulse, Gardiner argues, is essentially an institutional force or "will to create and manage a *canonicity*—not just a canon or set of texts but an ordering principle based on values which seem to pre-exist and are presented as natural" (3). In other words, English literature as a discipline and a body of works rests on the assumption that there is a timeless and universal tradition that embodies—to misquote Matthew Arnold—"the best which has been thought and said in the world" (190). Disseminating Englishness, in both the long nineteenth century and the contemporary present, often involves disseminating the notion that British culture in general and English literature in particular constitute a canonical tradition. My book thus draws on the important work that has been done by Baucom, Gikandi, Jed Esty, and Gauri Viswanathan on the globalization of Englishness and English literature under British imperialism, while taking this work in the direction of the globalization of cultural commodities and the trans-imperial dynamics that structure this phenomenon today. As Viswanathan argues in *Masks of Conquest*, the dissemination of Englishness, especially via English literature, exerts a unifying force. This book seeks to understand this unifying force not in terms of political domination over the (former) colonies, but in terms of the production, distribution, and consumption of cultural commodities at a time when culture is being instrumentalized as a source of economic revenue in a late capitalist creative economy.

Bourdieu begins *Distinction* with the statement that "[t]here is an economy of cultural goods" (1). Since the 1980s and 1990s, this economy of cultural goods has rapidly become an increasingly attractive source of revenue, especially in post-Fordist economies that are moving away from manufacturing towards a greater emphasis on services. The monolithic "Culture Industry" of Adorno and Horkheimer is now better understood as a variety of cultural industries specializing in film, television, and digital media; publishing; pop music; heritage tourism; advertising; graphic design; and many other fields of cultural commodity production. The success of these industries, especially in the US and Britain, has over the last two and a half decades inspired a celebratory discourse on the creative economy, which in turn promotes the further expansion of the cultural industries. While the Thatcher government in the 1980s was arguably the first to focus attention on the economic value of culture in Britain, the New Labor government headed by Tony Blair in the late 1990s played a major role in conceptualizing this marketization of creativity. The idea was then taken up by John Howkins in *The Creative Economy* (2001) and Richard Florida in *The Rise of the Creative Class* (2002). Howkins, Florida, and the Department of Culture, Media and Sport (DCMS) set up by New Labor in 1997 all have slightly different definitions of what counts as a cultural or creative industry. Nevertheless, the discourse that they and others have collectively produced fundamentally assumes that art or culture (broadly understood) is a particularly profitable area for economic development, and that the state should actively steer the economy in this direction (Brouillette

1). In his 1998 manifesto *Creative Britain*, DCMS Minister Chris Smith championed the government's role in nurturing "the growing importance to the modern economy of Britain of all those activities and industries that spring from the creative impulse" (1). Under Smith's direction, the DCMS set up the Creative Industries Taskforce to establish the scale and potential of the cultural industries in Britain. The taskforce published its findings in the 2001 *Creative Industries Mapping Document* which, together with Howkins's and Florida's highly influential books, inspired governments in Europe, South America, and especially East Asia (including Japan) to look to cultural commodity production and export as a lucrative new industrial sector (O'Connor 49). The neo-Victorian narratives discussed in this book comment on this contemporary context, in which they also participate as globally circulating cultural commodities. In employing the image of Victorian Britain to discuss contemporary concerns, these narratives signal that the turn to cultural commodity production and export in Britain, the US, and Japan is refracted through the earlier globalization of Englishness and English literature in the long nineteenth century.

We might extrapolate from Jed Esty's line of reasoning in *A Shrinking Island* and claim that the Englishness that the British cultural industries have been exporting worldwide since the 1980s is motivated by a post-imperial desire for a uniquely English national identity. If this is the case, we also need to recognize that this export of a distinctive Englishness draws upon the traces of former imperial networks and the earlier dissemination of Englishness as canonical culture, or what Esty calls "the primary universalism of the metropolitan era" (14). The late modernist writers that Esty discusses implicitly inscribe universalism back into the language of English particularism by representing Englishness as paradoxically unique and representative of modern nationalism at the same time (14). *Empire of Culture* demonstrates that this ideology of simultaneous universality and particularity was already present in the globalization of British culture in the long nineteenth century, and that it continues to shape the global creative economy in the late twentieth and early twenty-first centuries. As the library scene in *Viceroy's House* indicates, Englishness presents itself both as a standard of civilizational progress that is shared by all, and as a prized possession that belongs to a specific group of people. The export of Englishness in the global creative economy today intertwines the particular with the universal and vice versa to create a new cultural empire for the British, one that is founded on the transnational circulation of heritage and other high-culture commodities.

∽

Like its nineteenth-century precursor, the British cultural empire in the late twentieth and early twenty-first centuries is only one amongst several. Drawing on Caroline Levine's "From Nation to Network" as well as polycentric models in world systems and world literary theory, *Empire of Culture* approaches the global creative economy as a vast network connecting multiple centers and peripheries. This book interrogates the relations between three major centers of cultural production and one peripheral site of consumption: Britain, the United States, Japan, and Singapore. The picture that emerges from exploring these relations is not quite a totalizing world-literary system that is—in Franco Moretti's pithy formulation—"simultaneously *one*, and *unequal*: with a core, and a periphery (and a semi-periphery) that are bound together in a relationship of growing inequality" (46). Instead, my readings of neo-Victorian texts and practices map a world of multiple cultural empires formed out of networks, which are autonomous at some points and intersect at others. These cultural empires coexist, and often compete and cooperate with one another in commodifying culture. Although this book focuses on Britain, the US, Japan, and Singapore, these four locations exemplify trans-imperial and transhistorical dynamics that can also be seen in other rising cultural production powerhouses in East Asia, such as South Korea and mainland China.

In examining the relations between multiple cultural empires, this book responds to recent scholarship in literary and East Asian studies that posit a polycentric approach to understanding the production and circulation of world literature and East Asian popular culture respectively. Debjani Ganguly, for example, draws on Muhsin al-Musawi's work on the Arabic Republic of Letters to propose a "polysystemic" model of world-literary production (272–73). Similarly, scholars of East Asia including Chua Beng Huat and Joseph Tobin often employ polycentric models in analyzing the "rogue flows" (Iwabuchi, Muecke, and Thomas) of popular culture between Japan, South Korea, China, Taiwan, Hong Kong, Singapore, and other locations in the region. Besides engaging with scholarship on world literature and East Asian popular culture, this book also speaks to the growing interest in trans-imperial relations in Victorian studies, as well as in the field of world history. In her contribution to the 2018 "Keywords" issue of *Victorian Literature and Culture*, Sukanya Banerjee contends that the term *trans-imperial* is less anachronistic and more appropriate than *transnational* in describing cross-border interactions in the nineteenth century (926). Not only does *trans-imperial* recognize that Britain and its empire are mutually constitutive and therefore coeval, it also draws attention to Britain's relations with other imperial powers (Banerjee 926). Likewise, in the coda to *Empire in Question*, Antoinette Burton critiques the tendency in historians to assume that Britain (especially Victorian Britain) represented the very essence of what it means to be global (277). Following Dipesh Chakrabarty, Burton provincializes the British Empire by revealing its intersections with other empires in the world (279). "[R]ematerializing the histories of other contemporary empires," Burton argues, "makes that globality [in British imperial history] look like a co-production rather than a distinctively English/British phenomenon" (289). In a similar vein, Laura Doyle proposes "inter-imperiality" as a productive critical framework that sheds light on the kinds of affiliations and locations in global history that cannot be neatly reduced to a single core and a single periphery (and a single semi-periphery) (161, 163).

Empire of Culture adopts this polycentric, trans-imperial framework proposed by Burton, Doyle, and others to explore relations of competition and collaboration between multiple empires both past and present. These relations cannot be reduced to the conventional binaries of colonizer and colonized, domination and subjugation, and even domination and resistance; binaries which structure much of existing scholarship in both postcolonial and Victorian studies. Not only is global cultural production today organized around several major centers, the historical transmission of British culture that has informed these contemporary relations of cultural production was likewise more than a unilateral process of core-peripheral domination. The US and Japan certainly came under British imperial influence in the second half of the nineteenth century, even though by that time the US had gained its independence, and Japan had not been formally colonized by any Western power. However, the US and Japan were also becoming imperial powers in their own right towards the end of the nineteenth and into the twentieth century. Japan acquired its first overseas possession, Taiwan, after defeating China (once the foremost imperial power in the region) in the 1894–1895 Sino-Japanese War. Japan and China had gone to war over Japanese intervention in Korea, which had begun twenty years earlier with the signing of the Kanghwa Treaty in 1876. This treaty enabled Japan to gain a foothold in the Korean peninsula, and to impose the same system of unequal trade treaties on Korea that the Western powers were subjecting Japan to at the same time. After defeating Russia in 1905, Japan went on to exercise even greater control over Korea, eventually annexing the entire country in 1910. Back in 1898, as a result of the Spanish-American War, the US took over the Spanish colony of the Philippines and used its newfound base in the Asia-Pacific to expand its influence, while ceding its interests in Korea to the Japanese, who were in turn supported by the British against Russia in the Anglo-Japanese Alliance of 1902–1921. As the colonial history of Korea demonstrates, the imperial project in the long nineteenth century was a tangled web of declining and aspiring imperial powers, inter-imperial rivalry, and shifting allegiances, whose complexity calls on us to look beyond the usual dichotomies.

Exploring trans-imperial dynamics also requires us to rethink the periodizing categories that we use to frame our study. The *long nineteenth century* conventionally refers to the period beginning with the French Revolution in 1789 and ending with the onset of the First World War in 1914. For the purposes of this book, however, the long nineteenth century begins with the British colonization of Singapore in 1819 and then the opening of Japan to Western trade in 1853. It incorporates the rise of Japanese imperialism in East and Southeast Asia from the 1870s to the 1940s and ends with the conclusion of the Asia-Pacific War in 1945. This book's version of the long nineteenth century also extends from the emergence of *heritage* as a concept and practice in 1830s Britain, to Anglo-American competition over heritage ownership at the turn of the century, and lastly to P. G. Wodehouse's attempts to preserve a rapidly disappearing Victorian heritage for Anglo-American audiences in the early to mid-twentieth century.

As these time frames suggest, this book foregrounds the longue durée, rather than seeking out clear-cut continuities and disjunctures between the Victorian past and the contemporary present. Although many of the neo-Victorian narratives discussed in this book are set during Queen Victoria's reign (1837–1901), the historical contexts that they engage with far exceed the regnal temporal markers that we habitually use to designate the Victorian period. In emphasizing the longue durée, this book departs from critical works on neo-Victorianism that approach the relation between the Victorian period and the neo-Victorian context of production in terms of sameness and difference. In their 2014 edited collection *Neo-Victorian Literature and Culture*, Nadine Boehm-Schnitker and Susanne Gruss define the "neo-Victorian project" as "an ongoing cultural and academic venture to analyze the manifold overlaps and intersections, the continuities and the breaches between 'us' and 'them'" (1). Similarly, in Diane Sadoff and John Kucich's *Victorian Afterlife*, neo-Victorianism (or "post-Victorianism" as they prefer to call it) locates postmodernism's origins in the nineteenth century, while acknowledging the gap between the nineteenth-century past and postmodernism's discursive production of its origins in that past (x–xvi, xxv–xxvii). Likewise, Cora Kaplan states that the term *Victoriana* encompasses a wide range of representations and reproductions that take the Victorian as their referent, "whether as the origin of late twentieth-century modernity, its antithesis, or both at once" (3). These approaches to neo-Victorian fiction and culture are based on an analogous mode of thinking, in which the scholar of neo-Victorian studies seeks to determine how closely the contemporary present parallels, or does not parallel, the Victorian past. Although the "palimpsestuous" nature of the neo-Victorian undoubtedly encourages the reader/viewer to read the past and the present analogously (Jones, "'Palimpsestuous' Attachments" 38), this book suggests that we also need to examine how material trans-imperial connections in the long nineteenth century have shaped our present through multiple twists and turns in the longue durée.[6] The global history of British imperialism does not parallel the global creative economy today; the nineteenth century is not in some way already postmodern. Rather, the past shapes the present through a series of historical developments extending outwards from the nineteenth into the mid-twentieth century. In particular, the escalation of Japanese imperialism from 1895 to 1945 intersected with its British counterpart to give rise to many of the developments that this book discusses. In foregrounding the longue durée, *Empire of Culture* diverges from the conventional Eurocentric conceptualization of the long nineteenth century. By shifting the timeframe from 1789–1914 to 1819–1945, this book reformulates the long nineteenth century so that it becomes appropriate to the study of Britain's engagements with the US and especially East Asia, as seen through the eyes of neo-Victorian fiction and culture.

Empire of Culture is divided into three sections that discuss Britain's relations with the US, Japan, and Singapore respectively. The enduring belief in British culture's canonicity and universality fuels the British heritage industry today, while bringing it into competition and collaboration with the American and Japanese cultural empires. The first two sections of the book examine these trans-imperial interactions. The struggle in *Possession* over who gets to "possess" a collection of fictional Victorian letters underscores Anglo-American rivalry *and* cooperation in commodifying British heritage since the 1980s. *Possession* traces this ambivalent transatlantic relationship back to the sense of a shared Anglo-American literary inheritance in the late nineteenth and early twentieth centuries, and to the anxieties that surrounded this shared heritage at a time of rising American wealth, tourism, and the purchase of British heritage properties. Japanese neo-Victorian manga and magazines likewise point to how the positive reception of British culture and English literature in the second half of the nineteenth century has left its mark on Japan's current position in global cultural commodity flows. Certainly, contemporary Japanese popular culture, as well as Japanese intellectual life in the long nineteenth century, has often engaged with countries and historical contexts besides Victorian Britain, from Mori Ōgai's (1862–1922) reading of German literature to Ikeda Riyoko's *shōjo* manga *The Rose of Versailles* (1972–1973). Japan in the nineteenth century did not become the colony of any particular power, and it was open to a multitude of Western influences. Nonetheless, the second section of the book zooms in from this broader context to focus on Japanese attitudes towards Britain both in the past and in the present. In the neo-Victorian manga series *Kuroshitsuji*, the aristocratic protagonist's penchant for English tea and delicate pastries signifies "English" taste and refinement, but during a curry-cooking competition, the protagonist's "Japanese" butler creates a fusion concoction that wins Queen Victoria over with its hybrid and populist sensibility. As this example shows, Japan's historical encounter with Britain and the West has since generated a long-standing desire for an aristocratic form of Englishness that is associated with an idealized image of Victorian Britain. On the one hand, the Japanese manga and magazine publishing industry supports the British heritage industry by channeling young Japanese women's desire for this Englishness into tourism and other consumption practices. On the other hand, the products of this publishing industry, such as *Kuroshitsuji*, draw upon Japanese imperialist discourse from the 1930s and early 1940s to position Japanese manga, anime, and other cultural commodities as a proudly popular alternative to the British high-cultural empire.

The last section of the book turns from texts to the people who consume them, focusing on young Singaporean women who dress up in Victorian-inspired outfits as followers of Lolita fashion from Japan. The historical circulation of British culture as canonical culture informs not only cultural commodity production but also consumption in places such as Singapore, where it forms the backdrop against which consumers negotiate between the diverse offerings of the three cultural empires. Why do these women invest time, effort, and money in performing this highly mediated form of Victorian-ness, and how does Singapore's doubly colonial past as a former British and Japanese colony shape the fashion practices of these women? As they negotiate between the British and Anglo-American cultural industries on the one hand and "Cool Japan" on the other, these young Singaporean women reaffirm the intertwined legacies of English literature and race, while finding a space within these legacies to perform an imaginary Victorian self that can accommodate their non-white bodies. *Empire of Culture* concludes with a coda that extends its central arguments to (South) Korea: a rising center of global cultural production and yet another node in the trans-imperial networks that this book is concerned with. Park Chan-wook's film *The Handmaiden* reveals what is at stake when we use the category of the neo-Victorian to talk about historical fiction and practices such as historical costuming. In adapting Sarah Waters's novel *Fingersmith*—itself a mashup of Victorian novels—*The Handmaiden* transposes the Victorian Britain of *Fingersmith* to Korea under Japanese rule in the 1930s. In doing so, the film calls the very meaningfulness of the term *neo-Victorian* into question. *The Handmaiden* demonstrates that, by shifting our gaze from the narrowly national neo-Victorian to trans-imperial connections in the long nineteenth century, we can expand the number and kinds of networks available for study, networks that exceed not only the grasp of formal British imperialism, but also the compulsion to tie our understanding of global circuits of power back to Britain.

Yet, at least for the time being, Britain retains its hold over the postcolonial imagination. As a scholar of English literature born and raised in Singapore, I have long been fascinated by how those of us whose countries and lives have been touched by the British Empire look back on the colonial encounter. What are the ways in which the past (including our perception of it) informs not only how we conduct politics or do business, but also how we enjoy our leisure: where do we travel to when we are on holiday, what do we do when we get there, where do we shop, what do we eat, what books do we read (if we still read books), and what films and TV shows do we watch? How does our seemingly inconsequential involvement in the global marketization of culture reaffirm and/or disrupt former imperial structures of power in a post-imperial present? This book is an attempt to answer these questions. In 2019, the Singaporean state and numerous community organizations rolled out a series of events to commemorate the two-hundred-year anniversary of Sir Thomas Stamford Raffles's landing on the island and the subsequent colonization of Singapore under British rule. The 2019 bicentennial marked a turning point in the country's history in a double sense. Firstly, it marked the British arrival on the island in 1819. Secondly, in stretching the time frame to five hundred years before Raffles, the so-called bicentennial also marked the first time that Singaporeans were encouraged on an unprecedented scale to rethink the conventional privileging of Raffles's "founding" of Singapore as the starting point for Singapore's transformation from a fishing village to a modern metropolis. The bicentennial program, which the organizers insisted was to be a commemoration rather than a celebration, sought to decenter the place of Raffles in Singapore history by drawing attention to the contributions that other individuals and groups have made pre- and post-1819, as well as to the unsavory aspects of British colonial rule.[7] To signal their revisionist intentions, the Singapore Bicentennial Office (SBO) commissioned local artist Teng Kai Wei to paint over the white polymarble statue of Raffles located at the historic landing site in Boat Quay, so that the statue looked as if it were disappearing into the skyscraper behind it (figure I.2).

Figure I.2. The iconic statue of Sir Thomas Stamford Raffles at Boat Quay, 21 June 2023. *Source:* Photo taken by the author.

However, as one commentator predicted in January 2019, the long-standing notion that Raffles and British colonialism paved the way for Singapore's present-day success has proven difficult to dislodge (Tee). While both organizers and commentators claimed that the bicentennial did not set out to either glorify or vilify the country's colonial past, the discourse surrounding the commemoration repeatedly invoked the *precious gifts* and *assets* that the British have left Singapore, whether intended or otherwise: the rule of law, parliamentary democracy, systems of civil administration, and the English language, to name a few (Fernandez, "Instead of Angst"). "The British left us with a rich and positive legacy," veteran diplomat Tommy Koh declared at the book launch of *200 Years of Singapore and the United Kingdom*, which was published in conjunction with the bicentennial (qtd. in Tay).[8] If there is a specter haunting the Singapore bicentennial, it is certainly not the present/absent Raffles statue with its surrounding crowds of smiling tourists and locals busily snapping photos. Like a Victorian Gothic novel, the bicentennial implies that it is the *pre-nineteenth-century past* that returns from the dead to terrify Singaporeans with the possibility that the island might once again be violently "besieged and brought down," as it had been in the centuries before Raffles arrived (Hussain). In his opinion piece for the *Straits Times*, Zakir Hussain argues that this pre-1819 history reminds Singaporeans not to take their present-day security and prosperity for granted. In comparison to the bloodshed and turmoil of the precolonial past, British rule in the nineteenth century seems like a positively genteel affair. Until the Japanese invasion in 1942, the British did not have to enforce or defend their interests in Singapore through war and conquest. In recent years, neo-Victorian studies has employed the trope of the specter to conceptualize how neo-Victorian fiction engages with the various traumas of the nineteenth century that return to haunt us in the present, including the trauma of imperialism.[9] This book charts a different terrain, one in which neo-Victorian texts and practices register the British colonial inheritance, including the gift of English literature, not as traumatic, but as enlightening, civilizing, and even pleasurable.

Part I

Chapter One

Who Owns the Victorians?

A. S. Byatt's neo-Victorian novel *Possession: A Romance* (1990) opens with an epigraph from Nathaniel Hawthorne's *The House of the Seven Gables*, as a means of explaining why the novel is subtitled "A Romance" rather than "A Novel." The quoted passage from Hawthorne states that the romance form, unlike the more realistic novel, gives the author greater artistic license to "connect a bygone time with the very present that is flitting away from us." With half of its narrative set in nineteenth-century Britain and the other half in the 1980s, *Possession* makes connections between the Victorian past and the novel's contemporary present. In particular, the novel speaks to the increasing commodification of the past, including the Victorian past, as a result of the Thatcher government's neoliberal economic policies. The 1980s in Britain was a moment in which heritage became especially prominent in government policy and public life. The Thatcher government founded English Heritage in 1983, followed by numerous local councils, which set up their own agencies to preserve historic monuments and to convert these monuments into revenue-generating heritage tourist attractions. During this time, the number of museums and country houses open to the public also grew exponentially with state support (Hewison 73, 99–102). Today, the concept of heritage has become ubiquitous, taking the form of diverse things and practices ranging from stately homes and Battle of Bosworth reenactments to Laura Ashley prints and heritage soap dishes.

Possession is, amongst many things, a story about rival British and American scholars laying claim to heritage. The trope of possession in Byatt's novel has multiple meanings, not least of which is the possession or ownership of objects inherited from the past. The plot of the novel revolves around two groups of academics, one British-led and the other American-led, competing to acquire a collection of secret love letters exchanged between two fictitious Victorian poets, Randolph Henry Ash and Christabel LaMotte. This transatlantic rivalry takes on an added dimension when we consider how interchanging flows of British literary works and American tourism in the long nineteenth century have helped to construct English literature as a canon that appears to belong to both Britain and the US. This sense of a shared heritage has since given rise to Britons and Americans staking competing claims on British high culture, first from the mid-nineteenth to the early twentieth century, and more recently in their bid to monetize what we might call *cultural property* in global cultural commodity flows. In making the ownership of cultural property a central focus of narrative interest, *Possession* parodies the burgeoning of what Robert Hewison calls the "heritage industry" and its notion of patrimony in 1980s Britain. The novel pokes fun at Anglo-American competition over cultural property in this relentless commodification of British heritage, not only since the rise of free-market economics in the 1980s, but also in the Victorian past that the novel depicts. Reading *Possession* alongside heritage conservation legislation, periodical press journalism, and Henry James's 1875 short story "A Passionate Pilgrim" demonstrates that the concept of national cultural property gained credence in Britain over the course of the nineteenth and early twentieth century with the emergence of the heritage industry. Far from being a purely national phenomenon, the growing British attachment to national patrimony was, and still is, motivated by an extra-national force: the perceived threat of the American millionaire and his/her claim to British heritage via the shared reading of English literature.

Before I begin, I want to clarify how I use the term *heritage* in the following discussion. Heritage, as Peter Howard explains, is related to the concept of inheritance (6). Heritage refers to "circumstances or benefits passed down from previous generations" (Howard 6), and it includes not only human-made artefacts and buildings, but also natural environments and intangible ideas and practices. As the word *benefits* implies, most people think of heritage as something that has not only been handed down from the past, but which is also valuable and hence worth preserving for future generations (Howard 1).[1] As a kind of inheritance, heritage—like real estate and family heirlooms—is tied up with questions of property ownership.

The British Heritage Industry, 1980s–Present

Admittedly, *Possession* is primarily concerned with the textual interpretation of the past, and its possibilities and limitations for human historical knowledge. The novel has certainly been treated as such in much of the existing scholarship. Many critics including Suzanne Keen and Louisa Hadley treat *Possession* as an example of what Linda Hutcheon calls "postmodern historiographic metafiction." John Su and Kate Mitchell briefly mention the British heritage industry, especially Hewison's analysis of it, but they are ultimately concerned with *Possession*'s stance on whether collecting historical artefacts can lead to a truthful understanding of the past. This chapter takes a different approach. Rather than examine *Possession*'s epistemological meditations on history and textuality, this chapter considers how *Possession* engages with heritage as a material object and as an industry within a wider tourism economy. At several points in the narrative, *Possession* mentions, almost in passing, several real and fictional historic buildings that have become tourist destinations within the world of the novel. In this way, the contemporary half of *Possession* situates its tale of transatlantic rivalry within the wider context of heritage commodification that was happening in the 1980s. In their attempt to retrace Randolph Henry Ash's 1859 expedition to North Yorkshire, Roland and Maud (the two protagonists of the novel and leaders of the faction that claims British ownership of the poets' letters) book a room at the fictitious Hoff Lunn Spout Hotel, which, the omniscient third-person narrator explains, had in fact existed when Ash made his journey in 1859. Maud "had found" this historic hotel "in the Good Food Guide, where it was recommended for 'Uncompromising fresh fish dishes, and unremitting if unsmiling good service'" (242). At the end of the novel, all of the characters put up for the night at the Rowan Tree Inn, another historic building that has been turned into a tourist destination "mentioned in all the Good Food guides" (487). Ash's house in Bloomsbury has also been transformed into the "Ash Museum," which sits alongside numerous real museums, galleries, and libraries whose names appear sporadically throughout the novel. Roland, Maud, and their colleagues visit, or own souvenirs previously purchased at, various well-known cultural institutions including the British Museum, the Tate, and the National Portrait Gallery. Many of these institutions are nonprofit organizations that serve the public good, but they function as major tourist attractions as well. While these institutions receive some funding from the state, they also derive part of their income from selling tourists the experience of coming into close proximity with the historical artefacts that they preserve. The repeated references in the novel to historic buildings that have been converted into hotels and F&B establishments, and to museums that have been turned into tourist attractions, signal that the growing marketization of heritage in 1980s Britain shapes the characters' struggles to "possess" the Victorian poets' letters.

In *Possession*, the desire to possess historical artefacts is closely intertwined with the desire to make money out of them. Ownership of the letters, the novel implies, is desirable at least partly because it would enable the owner to exploit their economic potential. The lawyer Euan MacIntyre advises Maud that, when she acquires legal ownership of all the letters, she should sell the documents "to the British Library or somewhere acceptable" (437). Although Maud resists the idea of selling the letters and wants to donate them to the university she works in instead, her decision is still motivated by financial considerations. Archiving the letters in the Women's Resource Centre, Maud argues, would attract funding to the centre. On the other side of the ownership debate, Maud's distant relations, the Baileys of Seal Court, seek to establish their ownership of the letters so that they might sell them for a princely sum to Professor Cropper, a wealthy American academic who has made a career out of buying and transporting historical artefacts from Britain to his museum in New Mexico.

This desire to possess the letters in order to monetize them echoes the Thatcher government's championing of heritage and its rhetoric of enterprise. As part of the government's campaign in the 1980s to replace the declining manufacturing industries with a new service-oriented economy, local economic development agencies turned increasingly to cultural objects, including heritage, to generate revenue for flagging local economies (O'Connor 31).[2] In particular, local authorities began to link state investment in historic sites and museums to an economic agenda of developing visitor attractions (O'Connor 32). Local government officials actively encouraged tourists to visit historic sites and museums because, even though tourism does not by itself provide all the funds necessary to preserve heritage, it greatly benefits the service industries that are centered around tourist attractions such as transport, accommodation, catering, and retail (Hewison 99). On the national level, the Historic Buildings and Monuments Commission for England (more commonly known as English Heritage) received government funding to market the properties that it was responsible for as tourist destinations (Hewison 101). Using the language of enterprise, the first *Annual Report and Accounts* of English Heritage outlined the various "market research" and "marketing and sales promotion activities" to which the organization "attaches high priority" (*Report and Accounts 1983–1985* 12). The report states that English Heritage has, in its first eighteen months, "improv[ed] contacts with the travel industry" by advertising in tour operators' trade publications and attending trade shows (12). It also explains that the organization has "improv[ed]" ticket and sales offices "to supply all the monuments open to the public with an increased basic selection of popular, inexpensive items, as well as more specialized souvenirs," thereby increasing on-site sales (12–13). From its inception, English Heritage has evidently sought to carry out its duty "to promote the public's enjoyment of . . . ancient monuments and historic buildings" (*Report and Accounts 1983–1985* 4) by turning heritage sites into tourist attractions complete with souvenir gift shops.

In transforming heritage into a tourism business, the Thatcher government also sought to reduce the heritage sector's reliance on government funding in the long run. This privatization of heritage was part of the Thatcher government's wider neoliberal reforms aimed at downsizing the civil service, reducing state regulation, and, as Thatcher described it in her memoirs, "channel[ing] more of the nation's talent into wealth-creating private business" (Thatcher 45–46). It is important to note here that most public heritage organizations in the 1980s, including English Heritage, continued to receive government funds, and were not sold off to private corporations in the same way as British Rail passenger services (in the 1990s) and more recently, the Royal Mail. However, the Thatcher government expected these public heritage organizations to behave as if they were private corporations, and to expand their commercial income so as to rely less on government funds in the future. Successive governments after Thatcher appear to have achieved her administration's goals. In the early years of English Heritage, the great majority of the organization's income came from government grants-in-aid, and only a small proportion came from commercial activities. In the period 1983–1985, English Heritage received £49,910,000 as grant-in-aid, and only £2,460,000 from admissions and sales, and £151,000 from membership subscriptions, sponsorship, and donations. By 1989, English Heritage's commercial income had risen to £6,621,000, but the grant-in-aid it received had also risen to £66,249,000.[3] The proportions have since been reversed. In April 2015, English Heritage ceded its statutory functions to a separate government agency called Historic England, and became a private registered charity, whose aim is to become completely self-financing by 2023.

The website of English Heritage in 2015 showed that over the past decade, the organization had doubled its commercial income and now depended on government grants for only fourteen percent of its total income.

Possession parodies this heritage-enterprise culture that has now become the status quo in the early twenty-first century. Roland and Maud are joined in their battle by Roland's Scottish supervisor, Professor Blackadder. As far as Blackadder is concerned, the Victorian poets' letters are part of Britain's national heritage and hence should not be sold to the American Professor Cropper, who intends to display the letters in his museum in the US. As a British nationalist, Blackadder firmly "believe[s] British writings should stay in Britain and be studied by the British" (10). He therefore lobbies the Ministry for the Arts to buy the letters for the British Library, while also making a clumsy appeal on television to the public. Feeling completely out of place in front of the camera, Blackadder finds himself rambling on about Ash's love poetry before concluding that the letters "have got to stay in our country" because "they're part of our national story" (404). Despite speaking the language of national heritage, Blackadder fails to convince the Ministry for the Arts because he neglects to speak to the Thatcher government's free-market approach to heritage. *Possession* thus presents the reader with a hilarious contradiction: how can heritage function as a free-market enterprise if the free market will not preserve heritage in the first place? Blackadder is turned away by a government bureaucrat, who informs him that the Minister for the Arts "d[oes] not believe that it [the discovery of the letters] warrant[s] interfering with Market Forces," and that "[i]f the retention of these old letters in this country is truly in the national interest, . . . then Market Forces will ensure that the papers are kept in this country without any artificial aid from the state" (398). By poking fun at Blackadder's dilemma, the novel responds with humor to Hewison's lament in 1987 that museums, once seen in the Victorian period as "sources of education and improvement [that] were therefore free," are now "treated as financial institutions that must pay their way, and therefore charge admission fees" (Hewison 129). Barbara Kirshenblatt-Gimblett makes a similar observation in her 1998 book *Destination Culture*, in which she argues that museums are increasingly expected to pay for themselves as attractions in a wider tourism economy (7).

Possession is still relevant today because the heritage industry that it parodies in 1990 continues to thrive in the twenty-first century. In his 2008 book *The Heritage Obsession*, Ben Cowell states that more than two-thirds of the population in England visit heritage sites each year, and membership of the National Trust and English Heritage combined has reached more than four million (127). The size of the heritage economy is not easy to quantify (Cowell 133), but statistics from the *Heritage Counts* reports produced annually by English Heritage (up till 2015) suggest that the heritage industry is indeed big business for the British economy.[4] The 2010 report states that heritage is the key driver of inbound tourism to the UK, with more than fifty percent of inbound tourists visiting castles, churches, monuments, and historic houses (10). According to the report, the estimated tourist spending in the UK that can be attributed to heritage (including spending on food, accommodation, and admission fees to attractions) generates £7.4 billion of gross domestic product (GDP) per annum and supports employment for 195,000 people (10). The 2014 report states that in 2011, heritage tourism in the UK created 393,000 jobs (742,000 jobs including natural heritage tourism) and £14 billion of economic output (£26.4 billion including natural heritage tourism) (11). Tourist spending in general is in fact the largest market in the British economy. According to the *United Kingdom Tourism Report* for quarter four in 2014, international tourism receipts for "travel items" (i.e., goods and services purchased by, or on behalf of, the traveler to use or give away) totaled £21.8 billion in 2011 (21–22). As a major component of the wider tourism economy, heritage tourism apparently "contributes more to the UK economy than the advertising, car manufacturing or film industries" (*Heritage Counts 2014* 11), although period film and television production is an important part of the heritage industry, as chapter two will show.

Because the heritage industry in Britain is so lucrative, government agencies, public institutions, and private organizations are often keen to claim ownership of heritage, not only in order to protect it, but also to exploit its economic potential. This desire to claim ownership for economic reasons is clearly manifested, for example, in the British Museum's attempts to keep the Elgin Marbles in the face of Greek demands that the friezes be returned. Most supporters of the British Museum contend that the museum is protecting the Elgin Marbles on behalf of humanity, and they say nothing about how the artefacts draw large numbers of tourists to Britain. However, when New Labor came to power in 1997 with a campaign to cultivate Britain's cultural industries, then-Heritage Secretary Chris Smith (who would later become DCMS Minister and the author of *Creative Britain*) made clear the new government's stance on the Elgin Marbles, and his remarks are telling. Smith asserted that the Labor government would keep the friezes in Britain because "[m]illions of visitors come every year to see them, not just from Britain but from everywhere around the world, and it would make no sense at all to split up the British Museum's collection in that way" (qtd. in H. Smith 7).

On the other hand, *Possession* challenges the idea, implicit in the Elgin Marbles debate, that heritage can be said to belong to a particular person, group of people, or nation-state. The novel symbolically undermines attempts to claim ownership of heritage and to appropriate the economic capital that comes with ownership. It thereby challenges the very notion of cultural property that underpins the British heritage industry in the global creative economy today. By the end of the novel, *Possession* implies that the letters ultimately do not belong to anyone. The narrative encourages the reader to identify with Roland and Maud's efforts to prevent Professor Cropper from gaining possession of the letters, but in the end it does not support either side's claim to ownership. After the main characters have discovered and read the final letter written by the female poet Christabel LaMotte, the novel gives no further information about the characters' struggles to lay claim to the documents. By not telling the reader which character eventually gets to own the letters, the novel leaves the reader to be satisfied with possessing the knowledge gained from reading the letters, rather than possessing the letters vicariously through the characters. Maud's American colleague Leonora encapsulates this sentiment when she declares: "I can swear in advance I'm not out to snatch any manuscript, covertly or openly. I only want to *read* the damn things." (478) The letters belong to no one and to everyone, as they are shared in the form of knowledge amongst all the characters who read the letters, and with the readers of the novel as well. In privileging the shared possession of knowledge over the exclusive possession of property, *Possession* refutes the idea that an individual or group, and especially a nation-state, can truly possess the remains of the past as its own property. The novel thereby strikes at the heart of the British heritage industry's understanding of heritage as a kind of property, whether owned individually or collectively. This notion of cultural property (especially that of the nation) had actually emerged much earlier in the long nineteenth century, finding its first popular expression in Britain in the expanding public enthusiasm for historic monuments and artefacts, and in the accompanying fear that wealthy American buyers would compete with the British for ownership of these objects. Reading *Possession* in relation to an earlier body of literary and historical sources—including Henry James's travel writing and debates about heritage conservation legislation—helps us connect the British heritage industry in the present with the development of cultural property as a concept in the nineteenth and early twentieth centuries. This notion of cultural property, these texts reveal, gained credence in Britain over the course of the long nineteenth century partly in reaction to the threat of wealthy Americans purchasing heritage buildings and artefacts that the British felt were rightfully theirs.

The Concept of Cultural Property, from Walter Scott to Lord Curzon

Despite ironizing the heritage industry, *Possession* suggests that there might still be something worthwhile in the heritage mode of relating to the past. For all its skepticism about heritage, the novel celebrates how the materiality of Ash's and LaMotte's letters helps Roland and Maud to put aside their intellectualizing tendencies and allow themselves to be "possessed" by the sensual love that emanates from the letters. Likewise, there is one instance in the nineteenth-century half of the novel that reveals a corporeal mode of engaging with the past that anticipates Roland's and Maud's (and our) fascination with the materiality of historic objects and places in the late twentieth and early twenty-first centuries. During his 1859 expedition to North Yorkshire, Ash writes a letter to his wife Ellen describing how he visited historic sites in Whitby. In this letter, Ash departs from his usual concerns with interpreting and representing the past through language and writing to dwell at length on knowing the past through the materiality of ancient sites and artefacts. He invokes the idea that the past inheres in the present in the form of these archaeological remains:

> The past lies all around, from the moorland graves and supposed Killing Pits of the Ancient Britons to the Roman occupation and the early days of Christian evangelism under St. Hilda. . . . Certain details may bring these long-vanished folk suddenly to life in the imagination. Such are the finding hereabouts of a heart-shaped ear-ring of jet in contact with the jaw-bone of a skeleton; and a number of large jet beads cut in angles, found with a similar inmate of a barrow, who had been deposited in the houe with the knees drawn upward to the chin. (255)

For the first time, Ash's imagination of the past is sparked off not by the words of writers from preceding generations, but by objects left behind by people who had lived in the area centuries ago. The skeletal remains and pieces of jet jewelry buried in the ancient tombs seem to speak directly to him of the past lives of these inhabitants. In invoking the concept of heritage, Ash also speaks of the need to preserve it. In the letter, he laments how "the stones of the Roman road [have] go[ne] to the construction of the dry stone walls, to the loss of archaeology and the preservation of our sheep," and how "the huge boulder on Sleights Moor" was broken up for mending the very road that he had used for traveling (255–56). Although Ash remains committed to engaging with the past through his poetry, this anomalous trip to Whitby offers a glimpse into the widespread phenomenon of sightseers visiting historic monuments in Britain in the long nineteenth century. Some of these sightseers were American tourists, as we shall see in this chapter's third section on Henry James, conservation legislation, and the "American Peril." In other words, the concept of cultural property, and especially *national* cultural property, first gained credence in Britain in the context of the historical emergence of what is now known as the British heritage industry.

Reading *Possession* vis-à-vis this earlier history helps us to approach the relationship between property and the (neo-) Victorian novel from a different angle. The concept of property in nineteenth-century Britain encompassed not only the kinds of property owned by individuals, but also national cultural property or patrimony, which is owned collectively by the nation-state and not (or not only) by an individual. Historic monuments and artefacts are not quite the same as the commodities displayed in shop windows that Andrew Miller discusses in *Novels behind Glass*. Neither are they quite like the household goods gracing domestic spaces that are the central objects of study in Jeff Nunokawa's *The Afterlife of Property* and Deborah Cohen's *Household Gods*. They are not even particularly "portable," as Wemmick puts it in *Great Expectations*. Unlike forms of property that are clearly tied to individual ownership, national patrimony often raises conflicts between the legal definition of property that prioritizes the individual owner's rights, and an ethical conception of property that emphasizes communal ownership and state guardianship.[5]

Despite these differences, national cultural property in nineteenth-century Britain was subject to the same forces of commodification that impacted other forms of property. As Ash's trip to Whitby in *Possession* suggests, historic monuments and artefacts became tourist attractions over the course of the nineteenth century. In this sense, historic monuments and artefacts were part of the same culture of display that Miller describes in

Novels behind Glass. They were also subject to the same tensions between fungibility and fetishism that John Plotz sees as characteristic of "portable property" in the Victorian period. While historic places and objects were often fetishized as irreplaceable embodiments of the nation's history, culture, and identity, they were also fundamentally exchangeable with other attractions that competed for the tourist's attention, such as seaside resorts, fairgrounds, and country houses with no special historical associations. Last but not least, historic monuments and antiques in the nineteenth century were often privately owned. As such, they were fraught with the potential to be "lost" to other owners, just like the household goods that Nunokawa discusses in *The Afterlife of Property*. With the spread of the commodity form into the domestic space of the home, one's possessions, Nunokawa contends, were no longer safe from being bought and sold on the market. This domestic insecurity, Nunokawa argues, generated anxieties about "the inevitable loss of property in the nineteenth-century imagination" (7). Likewise, from the middle of the nineteenth century onwards, the British public and the state became increasingly worried that American investors and collectors were buying up and taking away properties that they felt belonged to the nation and which therefore should have been protected, like the domestic home, from market forces. These anxieties about the vulnerability of British national heritage in an international free market helped to define the concept of national cultural property as it emerged in Britain during the nineteenth century and into the twentieth.

The concept of national patrimony took on a recognizable form in Britain in the early decades of the twentieth century, but it had actually begun to take shape about a century earlier. In 1913, the British government passed the Ancient Monuments Consolidation and Amendment Act. In creating this piece of legislation, the British government effectively acknowledged for the first time that the state was responsible for collecting and preserving the physical remains of the nation's history (Thurley 82–83). In the parliamentary debates leading up to the 1913 act, Lord Curzon argued that historic buildings such as Tattershall Castle in Lincolnshire "are part of the heritage of the nation, because every citizen feels an interest in them although he may not own them; and they are part of the history of the nation, because they are documents just as valuable in reading the records of the past as is any manuscript or parchment deed to which you can refer" ("Lords Sitting of 30 April 1912" 871–72). Curzon's speech indicates that, by the second decade of the twentieth century, a clearly defined notion of national cultural property—owned by the people and protected by the state—had taken root in the British public imagination. Curzon's speech also marks a paradigm shift in how the nation-state approaches its history. British citizens, Curzon argues, should now learn about their past through a physical encounter with historic sites, rather than contenting themselves with the knowledge gained from reading old documents such as manuscripts and parchment deeds. These developments in the 1910s were not entirely new. Before I discuss how the threat of the American buyer contributed to the conceptualization of national cultural property in Britain, I would like to briefly outline how the notion of national cultural property developed in tandem with the origins of the British heritage industry, from Walter Scott's historical novels in the 1810s to the passing of the Ancient Monuments Act in 1913.

Scott's historical fiction was largely responsible for establishing the connection between history and place that has become so familiar in the British heritage industry today. In *Men from the Ministry: How Britain Saved Its Heritage*, Simon Thurley attributes the first expression of popular enthusiasm for history in Britain to Scott's historical novels in the 1810s and 1820s (7–8). Scott's novels, Thurley argues, made the past seem tangible and real in an unprecedented way (7–8), thereby paving the way for the development (in Thurley's account) of state intervention in preserving historic monuments for the public good. Scott's realism consists of embodying an intangible past—what Ash in *Possession* calls "the bloodless cries of the vanished" (104)—in the form of tangible historic sites and objects. *Kenilworth* (1821), for example, situates the history of Robert Dudley's courtship of Queen Elizabeth I and his subsequent downfall in the stone walls and towers of Kenilworth Castle. Through lavish descriptions of Kenilworth Castle and other historic buildings, Scott's historical novels promote the idea that history manifests itself in physical buildings and artefacts, which can then be "possessed" by the nation-state as embodiments of its history. The popularity of Scott's historical fiction across Britain, together with increasing tourism to historic monuments in the early nineteenth century, gradually encouraged the public to perceive these monuments as national cultural property. Scott's novels and his earlier poetry, Nicola Watson argues, actively solicit tourism (12, 156–57). The narrator in *Kenilworth* invites the reader to visit Kenilworth Castle in order to compare his detailed descriptions of the castle during the reign of Queen Elizabeth I with the actual castle, which in Scott's time was already in ruins: "We cannot but add, that of this lordly palace, where princes feasted and heroes fought, now in the bloody earnest of storm and siege, and now in the games of chivalry, where beauty dealt the prize which valor won, all is now desolate. The bed of the lake is but a rushy swamp; and the massive ruins of the Castle only serve to show what their splendor once was . . ." (429). Earlier in the novel, the narrator similarly encourages the reader to seek out an ancient mansion called Cumnor Place in Oxford, "of which the ruins may be still extant" (35). As Scott's popularity grew, the historic sites featured in his works became sightseeing attractions, of which Kenilworth Castle was one of the foremost (Thurley 7–8). With the expansion of the railway and the growth of middle-class tourism, the idea of national patrimony began to gain momentum in the 1830s and 1840s, as Thurley, Peter Mandler, Adrian Tinniswood, and other historians have documented in their accounts of heritage sightseeing in the nineteenth century. William Harrison Ainsworth, for instance, expressed this growing sense of national ownership in the preface to his historical novel *The Tower of London* (1840), in which he called for more areas of the tower to be opened to the public. These historic features of the tower, Ainsworth proclaimed, "are the property of the nation, and should be opened to national inspection" (iv).

As public demands for widening access to historic sites rose over the course of the nineteenth century, the British state became increasingly involved in preserving and managing these sites. This increase in state intervention fed back into the growing sense that these sites were indeed "the property of the nation," as Ainsworth had put it. In 1869, Austen Henry Layard, who was first commissioner of the Office of Works and Public Buildings at the time, set out to protect historic sites "of great national as well as archaeological value" by asking the Society of Antiquaries to compile a list of sites that the state should protect ("Commons Sitting of 2 April 1869" 28). This list was in effect the precursor of the National Heritage List maintained by English Heritage in the 1980s and now by Historic England. In 1882, parliament passed George Shaw Lefevre's Ancient Monuments Protection Act, which was then extended in 1900. The 1882 and 1900 bills primarily sought to persuade private owners of historic monuments that were on the list of protected sites to pass these monuments over to the Office of Works, which would look after them on behalf of the nation (Thurley 41). By the end of the nineteenth century, the concept of national patrimony—including the assumption that the nation's claims to property were as valid, if not more, than the individual owner's rights—had become entrenched in the public imagination. In the early 1890s, Octavia Hill, Hardwicke Rawnsley, and Robert Hunter proposed to set up a corporation capable of holding land so that "landowners and others may be enabled to dedicate to the nation places of historic interest or natural beauty" (qtd. in Waterson 37). The National Trust was thus founded in 1895, and in 1907 parliament granted the trust the unprecedented power to hold land in perpetuity, thereby protecting the nation's cultural property from being sold, mortgaged, or compulsorily acquired by other parties except by an act of parliament (Thurley 64).

The period stretching from Scott in the 1810s to the Ancient Monuments Act in 1913 was thus an important period in the development of the concept of national cultural property in Britain. Strictly speaking, the term *cultural property* was used in English in a legal context for the first time only in 1954 at the Hague Convention for the Protection of Cultural Property in the Event of Armed Conflict (Bailkin 5).[6] Although the Hague Convention defined the term on the principle that heritage ultimately belongs to humanity in general, legal scholars have since used the term *cultural property* to designate objects and practices that supposedly express the collective identity of a particular social group, and to which the group consequently has an inalienable right (Barkan 21–22). Although it is therefore technically anachronistic to speak of national cultural property in Britain before the mid-twentieth century, the popular perception in the long nineteenth century that historic sites embody the history of the nation and hence belong collectively to the people anticipates the current understanding of cultural property. This nineteenth-century conception of national patrimony also prefigures the British heritage industry in the late twentieth and early twenty-first centuries in terms of state intervention and the commodification of historic sites in the context of a wider tourism economy. To borrow Jordanna Bailkin's expression, the nineteenth century constitutes "a prehistory of cultural property" in Britain (7).[7]

Besides being the forerunner of the British heritage industry today, the popular passion for historic monuments and artefacts in Britain from the early nineteenth to the early twentieth century also anticipates the educational dimension of heritage tourism today. Self-education through tourism and other forms of pleasurable consumption is a recurring theme in the following chapters. Heritage tourism is an important part of what we now call *cultural tourism*, a kind of tourism that, unlike the typical sand, sun, and sea holiday, seeks to educate the tourist while entertaining him/her (McKercher and du Cros 1–10). Whereas the concept of *culture* in cultural property performs inclusiveness in foregrounding collective ownership, the pedagogical impulse in cultural tourism derives from an elitist Arnoldian conception of culture as "the best which has been thought and said" (Arnold 190). This elitist conception of culture, Raymond Williams contends in

Culture and Society, gives rise to the predominant but mistaken view that culture is that which should be taught to the unruly masses in order to elevate them (297–312). Like the concept of national cultural property, this desire to educate the masses has its roots in the origins of heritage tourism in the long nineteenth century. The heritage and museum movements in Britain in the second half of the nineteenth and early twentieth centuries envisioned historic sites and museums as places where tourists could engage in learning and self-improvement. Moreover, as history became more widely taught in schools in the 1890s and 1900s, educators became increasingly invested in teaching national history through historic monuments (Thurley 76–77). Charles Trevelyan, parliamentary secretary to the board of education, spoke out in support of the 1913 Ancient Monuments Act, proclaiming that "the idea has really got into our system of education that the nation ought to learn about its past through what is left of its monuments" (qtd. in Thurley 76).

While proponents of heritage often spoke of learning about the nation's past, proponents of museums promoted a different kind of learning premised on an even more overtly elitist understanding of culture. Advocates of public museums envisioned tourists visiting museum collections not so much to learn about national history as to cultivate their tastes in art and design by viewing humanity's *best* creations on display. In the eighteenth century, upper-class tourists visited each other's country houses to find out about the newest trends in art, architecture, and furnishing (Mandler 7–9). While middle-class country-house visitors in the nineteenth century moved away from this practice to focus on the houses' historical associations instead, the museum movement appears to have incorporated this earlier desire to combine tourism with an education in good taste.[8] Museums proliferated in Britain with the passing of the 1845 Museums Act and the 1850 Free Libraries and Museums Act. Those who argued in favor of the widespread establishment of public museums claimed that these museums would help reform the "uncivilized" masses through education and self-improvement, especially via an aesthetic experience (Woodson-Boulton 117–18, 124–25). John Ruskin's museum at Walkley, Sheffield, for instance, aimed "to teach aesthetics, ethics, even politics . . . through the study and enjoyment of beautiful objects" (Barringer 137). Henry Cole, founding director of the South Kensington Museum (now known as the Victoria and Albert Museum), similarly called for museums to elevate the aesthetic tastes of workers, factory owners, and consumers so as to improve the design of British manufactures, although he was less interested than Ruskin in art's impact on social relations

(Burton, *Vision and Accident* 29). For Cole, the museum as an institution was not meant to be a repository for historical artefacts as such, but a way of improving the tastes of the people (Burton, *Vision and Accident* 30). In contrast to Ruskin and William Morris who believed that art should be part of everyday life, the South Kensington Museum under Cole's direction consciously promoted an aristocratic form of taste that prioritized aesthetic beauty over functionality. Cole steered the museum away from everyday objects towards rare, expensive, and luxurious artefacts (Burton, *Vision and Accident* 79), so as to "place objects of the highest art within reach of the poorest person" (Cole, qtd. in Burton, *Vision and Accident* 80). Cole's association of heritage tourism with acquiring aristocratic cultural capital would later become a prominent theme in the British heritage industry in the late twentieth and early twenty-first centuries, as later chapters will show.

The American Peril

Over the course of the nineteenth and early twentieth centuries, museums in Britain, and the British Museum in particular, amassed large collections of artefacts from around the world, many of which came from places under British colonial rule and imperial influence. Many of these artefacts, such as the Elgin Marbles, have since been classified as British national property, resulting in the paradox that the British Museum "displays everything but British artefacts," as Elazar Barkan puts it (29). The British Museum is a frequent advocate of the "universal museum," where "the cultural productions of the whole world are assembled under one roof with public access, allowing all cultures to be represented and placed in meaningful relationships with each other" while being "held in trust for humankind" (Skrydstrup 523–24). The universal museum, in other words, is at odds with the notion of cultural property. It does not recognize that objects taken from places around the world constitute the cultural property of particular nations and communities rather than humanity in general, and that these objects should therefore be repatriated to their rightful owners. In *Possession*, however, it is the American scholar Professor Cropper who employs the concept of the universal museum to stake his claim on the Victorian poets' letters, and it is the British-led team of academics who have to defend their cultural property from this foreign threat. Echoing the British Museum's own rhetoric, Cropper claims that he will "preserve [the letters] [in his museum] in Harmony City and make them accessible to all scholars of all nations" (321). The letters "would join their fellows in perfect conditions—air pressure, humidity, light—our conditions of keeping and viewing are the best in the world," Cropper boasts (321). This reversal of fortunes in *Possession* points to the anxieties induced by the alienability of Britain's own national patrimony, anxieties which too had their precedent in the long nineteenth century.

Anxieties about wealthy Americans buying and taking away British heritage monuments and artefacts went hand-in-hand with the growth of heritage tourism in Britain in the long nineteenth century. These anxieties played a significant role in consolidating the concept of national cultural property in the country, especially from the mid-nineteenth to the early twentieth century. In other words, the British state and public placed increasing importance on national patrimony partly in response to competing American claims on what actually amounted to a shared heritage; a common cultural inheritance that had been engendered by preceding flows of British literary works to the US and American tourists coming to Britain to view heritage attractions. The rivalry between the British and American factions in *Possession* suggests that this earlier Anglo-American competition for cultural property ownership continues to characterize the marketization of heritage in Britain in the 1980s and beyond. As Barkan and Bush observe in their introduction to *Claiming the Stones/Naming the Bones*, a social group or nation's inability to fully possess cultural forms and practices as its own paradoxically fuels the desire to possess these things, so as to establish a firmer sense of collective identity (15). This is perhaps why, Barkan and Bush suggest, people only make claims on cultural property after it is lost (15). Such attitudes towards British heritage and the attendant American threat seem to have first appeared in Britain on a wide scale in 1847, with the auction of Shakespeare's birthplace in Stratford-upon-Avon. As Julia Thomas has shown in her account of the history of the bard's birthplace, the 1847 auction stirred up fears that Americans might purchase the birthplace and transport it wholesale to the US (39). These fears in turn fed into the growing public insistence that the birthplace and other historic relics constituted Britain's national heritage (Thomas 10). The fundraising campaign that urged the British public to buy Shakespeare's birthplace "for the nation" portrayed the potential American bidder as a threatening Other, "a particular type of speculator with no ethical values or, indeed, taste" (Thomas 52). This unscrupulous and uncouth American investor, the campaign insinuated, would transform Shakespeare's birthplace into a vulgar tourist attraction in America, itself "the birthplace of the showman and the speculator" (Thomas 52–57).

These anxieties came to the fore again in 1911 and 1912, when news broke out that an American syndicate was removing the medieval fireplaces in Tattershall Castle, Lincolnshire, for sale in the US, soon to be followed by the castle itself. Once again, the perceived American threat spurred the British public to strengthen its claims to what it saw as its national cultural property. The Tattershall scandal, together with the 1847 auction of Shakespeare's birthplace, gave rise to the myth of the "American Peril," which claimed that well-heeled Americans were buying up British heritage properties in droves and transporting them to the US to be, in the words of one British commentator, "[p]erked up in some Yankee domain" (Carey 449). British press journalism and parliamentary debates in 1911 and 1912 embodied this myth in the figure of the American millionaire. As in the earlier case of Shakespeare's birthplace, the discourse surrounding Tattershall traded in stereotypes of vulgar American investors and/or collectors who do not know how to genuinely appreciate historic monuments, and who consequently purchase these monuments simply to make a profit or to show off their newfound wealth. In particular, the British periodical press attacked the alleged American buyer of Tattershall for failing to understand that historic monuments are truly valuable only when situated in their original context. The *Times* editorial on 13 September 1911, for example, described the American syndicate that had removed the Tattershall fireplaces as "barbarian invaders who pillaged the treasures of their enemies" ("Fireplaces at Tattershall" 5). The editorial also proclaimed that the unknown American purchaser of the fireplaces "must be one of those strange people who are ready to ruin the glories of the past so that they may possess them, and who prove, therefore, that they have no understanding of what they are so eager to possess" ("Fireplaces at Tattershall" 5). In an opinion piece for *The Academy*, A. E. Carey contrasted the bad taste of the American millionaire who had allegedly planned to transplant Tattershall Castle in the US with the genuine knowledge of "the real beauty and ripeness of the old country" that one can gain from touring the English countryside judiciously:

> Our American cousins are some of them intent on the cult of the bizarre. It is rather pitiful to see what very little good the vast wealth of their millionaires is to them. A millionaire cannot eat two dinners a day; sometimes he dare not eat one. But his effort often is to start some futile demonstration of human ostentation. To spend thousands of pounds on a dinner to be eaten up in a balloon or down a coalmine is an exhibition of

poverty-stricken lack of ideas which makes the judicious grieve. A few years ago an American friend asked the present writer to lay out for him an English route by which he might see the real beauty and ripeness of the old country. We knew our man, and gave him an itinerary which by loitering along he could realize the mingled splendor and simplicity of large tracts of rural England—the noble sweep of our Down country, the homely attractions of villages almost unchanged in tone since the days of the Armada; the magnificence of our storied buildings. Our American went home with a wealth of reminiscence which he will not lose for the rest of his days. (449–50)

In contrast, the alleged American buyer of Tattershall Castle, Carey implies, would be spiritually much the poorer for having uprooted the historic building from its original location. Spurred on by the Tattershall debacle, in December 1911 Sir Schomberg McDonnell, secretary of the board of works, made an impassioned plea at the Society of Antiquaries to protect historic monuments from what he called "[t]he peril from America" (17). McDonnell's speech took the stereotype of the vulgar American millionaire and amplified it into a full-blown threat:

> One is very apt to think that because one mentions a building in a [conservation] report or schedule that therefore that building is safe. I believe the exact contrary to be the case, because in these days of millionaires and unscrupulous dealers everything of antiquity which is mentioned or carefully pointed out stands in the very greatest danger. The peril from America is, I think, immense. It was only the other day that we heard a rumor, happily unfounded, that some rich American had bought a beautiful castle in the Midlands, and was about to transport it stone by stone to the United States. (17)

Although McDonnell was referring to the unexpected dangers posed by heritage conservation lists, his reasoning also applies to the lists of historic monuments often found in tourist itineraries. Tourism, seen from this perspective, had become an opportunity for American millionaires to draw up shopping lists of British heritage properties that they would like to acquire.

Henry James's writing combines these two strands in the British perception of Americans, bringing together anxieties about American millionaires buying British heritage properties and prejudices against American tourists in Britain and other parts of Europe. These attitudes towards American tourists, investors, and collectors—at once anxious and contemptuous—helped to sharpen the notion of national cultural property in Britain from the mid-nineteenth to the early twentieth century. In James's fiction and travel narratives, the stereotype of the vulgar American investor and/or collector merges with that of the vulgar American tourist. From the mid-nineteenth century onwards, as it became easier for Americans to travel to Europe, British travel writing increasingly used the pejorative term *tourist* to denote not only the uncultured middle and working classes of British society, but also American visitors (Buzard 217). James participated in this anti-tourist discourse, criticizing his fellow American travelers for their ignorance and vulgarity (Buzard 217–28). In James's 1879 novel *The American*, the American protagonist Christopher Newman attempts to become "cultured" by buying large quantities of expensive artworks as he travels across Europe. "The world, to his sense," the narrator explains, "was a great bazaar, where one might stroll about and purchase handsome things" (103). In the opening chapter, Newman "stroll[s] through the Louvre" (33), unsure of how to understand "Raphael and Titian and Rubens" (34), until Noémie Nioche cheats him into buying her clumsily executed copy of Murillo's *The Immaculate Conception* at an exorbitant price. It is perhaps fortunate that the original painting in the Louvre was not for sale, although Newman's taste in art is so poor that he prefers the inferior copy to the original. James's disdain for American tourists in Britain and Europe reflects wider contemporary perceptions of the laughable yet threatening American tourist, investor, and collector, all rolled into one. These perceptions of American visitors paradoxically strengthened the sense of national ownership in Britain, by confronting the British with the unnerving possibility of losing their heritage treasures to an outsider, and a vulgar one at that. When the Tattershall scandal broke in 1911 and 1912, British commentators repeatedly asserted that the castle and its famous fireplaces belonged to the nation. The *Times*, for instance, reprinted a telegram on 22 September 1911 from a certain Colonel Sir Henry Knollys, who expressed "extreme indignation" on behalf of the county of Lincolnshire ("Tattershall" 6). "To hew [Tattershall Castle] into pieces for transport to some American city," Knollys lamented, "must needs wring the heart of any Englishman" ("Tattershall" 6). Knollys ends his telegram with calls for the public to protect the castle for its "national value" and to raise funds to effect "the rescue of the nation" ("Tattershall" 6). Likewise, parliamentary debates in the wake of the Tattershall case frequently invoked the prospect of losing historic monuments to American millionaires, which in turn helped to consolidate the British sense of ownership over its national patrimony. Parliamentary debates from 1912 onwards discussed the new threat of exportation in calling for enhanced state protection of historic monuments in Britain. On 30 April 1912, Lord Eversley pointed out that:

> When thirty years ago [he] was responsible for dealing with this subject and carried the first Ancient Monuments Act, practically the only danger which then existed to ancient monuments was the possibility of their neglect by the owners, a neglect due mainly to ignorance on the part of the owners of the value of them. But of late years a new danger has grown up, and that is the demand on the part of American millionaires to purchase these monuments and ship them across the Atlantic. ("Lords Sitting of 30 April 1912" 884)

The case of Tattershall Castle eventually prompted parliament to pass the Ancient Monuments Consolidation and Amendment Act in 1913, which extended the 1882 and 1900 Ancient Monuments Protection acts to prohibit the demolition of protected historic monuments, including for the purpose of exportation.

While the British state and public were trying to protect historic monuments in Britain from American buyers, American travel writers in the nineteenth century often asserted that Americans had a right to possess these monuments (at least metaphorically) because these monuments were as much part of America's heritage as they were British or English. These American writers staked their claims on the grounds of their deep-rooted familiarity with Britain's landscape, history, and ways of life, which they had acquired not only through their Anglo-Saxon lineage, but more importantly, through their reading of British literary works. Paul Westover argues that the travel narratives of Washington Irving, Nathaniel Hawthorne, Frederick Douglass, and many others indicate that nineteenth-century American tourists felt an affinity with Britain because of their exposure to British popular periodicals and famous works of British literature (185). While the discipline of English literature only began to be institutionalized in British and American universities towards the end of the nineteenth century, Westover observes that American exposure to British literary works from the early nineteenth century onwards encouraged American tourists of the period to see British literature as an Anglo-American canon of "English" literature, which belonged to them as much as to the British. They therefore traveled to Britain to view places associated with this canon as part of their shared cultural inheritance (Westover 184–85).[9]

While James criticized American tourists for their lack of taste, he simultaneously celebrated his fellow Americans appropriating British heritage, including the canon of English literature, even if it meant throwing one's money around like Christopher Newman in *The American* (Buzard 223–26). James's 1875 short story "A Passionate Pilgrim" clearly demonstrates how the flow of literary works from Britain to its former colonies in the US helped to elevate English literature and the historic sites associated with it into high-cultural forms that Americans desired to lay claim to, especially with the rise of American tourism to Britain in the latter half of the nineteenth century. Unlike the American travel writers Westover discusses, James treated the idea of taking possession of the "old country" not only figuratively, but also literally. Like *Possession*, "A Passionate Pilgrim" is a story about claiming ownership of objects that have been handed down from the past. The short story gives expression to the Anglo-American competition over heritage objects that had been growing since the 1847 auction of Shakespeare's birthplace, and which would later culminate in the Tattershall scandal and the 1913 Ancient Monuments Act, and again in Byatt's novel. In "A Passionate Pilgrim," New Yorker Clement Searle comes to England to claim (partial) ownership of an English country house. While the short story ironizes Clement for his rose-tinted view of England, it also suggests that Clement might have a right to claim a stake in Lockley Park. Firstly, Clement is related to the Searle family in England by blood. More importantly, however, Clement and his friend the narrator (another American tourist from Saragossa, Illinois) feel an intense sense of familiarity with places like Lockley Park because of their familiarity with British literary works. In the eyes of Clement and the narrator, the heritage fantasy of "old England" (117, 121) is colored by their reading of authors including Samuel Johnson (7), Tennyson (46), and Jane Austen (44). The coffee room in the Red Lion Inn looks familiar to the narrator because he has seen its type before "in books, in visions, in dreams, in Dickens, in Smollett, and Boswell" (8). On the journey to Worcester with Clement, the narrator "fe[els] like one of Smollett's pedestrian heroes, faring tavenward for a night of adventures" (44). Upon entering the town, he remarks that this is "where surely Miss Austen's heroines, in chariots and curricles, must often come a shopping for swan's-down boas and high lace mittens" (44). When Clement and the narrator arrive at Lockley Park, Clement speaks admiringly of the old country house as a repository of exciting tales from the past, much to the bemusement and scorn of the current owners. "You ought to have a book full of legends and traditions. You ought to have loves and murders and mysteries by the roomful. I count upon it," Clement tells his distant relations (60). For Clement and the narrator, England is "Story-book Land," a phantasmatic merging of reality and fiction that continues to characterize tourist experiences in Britain, as chapter five will show.

By reading British literary works, Clement and the narrator participate in the shared ethno-cultural heritage of English literature, which takes the form of a familial bond between the British and the Americans. This familial bond forms the basis for Clement's claim to the "family home" of Lockley Park, over and beyond Clement's blood ties with the Searles in England. To the American characters, England is "foreign" (26), with all the trappings of romance and picturesqueness, yet familiar and homely. The American characters repeatedly associate what they see on their travels in England with their memories of home and childhood in America, thereby implying that England is their home too. The narrator, for example, "had seen the coffee-room of the Red-Lion" in the books he had read "years ago, at home—at Saragossa, Illinois" (8). Wandering around the English countryside, Clement and the narrator "c[o]me to the common browsing-patch, the 'village green' of the tales of [their] youth" (43): "We greeted these things as children greet the loved pictures in a story-book, lost and mourned and found again. It was marvelous how well we knew them." (43) Although in this instance the narrator is alluding to the inborn knowledge of England that comes with belonging to the Anglo-Saxon race, it is very likely that Clement and the narrator did first encounter these impressions of England in "the tales of [their] youth"; namely, in the storybooks they read when they were children. To the narrator, this homely sense of familiarity makes England different from other tourist destinations for American travelers. "The latent preparedness of the American mind for even the most delectable features of English life," the narrator observes, "makes an American's enjoyment of England an emotion more fatal and sacred than his enjoyment, say, of Italy or Spain" (8). As longtime readers of English literature, Clement and the narrator have come to think of England in general, and Lockley Park in particular, as their home in a shared Anglo-American heritage.

In his travel writings, James likewise claims England as his home on the basis of his familiarity with the so-called English literary tradition. In his travels in Warwickshire, James sees the past coming to life in the form of scenes from Shakespeare and George Eliot. At "[a] quaintish village" near Kenilworth Castle, he "looked about for the village stocks; [he] was ready to take the modern vagrants for Shakespearean clowns; and [he] was on the point of going into one of the ale-houses to ask Mrs. Quickly for a cup of sack" ("In Warwickshire" 166). At an old rectory near Stratford, he sees a group of young women playing lawn tennis, who remind him of *Daniel Deronda*: "I remembered George Eliot's Gwendolen, and waited to see her step out of the muslin group . . ." ("In Warwickshire" 167) The town of Ludlow, with its old-fashioned air of "insular propriety," prompts James to imagine that "Miss Burney's and Miss Austen's heroines might perfectly well have had their first love-affair there; a journey to Ludlow would certainly have been a great event to Fanny Price or Emma Woodhouse, or even to those more romantically connected young ladies Evelina and Cecilia" ("Abbeys and Castles" 195). James's love for England, like that of Clement Searle, is mediated through his knowledge of England's literary and historical associations. Furthermore, like Clement, James desires to possess England's historic buildings and landscapes not only by gazing upon them as a tourist, but also by becoming their legal owner. In "Abbeys and Castles" (1877), James wryly notes that having property in a beautiful part of England is not necessary to appreciate the charm of the landscape, but "[a]t the same time having a little property would without doubt have made the attachment stronger" (185). James fantasizes about purchasing the country house that belongs to his friend's neighbor: "People who wander about the world without money in their pockets indulge in dreams—dreams of the things they would buy if their pockets were workable. . . . There was one [house] in especial, in the neighborhood I allude to, as to which the dream of having impossibly acquired it from an embarrassed owner kept melting into the vision of 'moving in' on the morrow" (185). In James's travel narratives, as in "A Passionate Pilgrim," the American tourist in England is not content with merely looking at heritage monuments and artefacts. He desires to make them his own private property as a rightful heir to a common Anglo-American cultural inheritance.

    James's writings suggest that culture ultimately plays a bigger role than blood ties or ethnicity when Americans identify with British literature and history as part of a shared cultural inheritance. After all, Paul Westover cites African American abolitionist Frederick Douglass as a key example in his account of American literary tourism to Britain in the nineteenth century (185). However, towards the end of the century, public opinion on both sides of the Atlantic increasingly viewed this Anglo-American cultural heritage as a distinctively Anglo-Saxon racial heritage, one which precluded the participation of non-white Americans. Some British commentators on the Tattershall Castle incident, for example, acknowledged that Britain and America shared a common racial heritage, while arguing that this did not mean that Americans were justified in purchasing British historic monuments. In his op-ed for *The Academy*, Carey acknowledges that "[t]he Anglo-Saxon race forms the backbone of the race inhabiting the United States," hence it is "but reasonable that a fair share of the common heritage of which we are equally proud should cross the sea" (449). Nevertheless, he claims that "to root up from their native soil historic buildings is another story" (449). Similarly, at the Lords Sitting of 30 April 1912, Lord Curzon called upon parliament to preserve historic monuments for the benefit of the greater Anglo-Saxon race dispersed in the US and the colonies. He welcomed American tourists to view their common heritage in Britain but drew the line at Americans taking historic monuments back with them (872). Although Reginald Horsman argues that the ideology of a superior Anglo-Saxon race bringing civilization to the world had already emerged in the US by the end of the 1846–1848 Mexican-American War, this ideology certainly became much more prominent in the late nineteenth century (1–2, 302–03). In the 1890s, Anglo-American relations moved towards a greater sense of a shared Anglo-Saxon lineage and, by extension, a shared imperial mission, which was perhaps most famously articulated in Kipling's 1899 poem "The White Man's Burden." Horsman observes that, while American Anglo-Saxonism in the first half of the nineteenth century was ambivalent about whether to include Celtic and other non-English Caucasian peoples, by the end of the century the theory of a specifically English Anglo-Saxon race had merged with that of a new "American" race composed of Western and Northern European peoples, to form a broader conception of a generically white "Anglo-Saxon" race pitted against the perceived threat of non-white immigration to the US (301–02). This conflation of Anglo-Saxonism with whiteness in the late nineteenth century expanded the usage of the term to refer to what Horsman calls "the white people of the US in contrast to blacks, Indians [native Americans], Mexicans, Spaniards, or Asiatics" (4); all of whom were effectively excluded from seeing themselves in, and much less claiming ownership of, a shared Anglo-American cultural inheritance.

With his big checkbook and sense of entitlement, *Possession*'s Professor Cropper is a late twentieth-century incarnation of the nineteenth-century (white) American appropriation of British cultural property, which James both ironized and championed. As the resolution of the Tattershall Castle scandal suggests, journalists and members of parliament at the turn of the twentieth century appear to have exaggerated the American threat to British heritage. In his 1911 speech at the Society of Antiquaries, McDonnell claimed to "have a list of [cases of threatened historic sites] literally as long as [his] arm" (17), but the examples he mentioned were either unfounded rumors or they were too vague to be credible. In 1912, Lord Curzon and Lady Blanche Gordon-Lennox wrote a letter to the *Times* revealing that unscrupulous dealers and estate agents often invented imaginary competing bidders—usually in the form of an American millionaire—to drive up the prices of historic buildings and artefacts (105–06). Curzon and Gordon-Lennox argued that this was what had occurred in the case of Tattershall Castle (106). Earlier in the year, the *Times* reported that "[t]he myth of the American millionaire who had bought the castle and was to remove it across the ocean, stone by stone, [had] vanished away, and no American was found to incur the odium of buying even the mantelpieces" ("Tattershall Mantelpieces" 9). Nonetheless, the stereotype of the vulgar American tourist, collector, and/or speculator has persisted from the mid-nineteenth through to the end of the twentieth century, and perhaps into the twenty-first. Chapter two examines how the 2002 Hollywood film adaptation of *Possession* attempts to counter this stereotype by changing Roland's nationality, so that the American villain is ultimately defeated by an American hero in the movie version of the story. On the one hand, the American threat helps to strengthen the sense of ownership that the British feel towards their national cultural property. On the other hand, this threat exists precisely because British culture is not exclusively national. Britain spread its cultural forms and practices, including English literature, to the US and other parts of the world through years of imperial expansion, especially during the nineteenth century. American claims on English literature and its associated artefacts and places reveal that the "dissemiNation" of British culture endangers British ownership of heritage properties, not only in the form of cultural hybridization—as Homi Bhabha has famously argued—but also in a very literal sense. Yet this dissemination enables the heritage industry in Britain to thrive, both in the nineteenth century and today, by drawing in large numbers of tourists from America and other places around the world, which have at one point or another come under the influence of the British Empire. This paradox has given rise to contradictory relations of competition and collaboration between the British heritage industry, American media conglomerates, and the Japanese popular culture industries in the late twentieth and early twenty-first centuries. This is the story that the following chapters unfold.

Chapter Two

All in the Anglo-American Family

The sense of a shared Anglo-American cultural inheritance centered on English literature continues to motivate American involvement in the British heritage industry in the late twentieth and early twenty-first centuries. In *Possession*, the American antagonist Professor Cropper will stop at nothing to gain ownership of the Victorian poets' letters, partly because he has a familial connection with the poet Randolph Henry Ash. Contrary to what one might expect, Cropper is not related to the Ash family. Instead of invoking the familiar rhetoric of blood, kinship, and the Anglo-Saxon race, Cropper stakes his claim to the letters on an intellectual appreciation of Ash's poetry, which has been passed down in his family since the mid-nineteenth century. Cropper's great-grandmother, Priscilla Penn Cropper, once received a letter from Ash declining her invitation to attend a discussion on spiritualism at her mansion in Chixauga, New Mexico (now Cropper's beloved family home). The letter was later preserved in the "Treasure Cabinet" (99) at the Cropper family home and subsequently donated, together with other family treasures, to the university museum collection that Cropper oversees. As a child, Cropper was strangely touched by Ash's letter, which he claims "gave rise to [his] life's absorbing interest" (102) in Ash: "I do not know why this one of the many treasures in our possession moved me most. . . . it may even be that Randolph Henry's rebuff to my ancestress's interest gave rise to my wish to show that we were, after all, worthy to understand, and, so to speak, to entertain him" (102). As far as Cropper is concerned, he deserves to "inherit" Ash's and LaMotte's secret letters because Ash is, in an intellectual rather than genealogical sense, part of his family history.

This notion of a common Anglo-American cultural heritage does not, however, result only in relations of competition between Britons and

Americans vying for the possession of heritage properties. It also encourages transatlantic collaboration in preserving and monetizing heritage properties in Britain for the shared benefit of both sides. Comparing Byatt's novel *Possession* with its 2002 Hollywood film adaptation helps us to see these relations of competition and collaboration at work in the British heritage industry today, especially in the field of period film and television production. In working together to commodify the past, the British heritage industry and American media conglomerates collectively (re)produce various stock images of Englishness, including that of the Victorian past. P. G. Wodehouse anticipated these developments in his Blandings Castle stories from the early twentieth century, drawing on the trope of the Anglo-American extended family to create and preserve an imaginary Victorian heritage for both British and American audiences.

Possessing *Possession*

In 2002, Hollywood movie studio Warner Bros. released the film adaptation of Byatt's novel *Possession*, starring Aaron Eckhart and Gwyneth Paltrow as Roland and Maud, and Jeremy Northam and Jennifer Ehle as the Victorian poets Ash and LaMotte. In this adaptation, directed by Neil LaBute, Roland has been rather jarringly transformed into a brash, cynical, and unrealistically handsome American, so that the rivalry between the British and American factions in the novel essentially becomes a conflict between an American antagonist and an American hero fighting for a just cause. While critics have bemoaned the "dumbing down" of Byatt's novel, this chapter takes what adaptation scholars call "fidelity criticism" in a different direction.[1] Comparing specific films and their literary sources to assess how faithful the former is to the latter used to be the dominant approach in adaptation studies, but scholars such as Thomas Leitch and Linda Hutcheon have since adopted a more nuanced approach to questions of fidelity. In the case of *Possession*, comparing key differences between the novel and the film brings to light the contradictory relations of competition and collaboration that exist between the heritage industry in Britain and media corporations based in the US. American media corporations undoubtedly exercise a great deal of influence in the global creative economy, prompting media scholars such as Herbert Schiller to characterize the export of American media products as a form of cultural imperialism. However, *Possession* and its film adaptation reveal that, when it comes to period film and television production from the 1980s to the present day, the American cultural empire does not and cannot operate unilaterally. In a global creative economy structured by multipolar rather than unilateral relations, the American cultural empire is in fact closely entwined with that of its erstwhile colonial overlord and "mother" country, thus forming an integrated Anglo-American media system that extends outwards beyond the boundaries of Britain and the US.

By changing Roland's nationality as well as his personality, the film adaptation of *Possession* downplays the competition between the British-led and American-led groups of academics, which was a central feature of the novel. Unlike the novel, the film explicitly affirms that the British rightfully own the Victorian poets' letters as part of their national heritage. In doing so, the film obscures the actual competition that occurs between British and American media corporations eager to gain possession of cultural property, not only in terms of national patrimony, but also in terms of intellectual property rights. In the film version of *Possession*, Roland is an all-American hero who respects and protects British ownership of the letters from the illegitimate claims of his fellow American, Professor Cropper. Unlike his British counterpart in the novel, the American Roland disclaims any form of ownership of the letters. He does not feel that the letters belong to him in a spiritual sense as the person who discovered them. As the "good" American, he leads the British scholars in their efforts to stop the "bad" American from gaining hold of the letters, thereby disrupting the Anglo-American dichotomy that structures the plot of the novel. At the end of the film, Roland assures Maud that he will hand over Christabel LaMotte's final letter, which Cropper had stolen from Ash's grave, to the British Museum. The film thus elides the legal struggles that feature so prominently in the novel. It creates the impression that the British nation-state's ownership of the letters is perfectly natural and incontestable.

In affirming that the British legitimately own the Victorian poets' letters, the film adaptation of *Possession* masks the fact that it in itself is a product of Anglo-American competition for cultural property, which in this case has resulted in the American appropriation of a novel by a British author. Shortly after Byatt's novel won the Booker Prize in 1990, Warner Bros. bought the film adaptation rights for an undisclosed, but probably very large, sum of money. As Byatt explains in her interview with Janet Watts for the *Guardian*: "They bought the book and I bought the swimming pool. People said take the money and run. So I did." Even though the studio then took more than a decade to release the film adaptation, Warner Bros.' acquisition of the rights to Byatt's novel effectively precluded the British Broadcasting Corporation (BBC) and other British film and television production companies from cashing in on *Possession*'s success. The happy ending in the Warner Bros. adaptation of *Possession* perhaps appeals to American audiences who want to see the US as a global superpower that defends the cultural property of others, rather than taking that property for itself. The novel version of *Possession* anticipates this reaction when Maud's American colleague Leonora pledges her support for Blackadder's public appeal to keep the letters in Britain. Leonora professes that she, as an American, is "not acquisitive" and that "[t]he days of cultural imperialism are over" (404). However, the fact remains that Warner Bros., as one of the major American players in global media production, has used its economic clout to purchase the intellectual property rights associated with a British novel, and to reap the economic profits that come from possessing that novel in its filmic form. Moreover, in taking possession of *Possession* as a form of intellectual property, Warner Bros. has also transformed *Possession* from a novel hailed as Britain's winning entry in the Booker Prize awards into an American media product complete with American protagonist, American director, and American movie stars.

Possession is only one of many examples of American media corporations appropriating British literary works as their own property by adapting these works for film and television. Warner Bros. released adaptations of Alan Moore's graphic novels *V for Vendetta* and *Watchmen* in 2005 and 2009 respectively. Moore had apparently sold the rights to his graphic novels willingly, but he later refused to endorse these and other Hollywood adaptations.[2] Under the Anglo-American system of copyright, once Moore had sold off the adaptation rights to his works, he could no longer exercise artistic control as the original author. The adaptations henceforth became the sole property of the new rights holders, namely, the movie studios.[3] Notwithstanding Moore's disparaging of Hollywood, Warner Bros. pocketed USD $132,511,035 in worldwide ticket sales for *V for Vendetta* (as of 6 July 2012), far surpassing the film's estimated production costs of USD $54,000,000 ("V for Vendetta"). These figures do not even include income from streaming services, DVD sales, and related merchandise. As Jennifer M. Jeffers argues, the contemporary American film industry has effectively "colonized" British literature by adapting it to fit American movie genre conventions and to serve the needs of American audiences (3–4).

Sharing *Possession*

Yet Jeffers's use of the expression *colonized* is perhaps too categorical. While American media corporations often claim ownership of British literary works through screen adaptations, these adaptations simultaneously support the British heritage industry in multiple ways. Whether classified as British-made, American-made, or coproduced (more on this later), the period films and television dramas that have proliferated since the 1980s often help to promote historic monuments in Britain as attractive tourist destinations. With the arrival of *Brideshead Revisited* on TV screens in 1981 and the rise of heritage films and costume dramas in cinemas in the 1980s and 1990s, period film and TV production has increasingly turned to what Andrew Higson calls a "discourse of authenticity" (42). This is a mode of film and TV production that is centered on achieving historical accuracy by paying careful attention to period details and by shooting at historic locations rather than in studios (Higson 42). This fetishization of historical "authenticity" intersects with a filmic "aesthetics of display" (another of Higson's terms) to present the viewer with beautiful images of historic locations in Britain (Higson 38–39), thereby encouraging not only American viewers but also viewers around the world to visit these locations as tourists. It is important to note here that American distributors and broadcasters have been showcasing period films and TV serials shot in Britain long before the 1980s. However, the growing insistence on location shooting and period detail since the 1980s has engendered an even greater degree of Anglo-American cooperation in commodifying, not only the literary heritage that these dramas often adapt or draw inspiration from, but also the physical heritage sites that feature prominently in these productions.

The film adaptation of *Possession* is a case in point. Whereas the novel encourages the reader to reflect critically on how we know the past, the film jettisons these epistemological concerns in favor of an uncritical, touristic attitude towards the past, one that is concerned primarily with "authenticity," spectacular display, and what Bella Dicks in *Culture on Display* calls "visitable history" (119). In the director's commentary included in the DVD release of *Possession*, Neil LaBute repeatedly invokes the idea of showing the audience "real" locations. The film was shot more often on location than on studio film sets because LaBute preferred to use the historic sites mentioned in Byatt's novel. When discussing the shot of Lincoln Cathedral seen from Maud's office window, LaBute explains that he tried to get landmarks like the cathedral on camera as much as possible to "give a sense of place." He adds that there is "[n]othing like a real view out of the window compared to a painted backdrop." Later in the commentary, he explains that filming near Thomason Foss in Yorkshire was difficult because of the rugged terrain, but he had chosen to film at that particular site because he "felt it was really important to be there" in the exact location which Byatt had specified in her novel. Although the film was not sponsored by the British Tourist Authority or local government tourism boards, LaBute's insistence on the value of "being there" in an actual location rather than on a film set fits neatly with the aims of the British heritage industry. Since Thatcher's neoliberal reforms in the 1980s, heritage monuments in Britain have increasingly become tourist attractions geared towards selling the experience of "being there" in a historic site—or in the words of English Heritage's marketing campaign—"stand[ing] where history happened" (*English Heritage*). Because LaBute was so committed to the specificity and reality of places, his adaptation of *Possession* effectively helped to advertise these places not only to American tourists, but also to tourists from around the world.

The cinematography in LaBute's adaptation of *Possession* further reinforces this unofficial marketing of historic sites as sightseeing attractions. In *English Heritage, English Cinema*, Higson describes the costume dramas of the 1980s and 1990s as a "cinema of attractions" (39). In these costume dramas, Higson claims, camera movement is less concerned with following the movement of characters than with showing the viewer period settings (38). As such, costume dramas generally make extensive use of long and medium shots, which show the viewer more of the background; as well as long takes, which give the viewer more time to look at the background (38–39). These aesthetic strategies, Higson contends, transform narrative space into "space for the display of heritage properties" (39). LaBute's *Possession* similarly puts heritage properties on display as spectacles for the viewer to admire. In *Possession*, establishing shots that indicate changes of location in the film narrative often depict historic monuments seen from afar, set amidst scenic landscapes. These establishing shots are divorced from character point of view and therefore are, as Higson describes, "displayed for the cinema spectator alone" (38). When the plot action moves to Lincoln, for example, the camera cuts to a high-angle, extreme long shot of the church where the Victorian poet Christabel LaMotte is buried (figure 2.1). The grey ruins of the church are framed slightly off-center by verdant green trees and fields and a shining lake in the foreground. The church appears as a picturesque pastoral idyll devoid of human figures and vehicles. Seal Court, the country

Figure 2.1. Establishing shot of the church in Lincoln where Christabel LaMotte is buried. *Source: Possession.* Directed by Neil LaBute, Warner Bros., 2002.

house in Lincoln in which LaMotte spends the last years of her life, appears in the film in a similar fashion (figure 2.2). Seen from a far distance, the white buildings of the country house stand out against a background of rolling green hills and blue sky shrouded in mist. Like the earlier shot of the church, there are no human figures or vehicles in this shot. This absence of objects such as clothing and motorcars, which would have connected the buildings to a particular time period, gives these historic monuments a distinctive heritage quality. In these establishing shots, the church and the country house possess an air of persisting through the centuries unchanged, from the past to the present and into the future. By directing the viewer's

Figure 2.2. Establishing shot of Seal Court, Christabel LaMotte's ancestral home. *Source: Possession.* Directed by Neil LaBute, Warner Bros., 2002.

gaze towards these romantic and seemingly timeless pieces of Britain's architectural heritage, the film encourages the spectator not to be satisfied with simply viewing these beautiful images on the screen. Through its emphasis on authenticity, the film urges the spectator to visit the actual locations featured in these images. Unsurprisingly, these shots of historic monuments in *Possession* bear a striking resemblance to images often found in heritage tourism marketing materials in Britain (figures 2.3 and 2.4).

In other words, while the film adaptation of *Possession* surreptitiously appropriates Byatt's novel as American cultural property, it also works with the British heritage industry to display history as a place that one can visit in the present. The aura of timelessness that surrounds historic monuments in the film not only positions these monuments as heritage, but also implies

Figure 2.3. Kenilworth Castle brochure. Obtained by the author at Kenilworth Castle on 30 May 2015. *Source:* English Heritage.

All in the Anglo-American Family   57

Figure 2.4. The main page of the official website of Leighton Hall, which stood in for Seal Court in *Possession*. *Source*: Leighton Hall website https://www.leightonhall.co.uk/

that one can visit the past that these monuments embody at any time, without any loss of authenticity. Whereas Byatt's *Possession* suggests that the past can be resurrected only as an imaginative representation, the film adaptation erases this gap between past reality and present-day interpretation. In the film, the Victorian past loses its distinctiveness and becomes "visitable history" (Dicks 119). It becomes a past that occupies the same time-space as the present, and which the film spectator can therefore slip into and experience in much the same way that visitors to heritage attractions experience the past through reenactments. The film dramatizes this idea of a seamless connection between past and present when it transitions between time periods by panning the camera from one part of the filming location showing the contemporary characters to another part showing the Victorian characters, and vice versa, in a single take. In the scene where Roland and Maud travel to Yorkshire to retrace Ash and LaMotte's journey in 1859, the camera first shows Roland and Maud's car traveling under the arch of an old railway bridge, and then pans upwards to show a steam engine crossing the bridge. The camera cuts to Ash and LaMotte in a railway carriage on the train that appears to have, in time-travel fashion, crossed the bridge seconds after Roland and Maud drive beneath it. Several shots later, when Ash and LaMotte walk out of their hotel room in Yorkshire, the camera focuses on the closed door and then shows a hotel staff member entering the room with Roland and Maud. The camera follows the characters as they move around the room, revealing that the layout of the room has changed since the Victorian characters walked out of it a few seconds earlier. All this action occurs within a single take. (In the director's commentary, LaBute reveals that he achieved this seemingly magical transformation by using a film set with moveable walls.) This flawlessly smooth transition between the contemporary present and the Victorian past creates the impression that the spectator, like Roland and Maud, can literally walk into the past as a "visitable" place and obtain unmediated knowledge of that past in the present. In encouraging viewers to immerse themselves in this audiovisual experience of the Victorian past brought back to life, LaBute's *Possession* and other period dramas like it echo and reaffirm what Robert Lumley has identified as the "heritage-center approach" in the British heritage industry (22). Since the 1980s, there has been a burgeoning of heritage attractions that, like their filmic and televisual counterparts, prioritize visitor enjoyment and emotional identification with the past over historical research and critical distance (Lumley 22).[4] In supporting this particular mode of relating to the past, the film adaptation of *Possession* enhances the "visitability" of the heritage sites that appear in the film—such as Bolton Abbey Priory and Leighton Hall, which stood in for the church in Lincoln and Seal Court respectively—many of which are business enterprises that stand to gain from film- and television-related tourism.[5]

These are only some of the ways in which the film adaptation of *Possession* and other similar period dramas complement the British heritage industry in the late twentieth and early twenty-first centuries. Period film and television production is a significant part of the wider heritage industry in Britain. While American media corporations sometimes compete with their British counterparts for lucrative adaptation deals, they also often collaborate with the latter to coproduce screen adaptations and original dramas inspired by canonical works of English literature. Although *Possession* was produced and distributed by three US-based studios (Warner Bros., Focus Features/USA Films, and Baltimore Spring Creek Productions), many of the period dramas that came before and after *Possession* are Anglo-American coproductions. In *Network Nations*, Michele Hilmes observes that the BBC had been developing the practice of coproduction as an effective means of financing programs as early as the 1960s (286–87). In more recent years, the 2011 film adaptation of *Jane Eyre*, for instance, was produced by Focus Features in association with BBC Films. The hit TV series *Downton Abbey* (2010–2015) was similarly coproduced by British commercial network ITV and American public TV station WGBH, which is best known for establishing the famous *Masterpiece Theatre* program on the Public Broadcasting Service (PBS) in the US. By the 1980s, Higson argues, the American market for

Hollywood movies had become so saturated that Hollywood began to invest heavily in films designed for foreign markets, including so-called British period films (121). As Claire Monk asserts, British cinema's subordination to Hollywood since the 1980s problematizes the seemingly self-evident British-ness of British period dramas (176–77). The desire for national self-affirmation, Monk argues, has led British media companies to produce and market period dramas as British products distinct from mainstream Hollywood fare (176–77). On the other side of the Atlantic, American distributors and broadcasters likewise market period films and TV dramas as uniquely British and as "something completely different" from American shows, as Jeffrey S. Miller puts it in the title of his book on British television in the US.[6] This branding of period dramas "as *particularly* 'British,' [and] as *particularly* characteristic of British cinema and television," Monk argues, obscures the fact that many of the period dramas of the 1980s and 1990s that are classified as British productions were actually made possible by American cofinancing, artistic collaboration, and distribution (176–77).[7] While Higson and Monk are primarily concerned with period films, these observations also apply to TV serials such as *Bleak House* (2005), *Jane Eyre* (2006), and *Cranford* (2007), all of which were jointly produced by the BBC and WGBH for *Masterpiece Theatre* (Butt 164).

As the anecdote that opens this chapter suggests, American investment in so-called British period dramas—like Professor Cropper's emotional investment in the Victorian poet Ash—stems at least partly from the assumption that Britons and Americans share a common cultural, and especially literary, heritage. Scholars of Anglo-American media studies have put forward many reasons for the abiding American interest in British period dramas, including the aforementioned drive for Hollywood market expansion; the low cost of British TV drama imports; nostalgia for a lost social order; and the long-standing association of British TV (and British culture more broadly) with quality and cultural capital, which chapters three and four will discuss in greater detail.[8] Nonetheless, the notion of a shared history and literature might be said to have motivated Anglo-American collaborations in media production and distribution, even before the current wave of period dramas began in the 1980s. When the American public television network PBS broadcast the BBC adaptation of John Galsworthy's *The Forsyte Saga* in 1969, the series proved such a success that WGBH set up *Masterpiece Theatre* on PBS to showcase dramas bought from or coproduced with British television corporations (Hilmes 278–80).[9] Since its inception in 1971, *Masterpiece Theatre*'s programming has focused predominantly on adaptations of canonical literary works by British authors and dramatizations of important events in British history. Although over the years *Masterpiece Theatre* has also featured adaptations of continental European literary works and American classics, British literature and history remain the mainstay of *Masterpiece Theatre*.[10]

At the beginning of each *Masterpiece Theatre* episode, the iconic opening sequence frames the chosen British literary work or historical event as a shared Anglo-American tradition. The camera pans over what appears to be an archetypal Victorian drawing room filled with bric-a-brac (Hilmes 282–83). As the fanfare from Jean-Joseph Mouret's "Rondeau" plays in the recording, the roving camera offers the viewer close-up shots of leather-bound books by Trollope, Hardy, Thackeray, and Henry James. The camera also highlights assorted knickknacks in the drawing room, including marble busts, war medals, framed photographs, and even a cocktail glass containing a martini; before cutting to the host of the show sitting in an armchair, presumably in the same room (Hilmes 282–83). On the one hand, the opening sequence plays up the British brand identity of *Masterpiece Theatre*, thus implying that the program is "something different from domestic [American] shows" (J. Miller xiii). On the other hand, its homely atmosphere suggests that the British literature and history featured on the program are perhaps not so different from American culture after all. The cozy intimacy of *Masterpiece Theatre*'s Victorian parlor echoes the homeliness experienced by Clement Searle and the narrator as they travel around England in James's "A Passionate Pilgrim." The opening sequence of *Masterpiece Theatre* positions British literature and history as something familiar to American audiences, not in the sense that American viewers know a lot about these subjects—in fact, *Masterpiece Theatre* had to employ hosts to provide contextual information at the start of each episode—but in terms of the familial feelings that the motif of home evokes. The opening sequence suggests that, while the literary works and historical events dramatized onscreen are distinctively British, they are also part of a wider Anglo-American family legacy. Moreover, in the same way that Anglo-Americanism was often conflated with Anglo-Saxonism in the late nineteenth and early twentieth centuries, this trope of an Anglo-American family legacy embodied in contemporary period dramas is predominantly presented as an exclusively white racial legacy. Up till *Bridgerton* surprised viewers in 2020 with its strikingly multiracial cast, the period film and TV drama industry had generally preferred to cast white actors in leading roles. *Wuthering Heights*' Heathcliff, for instance, had traditionally been played by Caucasian actors—until Andrea Arnold's 2011 adaptation, which sparked controversy for its portrayal of Heathcliff as a black man—even though Heathcliff's ethnicity in Brontë's novel is highly ambiguous. The collective imagination of the Victorian past in popular culture (and in the field of Victorian studies) is so deeply interwoven with an unspoken emphasis on whiteness that non-white peoples (including non-white Victorianists) find it very difficult to lay claim to this supposedly shared Anglo-American cultural inheritance, as the recent movement to "undiscipline Victorian studies" has revealed.[11]

In her reading of the *Masterpiece Theatre* opening theme, Hilmes argues that the opening domesticates the "foreignness" of British TV dramas by projecting a stereotypically "traditional" and "quaint" Englishness familiar to American audiences (283). Likewise, in discussing the export of British TV programs to the US, Miller foregrounds the difference of these programs and how some of this difference has become Americanized (*Something Completely Different* xiii). For example, his chapter "All in the Anglo-American Family: Hollywood Reproductions of British Originals"—from which this chapter has borrowed its title—examines how American TV production companies have adapted the format of British family sitcoms to address American concerns. While period films and TV dramas are certainly marketed and received as "something different" in the US, it might be useful to think of Anglo-American relations in the global creative economy not only in terms of difference and assimilation, but also in terms of a joint venture to conserve and commodify a shared racial and cultural heritage. This ethno-cultural heritage may seem foreign and distant to American viewers but, as the *Masterpiece Theatre* opening suggests, it is also close to home. P. G. Wodehouse's stories, which circulated widely on both sides of the Atlantic during his lifetime, draw on this paradox of the distant relation to preserve a rapidly disappearing Victorian past as an inheritance for both British and American readers in the twentieth century and beyond.

The Blandings Castle Family

Born in Surrey in 1881, Wodehouse wrote an astounding number of novels and short stories over a career that extended from the turn of the twentieth century to his death in 1975. Many of Wodehouse's works were published almost simultaneously in Britain and the US and were even written in transit during Wodehouse's frequent trips across the Atlantic (Damrosch 210–12). After the Second World War, Wodehouse moved permanently to the US and became an American citizen in 1955, but he continued to write of both Britain and the US, for both British and American readers. As works of popular fiction explicitly geared towards a wide Anglo-American readership, Wodehouse's stories, and especially his Blandings Castle saga, present a heritage fantasy of Britain that is at once Victorian and timeless, and which is inhabited by both British and American characters as a shared cultural inheritance. As Deepika Karle argues, while Wodehouse's fictional universe seems "exclusively English"—like "a pristine Garden of Eden that is more like Shropshire than Shropshire is"—it does include American settings and characters (32–33). Karle treats the American world in Wodehouse's fiction as a separate realm that complements its better-known English counterpart (33). In my reading of Wodehouse's Blandings Castle stories, I treat the English and American worlds in Wodehouse's fiction as a single entity, one that is unified by the idea of an extended Anglo-American family. In constructing a "jolly old world" (Voorhees 213) of Englishness shared by British and American characters as well as readers, Wodehouse's Blandings Castle stories combine two main discourses on Englishness that prevailed in the second half of the nineteenth and the first half of the twentieth century respectively. The Blandings Castle stories gesture on the one hand to Charles Wentworth Dilke's "Greater Britain," while expressing on the other a kind of nostalgia for a primeval English identity that Patrick Wright terms "Deep England." By presenting Englishness as both universal and distinctive, expanding and contracting, Wodehouse's Blandings Castle stories illuminate the central paradox that drives the export of British cultural commodities in the global creative economy today. While the images of Englishness articulated in the British heritage industry often claim to express a truly unique national culture, they simultaneously rely on Englishness's former imperial status as universal culture, as well as its former imperial networks of dissemination, to draw in audiences from the US and other places outside Britain in the late twentieth and early twenty-first centuries.

As the name suggests, Wodehouse's Blandings Castle saga is a long-running series of novels and short stories revolving around a fictional country house estate located in the county of Shropshire, England. The owner of Blandings is Clarence, ninth Earl of Emsworth, an absent-minded old man who enjoys pottering around his gardens and tending to his prize-winning pig, the Empress of Blandings. In each story, Lord Emsworth's tranquil life at Blandings is disrupted by the antics of his relatives, employees, and guests (which are in turn often exacerbated by his own absent-mindedness), until peace and order are restored at the end of the narrative. As many critics have observed, Wodehouse's fictional world is timeless in the sense that his characters do not age, nothing really bad ever happens, and his stories consistently avoid engaging substantively with the political and socioeconomic upheavals of his time.[12] If the world of Wodehouse's fiction is anachronistic in general, the figure of Blandings Castle stands out in particular as an anachronism within this already anachronistic world. Blandings stands for a Victorian as well as a more ambiguously ancient and feudal past in contrast to the world outside it, which in the stories frequently takes the form of London. The building itself dates from the Tudor period (*Something Fresh* 120), when "Queen Elizabeth, dodging from country-house to country-house in that restless, snipe-like way of hers, had last slept" in some of the castle's most magnificent bedrooms (*Summer Lightning* 594). The mental framework of Blandings' owner, however, is marked as Victorian. In *Something Fresh* (1915), the first novel in the Blandings Castle saga, the narrator informs the reader that Lord Emsworth has always been slow and unfocused since he was a schoolboy at Eton in the 1860s, where his classmates "had called him Fathead" (49). In *Leave It to Psmith* (1924), the reader is told that the Blandings library catalog has not been updated since 1885, and that Lord Emsworth does not understand why his sister, Lady Constance, insists that he rectify the situation:

> "Catalogue the library? What does it want cataloguing for?"
> "It has not been done since the year 1885."
> "Well, and look how splendidly we've got along without it," said Lord Emsworth acutely. (20)

In the 1947 novel *Full Moon*, one of the main characters comes to Blandings posing as an artist who specializes in painting animals. Despite the fact that the novel is ostensibly set in postwar Britain, Lord Emsworth believes that this imposter is the famous Victorian painter Sir Edwin Landseer (1802–1873), even though Sir Edwin "has been dead for years," as another character points out (190). Like its owner, Blandings is a Victorian relic that has somehow managed to survive untouched in the twentieth century, even as that fictional twentieth-century world outside Blandings becomes increasingly out of step with actual historical developments at the time of writing.

Yet Blandings Castle also possesses a timeless quality that cannot be pegged to any particular period. Many scholars of Wodehouse, and Wodehouse himself, have claimed that the old-fashioned world depicted in his works has a distinctively Edwardian tone.[13] In the preface to the 1974 edition of *Joy in the Morning*, Wodehouse claims that when he first started writing in the Edwardian period, his stories were "contemporary," but with the passing of time they had become "historical" (qtd. in Cannadine 473). However, on a deeper level, it does not really matter whether Wodehouse's fictional world is that of the Victorian period, the Edwardian period, the 1920s, the 1930s, and so on. The Blandings Castle stories evoke a vaguely ancient and feudal past that we now commonly refer to as *Deep England*. The term *Deep England*, which Patrick Wright coined in 1985, delineates a well-established tradition in British thought of defining Englishness as an inchoate collection of predominantly rural and seemingly primordial sights and sounds in the English landscape (Wright 77–83). While it might be argued that Wodehouse's oeuvre on the whole presents an "ahistorical world of an arcadia" (Mooneyham 133), the world of Blandings in particular is an especially idyllic pastoral paradise that embodies the nostalgic fantasy of Deep England. At Blandings Castle, the sun (almost) always shines, flowers bloom in abundance, the gardens and woods are perpetually at the height of their beauty, and Lord Emsworth never fails to grow the largest pumpkin or the fattest pig in the county. In *Summer Lightning* (1929), Sue Brown leans over the low stone wall that borders the castle and gazes at the vista that opens before her:

> The Castle had been built on a knoll of rising ground, and on this terrace one had the illusion of being perched up at a great height. From where she stood, Sue got a sweeping view of the park and of the dim, misty Vale of Blandings that dreamed beyond. In the park, rabbits were scuttling to and fro. In the shrubberies birds called sleepily. From somewhere out across the fields there came the faint tinkling of sheep-bells. The lake shone like old silver, and there was a river in the distance, dull grey between the dull green of the trees.
> It was a lovely sight, age-old, orderly and English, but it was spoiled by the [overcast] sky. (513)

Yet the storm passes quickly and Blandings is once again bathed in sunshine and verdant greenery in this story and others. Even the small town that surrounds the castle resists the passage of time: "Market Blandings had a comforting air of having been exactly the same for centuries. Troubles might vex the generations it housed, but they did not worry that lichened church with its sturdy four-square tower, nor those red-roofed shops, nor the age-old inns whose second storeys bulged so comfortably out over the pavements. . . . Nothing was modern in it [the town] except the moving-picture house—and even that called itself an Electric Theatre, and was ivy-covered and surmounted by stone gables" (*Summer Lightning* 221–22). Lord Emsworth too, like his beloved home, belongs to a primeval, pastoral, and—as Debra Rae Cohen has argued—a quintessentially feudal past ("Place of the Pig" 105). When the reader is introduced to Lord Emsworth for the first time in *Something Fresh*, the earl is described as being "as completely happy as only a fluffy-minded old man with excellent health and a large income can be" (48): "Other people worried about all sorts of things—strikes, wars, suffragettes, diminishing birth-rates, the growing materialism of the age, and a score of similar subjects. Worrying, indeed, seemed to be the twentieth century's specialty. Lord Emsworth never worried. . . . He was possibly as nearly contented as a human being can be in this century of alarms and excursions" (*Something Fresh* 48–49). While others in the twentieth century engage in "alarms and excursions," Lord Emsworth remains unscathed by these troubling conditions, secure in his feudal world of aristocratic wealth and privilege.

Beginning with *Something Fresh* in 1915 and ending with *Sunset at Blandings*, which Wodehouse was working on when he died in 1975, Wodehouse wrote the Blandings Castle stories at a time when the discourse on Deep England was gaining traction, and when country houses were increasingly perceived as emblems of national heritage and identity. For Jed Esty, this growing interest in Deep England was part of a wider turn to English cultural particularity in the 1930s and 1940s. This turn to a provincial Englishness, Esty contends, was occasioned by the decline of British imperial power in the early twentieth century (2–3). Undoubtedly, the myth of Deep England can be traced back further to Stanley Baldwin's *On England* in 1926 (Wright 78), or even to John Ruskin's championing of medieval Gothic cathedrals as embodiments of authentic Englishness in the nineteenth century (Baucom 49–69). Nevertheless, for Esty, the 1930s mark the pivotal moment when the "anthropological paradigms of the metropolitan [imperialist] era" turned away from studying native subjects towards studying the English, thereby "channel[ing] the potential energy of a contracting British civilization into a resurgent discourse of national particularism" (54). E. M. Forster's pageant-plays in the 1930s and 1940s, Esty argues, make a particular contribution to the discourse on Deep England. These plays represent Englishness not only as pastoral and archaic, but also as a delimited and knowable place that supersedes the almost infinite expansiveness of metropolitan and imperial space, which Forster had critiqued but failed to transcend in earlier works such as *Howards End* (Esty 77–81). As the British Empire contracted, Forster's "Abinger Pageant" and *England's Pleasant Land* paid tribute to "old rural England" by zooming in on narrowly defined locales within Britain: Forster's home village, the English countryside, a manor house (Esty 79–81). Likewise, although the Victorian public had already begun to view Tudor and early Stuart country houses as embodiments of national heritage in the nineteenth century, it was not until after the Second World War that the British public, the state, and NGOs began to take an interest in conserving country houses in general (Thurley 178–95).[14] While industrialization and the First World War had eroded the agrarian economy that underpinned country houses, the Second World War made country houses practically uninhabitable as a result of wartime requisitioning, postwar income tax and death duties, and the decline of domestic service as an attractive career option (Thurley 178). After the war, both the state and the National Trust began to acquire country houses from owners who could no longer afford them (Thurley 182–95), thereby paving the way for country houses to become the centerpiece of national heritage in Britain (Mandler 5). In this way, the discourse of Deep England became closely intertwined with the preservation of English country houses in the mid-twentieth century.

Wodehouse's Blandings Castle stories were shaped by these developments in the 1930s and 1940s, and to some degree even anticipated them. Like his contemporary Evelyn Waugh, Wodehouse admired the aristocracy for presiding over the feudal social hierarchy embodied in country house estates across the country. While Waugh and Forster mourned the twentieth-century disappearance of this Deep England in their novels about country houses, Wodehouse compensated for this loss by positioning Blandings Castle as an immutable past that has *not* disappeared. Whereas Howards End is threatened by suburbanization and Brideshead is irreparably damaged by war and the arrival of a new socialist order—what Waugh's narrator derisively calls "the age of Hooper" (351)—Blandings remains perfectly intact in the narrative present of each story. Like Wodehouse's characters who perennially return to their original state at the end of every narrative (B. Scott 91), the reader can always return to Blandings and find it unchanged, story after story. In this sense, Wodehouse's treatment of the past in the Blandings Castle saga cannot properly be called nostalgic because one can only be nostalgic about a state of affairs that has ceased to exist. The timelessness of Blandings, in other words, affords the reader the pleasure of returning to an ancient and feudal Deep England, which has supposedly been lost and yet remains "visitable" in the present. Seen in this light, the Blandings Castle stories, perhaps even more so than *Howards End* (1910) and *Brideshead Revisited* (1944), are closely aligned with the pleasures of "visitability" central to heritage tourism and period film and television production. Scholars often cite the screen adaptations of the Forster and Waugh novels as landmark examples of heritage film and TV drama, but Wodehouse's highly popular Blandings Castle stories deserve critical attention too as productive case studies of the British heritage industry.[15]

Moreover, the Blandings Castle stories suggest that the "visitable" heritage embodied in Blandings belongs not only to Lord Emsworth and his like, but also to Americans who marry into aristocratic families in Britain. The Blandings Castle stories thus reinscribe the contracted space of Deep England into the expansive space of what Charles Dilke in 1868 famously named "Greater Britain." As David Cannadine has pointed out, from the 1930s onwards and especially after the Second World War, Wodehouse's works increasingly feature impecunious landowners selling their country houses to American millionaires to be used as holiday homes or even to be transported to the US (488–89). These stories clearly capitalize on the by-now well-established myth of the American Peril (discussed in chapter one), but they do so for comedic purposes. In the Blandings Castle stories, however, Blandings remains the property of Lord Emsworth, whose source of wealth seems never-ending. Nonetheless, the castle welcomes Americans who acquire a spiritual, if not a legal, stake in the property through marriage and kinship relations. In *Something Fresh*, Lord Emsworth's younger son, the Honorable Frederick "Freddie" Threepwood, is engaged to Miss Aline, the daughter of "an American, a Mr. Peters, a man with many millions" (32), who has rented the country house estate next to Blandings. Lord Emsworth does not need Mr. Peters's money, but he is thrilled that Freddie's marriage will take the young man off his hands, for Freddie is an idle and idiotic troublemaker who has been racking up gambling debts and courting chorus girls. For Lord Emsworth, Freddie's marriage to "a girl with plenty of money and excellent breeding" (49), notwithstanding the fact that she is American, would render his "life . . . at last absolutely without a crumpled rose-leaf" (49). Much of *Something Fresh* revolves around the confusion and conflict arising out of Lord Emsworth absent-mindedly taking Mr. Peters's prized Egyptian scarab and mistakenly adding it to his own museum collection. At no point in the novel do the Threepwoods and Peterses clash over the latter's attempts to enter the ranks of the titled nobility in Britain by renting a country house and marrying their daughter to the son of a peer. In other words, the two families fight over the possession of a valuable but unattractive Egyptian antique, while they have no issues with sharing the British heritage embodied in Blandings as members of an extended Anglo-American family. At the end of the novel, Freddie does not marry Aline after all, but in "The Custody of the Pumpkin" (1935), Freddie marries the daughter of another American millionaire, who makes Lord Emsworth a happy man indeed by taking Freddie to the US to work for his dog biscuit manufacturing firm. In *Full Moon*, Lord Emsworth's sister Lady Hermione is eager to marry her daughter Veronica to Tipton Plimsoll, a young American millionaire who owns a large chain of stores in the US. Despite being an uncouth American with a commercial background, Tipton is welcomed into Lord Emsworth's extended family. By marrying Veronica, Tipton gains a spiritual share in Blandings, whose beauty, the narrator remarks ironically, prompts the young American millionaire to describe the castle poetically as "[s]ome joint!" (112). In other Blandings Castle stories, American characters with little money and status, such as *Summer Lightning*'s chorus girl Sue Brown, also become incorporated into the extended Threepwood family and its ancestral home, although some members of the family accept these new arrivals grudgingly. As Damrosch argues in his reading of Wodehouse as world literature, Wodehouse's works often exaggerate cultural differences between British and American characters as a means of interpreting British culture for American readers and vice versa (210, 213). Freddie's father-in-law Mr. Donaldson, for instance, is a stereotypical enterprising American tycoon who pushes his employees to sell more dog biscuits, and "who, when even slightly pleased, ha[s] a habit of spraying five thousand dollar cheques like a geyser" ("The Go-Getter" 95). Nonetheless, these cultural differences do not get in the way of the British and American characters forging harmonious marital and familial ties. Believing that Mr. Peters had given the Egyptian scarab to him as a gift, Lord Emsworth exclaims, "Really, there is something almost oriental in the lavish generosity of our American cousins" (*Something Fresh* 75), thus emphasizing both difference and commonality between the British and their distant relations in the US.

This invocation of an extended Anglo-American family in the Blandings Castle stories draws on the nineteenth-century notion of Greater Britain, which, as discussed earlier, gave way to the more parochial concept of Deep England with the onset of imperial decline in the twentieth century. In his account of Englishness in the nineteenth century, Ian Baucom argues that, as a result of the 1865 Morant Bay uprising in Jamaica, the British public began to view Britain's colonies not as faraway sites of production and trade, but as an integral part of Britain and its understanding of what it meant to be English (44). For Baucom, the debate that surrounded the Morant Bay rebellion prompted Britons to reconceptualize Britain as a space that was coterminous with its empire (44). Dilke's widely read 1868 travelogue *Greater Britain* was part of this centrifugal impetus in defining Englishness. From 1866 to 1867, Dilke traveled to various "English-speaking" and "English-governed lands," including the US, Australia, and India (1: vii). These travels, Dilke argues in his book, have proven to him that the "English race" is destined to achieve global dominance, although Dilke uses the word *race* to refer to both biology and culture. In celebrating what he sees as "the grandeur of our race, already girdling the earth, which it is destined, perhaps, eventually to overspread" (1: vii), Dilke applauds the global proliferation of both the English race and English culture. The trope of the Anglo-American extended family in the Blandings Castle stories echoes this dual conceptualization of Greater Britain. Firstly, it mirrors Dilke's claim that Britons and Americans are essentially members of the same biological race that extends beyond the boundaries of Great Britain to constitute a Greater Britain. In his travelogue, Dilke alludes to the biological dimension of race when he champions the English nation's supposedly superior ability in supplanting other races around the world through migration and settlement, crossbreeding, and the genocidal extermination of native peoples (1: 308–09; 2: 405–06). Dilke's vision of a globalized Englishness, in this sense, is closely aligned with the racial ideology of Anglo-Saxonism. "[T]he true moral of America," Dilke writes, "is the vigor of the English race. . . . Excluding the Atlantic cities, the English in America are absorbing the Germans and the Celts, destroying the Red Indians, and checking the advance of the Chinese" (1: 308). While echoing Dilke's emphasis on the racial affinities between the British and the Americans, the Anglo-American extended family in Wodehouse's fiction also reflects Dilke's assertion that the global triumph of the English race lies not only in the proliferation of its people, but also in the dissemination of its culture, although *culture* in Dilke's writings refers much more narrowly to liberal political and legal institutions. In *Greater Britain*, Dilke describes the United States of America as a melting pot of immigrants from around the world, who are all being "run into an English mold" (1: vii) through the widespread implementation of English liberalism's principles and practices. For Dilke, this "fusion" (1: vii, 312) of diverse peoples in America provides a testing ground that proves that English culture is a universal culture that can be fruitfully adopted by all peoples (1: 312, 318; 2: 407). Like Dilke's model Americans, American characters in the world of Blandings are anglicized insofar as they partake in the British heritage that Blandings Castle symbolizes as their common cultural inheritance.

However, the Blandings Castle stories also imply that acculturation works in both directions. Even Dilke expresses uncertainty over the future of the English race in *Greater Britain*: "Can the English in America, in the long run, survive the common fate of all migrating races? Is it true that, if the American settlers continue to exist, it will be at the price of being no longer English, but Red Indian?" (1: 309). In the world of Blandings, working as a dog biscuit salesman in the US transforms Freddie from a dissipated ne'er-do-well into a hardworking "[g]o-getter" ("The Go-Getter"). Similarly, in "Pig-Hoo-o-o-o-ey!" (1935), Lord Emsworth is surprised (and saddened) at how much working on a farm in Nebraska has changed his niece's fiancé James Belford: "Directness of this kind, he told himself with a pang of self-pity, was the sort of thing young Englishmen picked up in America. Diplomatic circumlocution flourished only in a more leisurely civilization, and in those energetic and forceful surroundings you learned to Talk Quick and Do It Now, and all sorts of uncomfortable things" (324). Hollywood movies also feature prominently in the Blandings Castle stories, as Freddie is a big fan of the motion pictures, often drawing inspiration for his harebrained schemes from the movies he watches. Upon moving to the US, Freddie even writes a screenplay and succeeds in persuading a Hollywood movie studio to pay one thousand dollars for it ("Lord Emsworth Acts for the Best" 307). As these examples indicate, if America in the world of Blandings is part of Greater Britain, Britain is just as much part of a Greater America. This two-way cultural traffic in the Blandings Castle stories signals that, with the decline of the British Empire and the rise of the US in the twentieth century and beyond, the project of (re)producing Deep England now requires Anglo-American collaboration; namely, collaboration between British and American corporations, institutions, government bodies, artists, agents, and so on in the heritage industry and the wider creative economy. Wodehouse himself collaborated with American scriptwriter Guy Bolton and composer Jerome Kern in writing hugely successful musical comedies for Broadway (Donaldson 109–10), and he went to Hollywood twice to write screenplays for MGM Studios (Donaldson 138–39, 158–60). His Blandings novel *Heavy Weather* (1933) was jointly adapted for television by the BBC and WGBH, and broadcast on *Masterpiece Theatre* in the US in 1995.

With their emphasis on Anglo-American kinship and collaboration, Wodehouse's Blandings Castle stories occupy a transitional phase that mediates between the idea of Deep England and the earlier model of Greater Britain. That said, we lose some of the insights that Wodehouse's stories offer if we think of Greater Britain and Deep England as a strictly chronological succession of discourses on Englishness from the second half of the nineteenth century to the first half of the twentieth. By combining these two conceptions of Englishness, the Blandings Castle saga illuminates the paradox at the heart of the British heritage industry and its transnational flows in the late twentieth and early twenty-first centuries. Together with its American partners, the British heritage industry constructs visions of English cultural particularity for export to other countries as a form of universal culture, thereby creating a new cultural empire of Greater Britain out of the vestiges of the old one. In the following chapters, I examine how several Japanese neo-Victorian narratives draw on certain familiar images of English culture (the country house, afternoon tea, shopping at Harrods, and so on) to create a fantasy of a specifically aristocratic kind of Englishness in conjunction with, but also in contradistinction to, the British high-cultural empire. There are some pleasures, these narratives suggest, which Cool Japan offers that Deep England cannot.

Part II

Chapter Three

Japanese Tourists in Victorian Britain

Through its network of enterprises linking tourist attractions, transportation, advertising, as well as film and TV production, the British heritage industry today draws visitors to Britain by exporting Englishness around the world. In doing so, it enters into relations of competition and collaboration not only with the US, but also with Japan, a cultural production powerhouse in its own right that had come under British influence in the nineteenth century but had never been part of Britain's formal empire. As Ross Forman has argued in his work on nineteenth-century Sino-British relations, examining Britain and China as "empires entwined" requires us to expand our understanding of imperialism to "the kinds of affiliations and influences that exceeded the grasp of formal imperialism" (5–6). The same can be said of Japan both in the long nineteenth century and in the global creative economy today. Jasper Fforde's 2001 novel, *The Eyre Affair*, provides an oblique but productive point of entry into unpacking the trans-imperial connections between Britain and Japan, then and now. Amongst other things, Fforde's tongue-in-cheek parody of *Jane Eyre* pokes fun at the Japanese enthusiasm for literary heritage tourism to Britain. Literary heritage tourism is a particular kind of heritage tourism that involves visiting places of birth, houses, graves, and other locations associated with famous writers and works of fiction in order to experience the environment that has supposedly given rise to literary genius. As discussed in chapter one, such literary-inspired tourism was and still is a significant part of the growing commodification of British heritage since Walter Scott in the early nineteenth century. Fforde's neo-Victorian novel provides a useful starting point for examining Japanese women's engagements with commodified

British heritage, especially heritage from the Victorian period. The protagonist of *The Eyre Affair* is a detective named Thursday Next, who teleports into the fictional world of *Jane Eyre* to hunt down a master criminal who is "disrupting" the narrative. While inside the world of *Jane Eyre*, Thursday encounters "a Japanese couple, dressed in period costume but with one of them holding a large Nikon camera [and] . . . a Brontë guidebook written in Japanese" (324). Thursday later discovers that Mr. Rochester does tours of Thornfield Hall for the Japanese tourists whom Mrs. Nakajima (the female half of the couple mentioned above) brings with her when she teleports into the novel. Rochester explains that he engages in this "extremely lucrative" business because "[c]ountry houses are not cheap to run . . . even in this [nineteenth] century" (331). Instead of depicting Japanese tourists visiting heritage attractions connected to Charlotte Brontë and *Jane Eyre*, *The Eyre Affair* features Japanese tourists wandering in and out of the fictional world of *Jane Eyre* as if it were a tangible tourist destination.

On the one hand, the absurdity of Japanese tourists walking around Thornfield Hall as if they were visiting a real country house satirizes the sheer pervasiveness of the tourism industry, or as Thursday puts it in *The Eyre Affair*: "there [are] very few places that the tourist business ha[s]n't touched" (325). On the other hand, it points to the fact that there are indeed many Japanese tourists visiting heritage sites in Britain, especially those associated with famous writers and literary works. For example, the 2007 *Japan Full Market Profile* report produced by the British Tourist Authority reveals that Japanese tourists frequently cited "heritage" as a key factor when choosing places to visit in Britain that year (Surman 196). While Japanese tourists are attracted to British heritage in general, they appear to be particularly interested in literary heritage. According to a 2009 study, the high volume of Japanese tourism to places associated with British books, films, and iconic characters such as Peter Rabbit has made literary tourism one of the most rapidly growing sectors within the British heritage industry (Surman 196–97). At the Brontë Parsonage Museum in Haworth, which regularly attracts large numbers of Japanese tourists, the guidebooks are written in both English and Japanese (Surman 197). In his account of his own literature-inspired travels across Britain in 2011, Simon Goldhill describes the crowds of Japanese tourists he sees at Haworth: "Well, this street looks exactly like a Victorian Yorkshire street. . . . Except that . . . in front of us [there is] a tour of thirty Japanese schoolgirls giggling and pointing. . . . it is hard to imagine what Emily would have made of a crocodile of Japanese girls coming up the parsonage path. Haworth is probably the only parish church in Britain with signs in Japanese" (72). The Japanese tourists wandering around Thornfield Hall in *The Eyre Affair* are an exaggerated representation of these Japanese tourists who come to Britain to visit the Brontë Parsonage Museum and other historic sites. Goldhill speculates that it is "our profound need to understand family dynamics, the search for self-expression and creativity, and the conflicts of gender, that keep us coming back to Haworth" (70). Perhaps the Japanese schoolgirls that Goldhill encountered came to Haworth for these reasons. However, a close look at some recent Japanese texts on Victorian Britain reveals that Japanese tourists, especially young women, might be traveling to British heritage attractions (including those with literary associations) for very different purposes.

The heritage industry in Britain explicitly targets Japanese women as potential tourists and consumers who have the time, money, and desire to travel for leisure. Scholars of contemporary Japanese consumer culture have long observed that what is conventionally called the *West* (*seiyō*) in Japan exercises a very strong appeal to Japanese women, an appeal that is often channeled into the consumption of luxury goods from high-end Western European and, to a lesser degree, American brands. Fashion studies scholar Yuniya Kawamura notes that, whereas teenagers in Tokyo are now hailed worldwide for their Japanese street styles, Japanese women in their twenties generally prefer European high fashion from Paris and Milan (31). In fact, in 2003 Louis Vuitton opened its largest store in the world in the Omotesando district of Tokyo, where more than a thousand people queued up to attend the grand opening (Kawamura 31). While Japanese female consumers clearly engage with a variety of Western countries, this chapter and the next focus on the particular appeal that the British heritage industry has for Japanese women who associate Englishness exclusively with the upper classes. In *English Heritage, English Cinema*, Andrew Higson momentarily digresses from his discussion of Anglo-American collaboration in period drama production to mention a trip to the United Kingdom organized by a Japanese travel agency. In conjunction with the release of the film adaptation of *Mrs. Dalloway* in 1997, H.I.S. Japan offered a seven-day package tour that included tours of a country house and some of the locations featured in the film, a flower arrangement demonstration, and afternoon tea at the Ritz. The package tour, marketed as the "English Lady Experience," promised its participants the opportunity "to experience the life of an English lady," to sample "the atmosphere of the good old England where *Mrs. Dalloway* is set," and to see "the traditional lifestyle, the noble culture, and a Victorian town" (qtd. in Higson 61). Evidently, the travel agency that devised this package tour, as well as the film studio that made the movie, have completely misunderstood Woolf's novel. The package tour evokes an idealized image of Britain and its culture of aristocratic Englishness, which the travel agency markets specifically to Japanese women.

This chapter explores Japanese women's engagements with the British heritage industry in the twenty-first century by reading two recent Japanese texts that are concerned with Victoriana, and which are targeted at young Japanese female readers. In 2003, the publisher of *Emma*, a popular manga series about a maid-of-all-work in Victorian Britain, published an accompanying guidebook to help readers better understand the manga's historical setting. The original manga series, which revolves around a forbidden romance between its domestic servant protagonist and a middle-class gentleman, contains many of the tropes and conventions of *shōjo* manga, a genre of comics in Japan that is predominantly targeted at young unmarried women. The guidebook, aptly called the *Emma Victorian Guide* [*Ema Vikutorian gaido*], seeks to provide its Japanese female readers with an accessible introduction to places and practices in nineteenth-century Britain, accompanied with beautiful illustrations of characters and scenes from the manga. In 2010, a Japanese publishing company called Takarajimasha published a *mook* (*mukku*, short for "magazine-book") on the Harrods department store in Knightsbridge, London. The mook, which is part product catalog and part lifestyle magazine, showcases the store's long history since its establishment in 1849. What these texts have in common, besides their interest in Victorian Britain, is the link that they draw between young Japanese women and the British heritage industry.

Reading these Japanese *heritage texts* reveals that the Japanese cultural industries work together with the British heritage industry to persuade Japanese female consumers that Japan continually lags behind the West, and especially Britain, in acquiring what might be called *aristocratic* cultural capital. In other words, the Japanese cultural industries are complicit in promoting what Harry Harootunian has theorized as a stadial understanding of world history, one in which Japan and other "late-developing" nations are always struggling to keep up with more "advanced" developments in the West.[1] While Japan had come into contact with multiple Western powers in the second half of the nineteenth century, the Victorian setting of the *Emma Victorian Guide* and the Harrods catalog prompts the reader to consider how the sense of belatedness expressed in these two texts might be shaped by the country's encounter with informal British imperialism in particular. With the forced opening of Japan's ports in 1859, British merchants began to introduce foreign goods and the cultural practices associated with these goods to Japanese consumers. On the other hand, Japanese officials and students traveled to Britain to learn from British civilization at its source. After the fall of the shogunate in 1868, the new Meiji state further intensified these efforts to learn from the West by embarking on an ambitious program of self-imposed Westernization. This history has given rise to a long-standing aspiration or yearning (called *akogare* in Japanese) to catch up with Great Britain and adopt its aristocratic tastes, manners, and social rituals. These aristocratic customs have since crystallized into a nostalgic vision of an English past that is paradoxically projected into the future—according to this stadial model of world history—as a universal ideal for the Japanese people, and especially young Japanese women, to emulate. The implicit whiteness of this vision, however, effectively limits young Japanese women to a mode of emulation that is not based on race or kinship, and which has historically been made readily available to them; that is, emulation through practices of consumption. The Japanese manga and magazine publishing industry in the early twenty-first century not only reaffirms these sentiments, but also exploits them to its own advantage, by channeling young Japanese women's desire for aristocratic cultural capital into the buying of both British heritage commodities and the Japanese heritage texts that promote these commodities. To put it another way, the Japanese publishing industry draws on the allure of British heritage to sell its manga and magazines, while facilitating the British heritage industry's expansion into the Japanese market. This situation harks back to the forced opening of Japan to Western trade in the second half of the nineteenth century, but this time the Japanese market is opened up to British products through entrepreneurial collaboration rather than gunboat diplomacy and unequal treaties. Whereas Britain in the nineteenth century exported manufactured goods and machinery to Japan, Britain in the twenty-first century exports the image of Victorian Britain to a cosmopolitan audience of young Japanese female tourists and shoppers. By helping to sell this image of Victorian Britain and its association with elite forms of cultural capital, the Japanese publishing industry feeds into the British heritage industry, thereby enriching the British economy long after the heyday of British imperialism in the nineteenth century. Whereas Japan then exported silk, lacquerware, fans, and other decorative objects to *Japonisme* enthusiasts in Britain and Europe, Japan today sends Japanese women to Britain on "English Lady" package tours where, in their pursuit of an unreachable ideal of English aristocratic culture, they supply foreign capital in visiting and shopping at heritage attractions such as Harrods.

Japanese Tourists in Harrods: Acquiring Cultural Capital

In the *Emma Victorian Guide* and the Harrods catalog, the Harrods department store appears as an icon of aristocratic Englishness, and as a major heritage attraction associated with the Victorian period. Historically, Harrods and the West End had emerged in the mid to late nineteenth and early twentieth centuries as shopping spaces catering predominantly to middle-class women, rather than the aristocracy. Nonetheless, the neighborhood became known as London's premier shopping district partly because of its older connections with the elite classes (Rappaport, *Shopping for Pleasure* 3–4, 8–9). Members of the royal family, the aristocracy, and the landed gentry had made the West End their home since the sixteenth and seventeenth centuries and had long practiced highly public forms of aristocratic consumption and self-display in the neighborhood (Rappaport, *Shopping for Pleasure* 8–9). The two Japanese texts draw on these historical associations of the West End to encourage Japanese female consumers to emulate the aristocracy and "become an English Lady" through shopping, in much the same way that British middle-class women did in the nineteenth century.

For those readers who are not familiar with Harrods's history, the *Emma Victorian Guide* explicitly locates Harrods's origins in Victorian Britain. Furthermore, the guidebook associates visiting Harrods with acquiring a particular form of cultural capital that is coded as aristocratic and English. In the section on shopping places and practices in nineteenth-century Britain, a character from the *Emma* manga series named Vivian Jones describes the nineteenth-century Harrods to the twenty-first-century reader. Vivian is the daughter of a nouveau riche merchant family that wants to enter the ranks of the nobility. Seen in the light of her family's attempts to join the aristocracy, Vivian's longing to shop at "the yearned-for Harrods" (*akogare no Harozzu*) (69) establishes Harrods not only as Victorian heritage, but also as the place to go to if one wanted to adopt the ways of the aristocracy in both the nineteenth and twenty-first centuries. However, informed by a scrupulous commitment to historical accuracy, the guidebook, through the voice of Vivian, tells the reader that Harrods is "slightly crass" (*sukoshi hin ga nai*) (69) because it puts price tags on its goods and sometimes holds bargain sales.

The Harrods catalog recuperates Harrods from this accusation of being "slightly crass" by representing the department store as a mecca of aristocratic Englishness to which the young Japanese woman should make her pilgrimage in order to "become an English Lady." The question of *taste* lies at the center of the catalog's portrayal of Harrods. Taste, as Bourdieu explains in *Distinction*, refers to specific sets of knowledge and skills that would enable one to consume certain kinds of commodities in the "correct" manner without appearing vulgar or ignorant. The Harrods catalog depicts the luxury goods sold in the department store as art objects that require the consumer to possess a particular type of taste that Bourdieu calls "the aesthetic disposition." This kind of taste, according to Bourdieu, encourages the consumer to prioritize the commodity's ability to please the senses over the commodity's practical function (3, 42). Those who adopt such an aestheticist attitude towards commodity consumption constitute a so-called cultural nobility, which, Bourdieu contends, has the potential to translate its cultural capital into social power, thereby distinguishing itself from the lower classes in the society it inhabits (22–26). The Harrods catalog appeals to its reader to acquire this aesthetic form of taste and thereby join the ranks of the cultural nobility. Harrods products, the catalog implies, are not simply very expensive commodities that the buyer can use to demonstrate how wealthy she is. The catalog repeats, almost ad nauseam, that Harrods products are "elegant" (*yūga*), "refined" (*jōhin*), "of high standing" (*kōkyū*), even "noble" (*nōburu*). The catalog encourages young Japanese women to emulate the aesthetic tastes of the English nobility by traveling to Harrods in London, purchasing its elegant and refined products, and immersing themselves on the whole in an "elegant shopping experience" (*yūga na shoppingu*) (4). The catalog thereby promotes heritage tourism to, and tourist spending in, Britain. The reader's introduction to Harrods begins with a virtual tour of the department store, with a Japanese model named KIKI-san standing in place of the young Japanese female reader whom the text addresses. Over an eleven-page photo spread, the reader follows KIKI-san as she walks around the store. The tour ends at the gift shop, which the catalog recommends as a must-visit destination for international tourists looking for elegant and refined souvenirs. This virtual tour seeks to inspire the intended Japanese female reader to follow KIKI-san's example and travel to Harrods to eat, drink, and shop like an "English Lady." It encourages young Japanese women to consume not only Harrods products, but also the Harrods department store itself as a heritage tourist destination that epitomizes an idealized English aristocratic lifestyle (figure 3.1).

Figure 3.1. The front cover of the Harrods catalog. *Source:* Reproduced with permission from TAKARAJIMASHA, Inc. 『Harrods』(宝島社) *Harozzu to Eikoku ryū jōshitsu sutairu* [*Harrods and Fine English Style*]. Takarajimasha, 2010.

Japanese Travelers in Victorian Britain: Learning Good Manners

Japanese people have in fact been traveling to Britain to emulate English aristocratic tastes and customs since the mid-nineteenth century. The Harrods catalog builds on a long-standing practice of Japanese travel to Britain that can be traced back to the last years of the Tokugawa shogunate and the early Meiji period. In 1862, the shogunate official Takenouchi Yasunori led a delegation to Britain and other Western countries to negotiate delaying the opening of the treaty ports of Hyōgo and Niigata and the port cities of Osaka and Edo (Tokyo). In 1863, five samurai from Chōshū escaped illegally to Britain to study at University College in London (Cobbing 24). Two years later, the Satsuma domain secretly sent nineteen samurai to study in Britain (Cobbing 24). Many of these early Japanese travelers became leaders of the new Meiji regime after the shogunate was overthrown in 1868. The Meiji state sent even more Japanese students to Britain in the 1870s as part of its reforms to "civilize" and "enlighten" Japan, as the famous slogan *bunmei kaika* ("civilization and enlightenment") put it at the time. By the late 1870s, Japanese students made up the largest Asian community in London (Cobbing 89, 110). Like many of the early Meiji reforms, this outflow of Japanese students to Britain and other Western countries was driven by the ambitious state-led program of "learning from the West," in which Japan sought to transform itself into the equal of the Euro-American imperial powers within a short space of time. Although Meiji Japan did not have a special relationship with any single Western power, the governing elite looked up to British cultural forms and practices in particular for their aristocratic connotations. This historical pursuit of aristocratic Englishness has engendered a deep-seated aspiration to catch up with this idealized vision of Britain, an aspiration which the Harrods catalog capitalizes on in order to market the Harrods brand to young Japanese female consumers.

Although most of the Japanese travelers in the 1860s and 1870s were not tourists on holiday, they acquired aristocratic cultural capital by traveling to Britain, in much the same way that the reader of the Harrods catalog is encouraged to do. These nineteenth-century travelers acquired cultural capital mostly as a by-product of their visits. The majority of these travelers went to Britain to study practical subjects related to government and industry. Along the way, they adopted aristocratic manners and tastes as a means to achieve the commercial and military power that they admired in Britain and its empire. As historians such as Olive Checkland and Andrew Cobbing have observed, early Japanese visitors to Britain felt embarrassed at their Japanese attire, and they came to the conclusion that, if Japan was to become "modern," the Japanese people would have to learn how to dress in Western clothes (Checkland, *Japan and Britain* 3). These travelers in the 1860s and 1870s kept diaries, which reveal how the travelers felt pressured to adopt British styles of dress on board the British ships they sailed in, at ports of call under British rule, and in Britain itself (Cobbing

82–85). The British exerted such social pressure on Japanese travelers even as late as 1913, when a Keio University professor of English literature called A. Kawabata wore a *yukata* on board a ship sailing to Singapore en route to Britain. In his diary, written in English and published as *A Hermit Turned Loose* in 1914, Kawabata describes how he "read in their [English passengers'] countenances their disapproval of this bold protestation by the smallest minority, and at once remembered the English idea of uniformity with majority" (51). Kawabata foregoes his *yukata* for "the air-tight European dress which was devised for colder climes of Europe [sic]" (51). Despite "fe[eling] constrained in [his] European suit," he feels "easy in [his] heart in company [sic] of those exacting English people" and congratulates himself on his "anglification" (51). Kawabata's capitulation, as well as that of earlier Japanese travelers in the mid-nineteenth century, suggests that these Japanese travelers were aware that, in order for them to be accepted into British society and for Japan to be recognized as Britain's equal, they had to acquire not only practical knowledge, but also English aristocratic manners and tastes. Meiji Japan thus saw a proliferation of etiquette guidebooks, beginning with Fukuzawa Yukichi and Katayama Junnosuke's *Seiyōishokujū* [*A Guide to Western Food and Attire*] in 1867.[2]

Much like the model Japanese tourist projected in the Harrods catalog, nineteenth-century Japanese travelers sought to learn English aristocratic manners, customs, and aesthetic sensibilities not only by reading guidebooks, but also by visiting heritage attractions in Britain. On the one hand, these Japanese travelers gained practical knowledge of government and industry by visiting new and "progressive" developments such as coal mines, factories, railways, the Bank of England, law courts, schools, and so on.[3] On the other hand, when it came to obtaining cultural knowledge, they turned to places where the aristocratic past was being preserved by the nascent heritage industry in Britain. The sons of elite families went to the ancient universities of Oxford and Cambridge "to study the training and character of the English gentleman," as the meeting notes of the Japanese club at Cambridge put it (qtd. in Checkland, *Britain's Encounter* 136). This was so that they would know how to interact with the British ruling class when they graduated and took up high-ranking posts in the Japanese government and diplomatic service (Checkland, *Britain's Encounter* 134–36). Japanese women too traveled to historic places in Britain to learn the ways of the aristocracy. Nabeshima Taneko, wife of the last feudal lord of Hizen, followed her husband to Oxford where, as Andrew Cobbing describes it, she "devoted her time abroad to learning the social graces of an English lady" (122). She also studied art as part of her efforts to cultivate all the "accomplishments" expected of aristocratic ladies in nineteenth-century Britain (Cobbing 136). Taneko's eldest daughter later became one of the few Japanese women who knew how to dance at the Western-style balls held by the Japanese government in the 1880s (Cobbing 127). Kawabata too made a trip to Oxford in 1913, writing in a letter that "[s]treet buses drawn by horses, 'New College' five hundred years old, were deeply interesting to see at the heart of a civilized country" (Kawabata 226). For these Japanese travelers to Britain in the nineteenth and early twentieth centuries, "civilization" was clearly not limited to the newest advancements. It included forms of aristocratic cultural knowledge such as good manners, ballroom dancing, and art creation and appreciation, handed down from the past and embodied in hoary historic places.

Driven by the desire to catch up with the West, Japanese travelers to Britain in the long nineteenth century threw themselves into an intensive process of self-education. The Harrods catalog similarly promotes autodidactic learning. Not only does it encourage its readers to learn how to behave like an "English Lady" by visiting the Harrods department store, but it also teaches these forms of cultural know-how, while intertwining its advice with the strategic marketing of items from the Harrods brand. The catalog thereby reassures its Japanese readers that even if they are unable to travel to Britain, they can still acquire English aristocratic cultural capital simply by learning from the editorial content in the catalog and buying the Harrods products that it recommends. In this way, the catalog draws on the historical project of "learning from the West" to serve the present-day interests of both Harrods and the publishing company behind the catalog. The Harrods catalog appropriates and amplifies the already existing *akogare* ("aspiration" or "yearning") for Englishness to sell not only Harrods products, but also "educational" publications like itself, which mediate between Western luxury goods and Japanese female consumers. In playing this mediating role, the catalog draws on the widespread understanding in Japan that the department store is an "acknowledged exper[t]" that teaches Japanese consumers about Western goods and the social practices that accompany these goods (Creighton 44).[4] Japanese department stores such as Mitsukoshi, Takashimaya, and Daimaru first emerged during the late nineteenth and early twentieth centuries as "display palaces for Western imports, which the Japanese were eager to see and buy" (Creighton 43). Many of these department stores had started out as dry goods stores during the Tokugawa period, but they began to remodel themselves along the lines of Western department stores in the 1890s and especially after 1900.[5] These new Western-style department stores played a pivotal role in introducing Western food and dress to the Japanese by offering instruction in cooking, the use of cutlery, and table setting; and by hiring sales assistants to teach customers how to wear Western garments (Creighton 46, 48). Most significantly, they sought to help their customers develop the ability to appreciate Western-style art (*yōga*). In 1907, the Meiji state launched the Monbusho Bijutsu Tenrankai, an annual art exhibition designed to "cultivate a refined artistic sensibility in the viewing public," and to thereby produce appropriately "cultured" citizens for the nascent Japanese nation-state (Oh 351). Department stores capitalized on the public interest in art generated by the state's cultural policy, positioning themselves as "leaders of fashion and taste" by holding art exhibitions and cultural events (Francks 114), and by opening new "departments" for selling artworks (Oh 352).[6] Japanese department stores today continue to offer classes on Western cooking, languages, art, and handicrafts, and to hold public exhibitions of Western art (Creighton 50–51). By encouraging its readers to learn more about Western aesthetic tastes, and by alluding to the established role of the department store in facilitating such learning, the Harrods catalog persuades young Japanese women to look to Harrods as an authoritative source of knowledge about English aristocratic culture.

Like a Japanese department store, the catalog teaches the reader how to consume Western luxury goods (Harrods products in this case) in an appropriately tasteful manner. The catalog includes an article entitled "Welcome to English Teatime: How to Relax with Tea in the English Style" ["Eikoku ryū tiitaimu no kutsurogikata"], which promotes Harrods tea blends by outlining the different times in a day when one can enjoy a cup of tea. One can, of course, drink tea whenever one wants to, but the article teaches the reader that there are specific times in a day when it is appropriate to have English tea (called *kōcha* in Japanese). These specific times for consuming tea constitute what the article calls "a tradition of English-style tea-time" (*dentō teki na Eikoku ryū tiitaimu*) (24). This "tradition," the article implies, is a form of intangible cultural heritage that the reader can learn to adopt by drinking tea at these specific times, and by drinking the specific Harrods tea blends that the article recommends. The article ends with a detailed, step-by-step guide that teaches the reader "how to make delicious tea, Harrods-style" (*Harozzu ryū, oishii kōcha no irekata*). The *Emma Victorian Guide* similarly teaches its readers how to consume Western luxury goods in the "correct" manner, but it does not intertwine its educational function with the promotion of particular products from particular brands. Nonetheless, like the Harrods catalog, it suggests that

Japanese Tourists in Victorian Britain

the art of making English tea is a form of English cultural heritage that Japanese women should learn in order to "become an English Lady." The guidebook features a lesson on "how to make perfect tea" (*kanpeki na kōcha no irekata*), which looks strikingly like the illustrated guide in the Harrods catalog (figure 3.2). This "educating" of the Japanese female consumer in

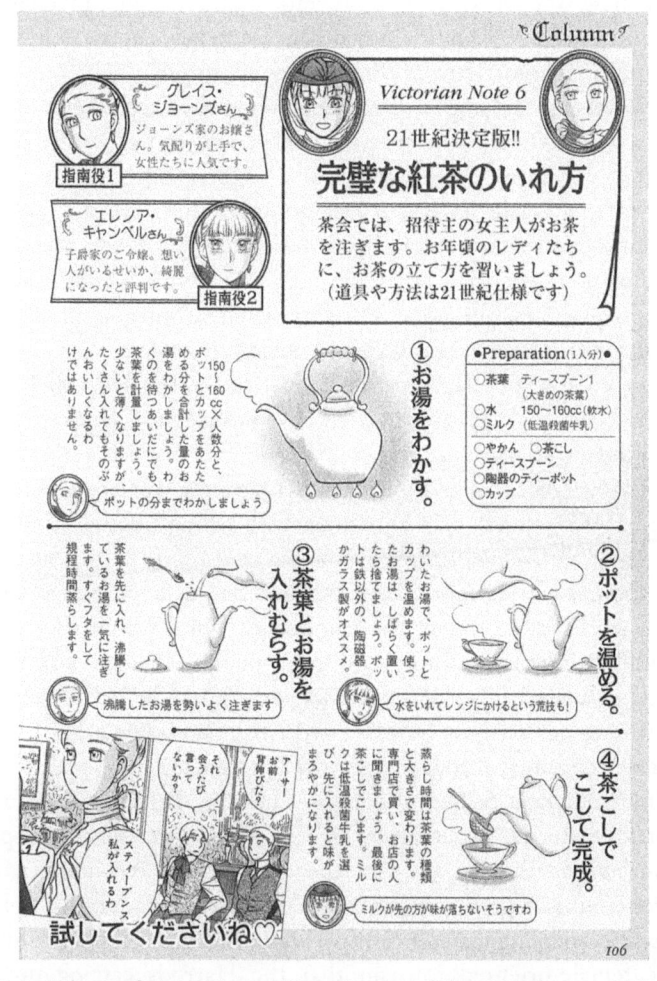

Figure 3.2. "The Definitive Twenty-First Century Edition!! How to Make Perfect Tea" ["21 seiki kettei ban!! Kanpeki na kōcha no irekata"]: Two young female characters from the *Emma* manga series teach the reader how to make the perfect cup of tea. The narrator refers to the two characters as "ladies" (*redi tachi*) (106). Source: Reproduced with permission from Kadokawa Corporation. *Emma Victorian Guide* ©Kaoru Mori 2003 ©Rico Murakami 2003 First published in Japan in 2003 by KADOKAWA CORPORATION, Tokyo.

effect channels her desire for aristocratic Englishness into purchasing two kinds of commodities: British luxury goods (such as Harrods tea) and the Japanese cultural commodities that teach her how to consume these luxury goods (such as the Harrods catalog and the *Emma Victorian Guide*). Buying both kinds of commodities, the two texts imply, will provide the young Japanese woman with the aristocratic cultural capital that she needs in order to distinguish herself from others (especially Japanese men), and to enter the privileged realm of "international" society.

In addressing this imperative to acquire cultural capital specifically to young Japanese women, the *Emma Victorian Guide* and especially the Harrods catalog perpetuate a much wider and ongoing discourse on Japanese women's "internationalism." Karen Kelsky argues that, with the aid of the media, young Japanese women in the 1980s and 1990s began to assert that they were more adept than Japanese men at learning Western languages and cultural practices, and were therefore better at integrating themselves into international (read: white Western) society (Kelsky 2, 123–24). Mass media representations of Japanese women in the early twenty-first century continue to claim that Japanese women have greater proficiency in English; are comfortable with traveling and studying abroad; and have cosmopolitan tastes (Bardsley 115). In the same way that Japanese women writers in the 1980s and 1990s wrote books on Britain with telling titles such as *Britain the Rich, Japan the Nouveau Riche* [*Yutori no kuni Igirisu to narikin no kuni Nippon*], the *Emma Victorian Guide* and the Harrods catalog urge Japanese women in particular to master the manners of white Western society, and thereby fulfil their potential for upward social mobility (Kelsky 124). Whereas upper-class Japanese women in the 1870s and 1880s adopted Western dress and etiquette to demonstrate how civilized Japan had become, the ideal Japanese female consumer of today endeavors to assimilate into idealized forms of Western aristocratic culture to empower herself.[7] The Harrods catalog in particular plays up the connotations of female empowerment by depicting the young Japanese woman as an independent traveler and shopper. KIKI-san ambles around Harrods on her own, talking to sales assistants, selecting souvenirs, and enjoying tea and cakes, without being accompanied by men.

The female-oriented tourism that the Harrods catalog promotes undoubtedly derives some of its impetus from developments in domestic tourism in Japan, especially the "Discover Japan" campaign of the 1970s and the more recent *rekijo* ("history fangirl") phenomenon. From 1970 to 1984, Japan National Railway conducted a hugely successful advertising campaign known as "Discover Japan," which encouraged young Japanese women to embark on solitary travel to relatively obscure places around Japan as a means of "discovering" both authentic Japanese-ness and their own sense of self (Ivy 39–41). In 2009, the Japanese mass media coined the term *rekijo* to refer to young Japanese women who are fans of historical personages portrayed in TV dramas, manga, anime, and other media narratives (Sugawa-Shimada 38). These women have been getting media attention in recent years because they often visit heritage attractions in Japan associated with their favorite historical figures (Sugawa-Shimada 39–40).[8] The Harrods catalog's promotion of outbound tourism certainly draws on these preexisting representations of young Japanese female tourists. However, the motivations for tourism in the Harrods catalog differ significantly from those championed in the "Discover Japan" campaign and *rekijo* heritage tourism. Unlike the *rekijo*, the figure of the Japanese female tourist in the Harrods catalog does not seek, as Sugawa-Shimada has argued, to make a personal spiritual connection with a historical figure (50–51). Neither does she travel in order to discover the "true" Japan in the remnants of its premodern past (Ivy 34). Compelled by the desire to catch up with the "cultured" West, this Japanese female traveler has more in common with the archetype of the cosmopolitan Japanese woman that has dominated the discourse on "internationalization" (*kokusaika*) in Japan since the 1980s. The Harrods catalog implies that young Japanese women, once equipped with the cultural capital that comes with the purchase of Harrods products, can join the ranks of the cosmopolitan elite and gain their independence from Japanese men.

The *Emma Victorian Guide* similarly suggests that, if the young Japanese woman wishes to be part of the cosmopolitan elite, she must be well-versed in the high culture of English literature. The guidebook's Further Readings list surprisingly recommends only literary works instead of books on the history of nineteenth-century Britain, even though the guidebook is designed to help readers understand the historical context in which the *Emma* manga series is set. Almost all the works recommended are canonical works of English literature (specifically novels) written between the early nineteenth century and the mid-twentieth century. The list includes familiar "Great Books" such as Austen's *Emma* (which incidentally has nothing to do with the manga of the same name), *Jane Eyre*, *Wuthering Heights*, and *Great Expectations*. The prestige of English literature in Japan, like that of other forms of aristocratic Englishness, has its roots in Japan's encounter with informal British imperialism in the second half of the nineteenth century. Like the Harrods catalog, the *Emma Victorian Guide* appropriates the long-standing desire for Englishness in Japan to serve the interests of the

British heritage industry, while promoting itself as an "educational" publication that provides the young Japanese woman with the cultural knowledge to succeed in international society. In the long nineteenth century, British literary works traveled not only to the US and to Britain's colonies, but also to Meiji Japan. The Meiji project of "learning from the West" consisted of, amongst other things, learning about the literatures of the West, including that of Britain. The educated middle classes in Japan came into contact with both "serious" literary works and popular fiction from Britain through rental bookshops (known as *shinshiki kashihon'ya*), which first appeared in Tokyo in the 1880s, and which in fact continued into the Taishō (1912–1926) and early Shōwa (1926–1945) periods.[9] Besides stocking academic texts and contemporary Japanese fiction, Meiji-era *kashihon'ya* provided access to a substantial amount of literary works in the original English language, including works by Shakespeare, Disraeli, Thackeray, Dickens, George Eliot, Captain Marryat, and M. E. Braddon.[10] English literature was also taught as an academic subject at Japanese universities by foreign and foreign-educated professors, including Lafcadio Hearn, who was the chair of English language and literature at the Imperial University of Tokyo from 1896 to 1902. Hearn was succeeded by Natsume Sōseki, who had previously spent two (unhappy) years studying English literature in London, and who would later become one of Japan's most famous novelists. Although the English language proficiency of Japanese university students has declined significantly over the last 130 years, the idea that, in order to ascend the ranks of international society, one should read English literature (or at least know something about it) remains influential. This equation of English literature with aristocratic cultural capital continues to hover over the Japanese publishing industry's investment in the British heritage industry today, as the *Emma Victorian Guide* makes clear.

The *Emma Victorian Guide* supports the heritage industry in Britain by affirming that English literature, unlike Japanese literature or other national literatures, is a universal cultural standard that the upwardly mobile young Japanese woman should familiarize herself with. *Jane Eyre*, according to the guidebook, is a "romantic love story that has been beloved by women around the world for more than a hundred years" (*100 nen ijō mo no aida, sekai jū no josei tachi ni aisarete kita rabu romansu*) (169). Likewise, Austen's *Emma* is an "entertaining novel that transcends time to bring enjoyment to the reader" (*jidai o koete tanoshimasete kureru goraku shōsetsu*) (168). The guidebook thus asserts that these novels have a universal and timeless appeal, which makes them must-read classics even in Japan in the twenty-first century. The notion of the *classic*—as we shall also see in this book's final chapter on Lolita fashion in Singapore—reifies English literature into a global standard of high culture, which young women in Japan and elsewhere are encouraged to acquaint themselves with, so that they may demonstrate their cultural sophistication. English literature's apparent universality, in this context, means more than the literary work's ability to speak to the "human condition" and other eminently relatable experiences. According to the *Emma Victorian Guide*, the Japanese female reader will be perfectly able to sympathize with the characters and situations in Austen's *Emma*, "while *Emma*'s world of dinner parties and balls is a far cry from our world in contemporary Japan" (*bansankai, butōkai, paatii nado, gendai Nihon de ikiru watashi tachi to wa kakehanareta sekai no hanashi de arinagara*) (168). It is significant that the guidebook uses the word *while* (*arinagara*) instead of *but* or *despite*. This implies that the difference between the aristocratic lifestyle depicted in *Emma* and the Japanese female reader's lifestyle in the present is not necessarily an obstacle to the latter's enjoyment of the novel. In fact, it is the very opposite. The guidebook cultivates and capitalizes on the existing idealization of aristocratic Englishness in Japan to reaffirm the canonicity of Austen's novel and of English literature in general. In doing so, it generates interest in historic places in Britain that are associated with well-known writers and literary works, thereby indirectly promoting the attractions of the British heritage industry to a Japanese audience. It is perhaps as much the *Emma Victorian Guide* as "profound" psychological needs that brought Goldhill's Japanese schoolgirls to the Brontë Parsonage Museum, where they might have spent an afternoon learning how to appreciate timeless and universal English literature, while spending their pocket money on *omiyage* ("souvenirs") at the museum gift shop.

Japanese Housekeepers in Thornfield Hall: Managing Other People's Heritage

In promoting British heritage brands and tourist attractions, the Harrods catalog and the *Emma Victorian Guide* effectively take on a "managerial" role in the British heritage economy. As managers of British heritage, these two texts help to (re)produce the paradoxical combination of universalism and particularism that is characteristic of discourses on Englishness. The two texts bring together Greater Britain and Deep England through their emphasis on invisibility and whiteness. Once again, *The Eyre Affair* provides a useful point of entry. At the end of the novel, Mrs. Nakajima and her husband move to the fictional world of *Jane Eyre* permanently and become the housekeepers of Thornfield Hall while Jane and Rochester live in Ferndean Manor: "My husband retired and he and I manage the house these days. None of us is mentioned in the book and Mrs. Rochester aims to keep it that way; much more pleasant than Osaka and certainly more rewarding than the tourist business" (354). While the Rochesters remain the owners of Thornfield, Mr. and Mrs. Nakajima are effectively in charge of running the estate. As *The Eyre Affair* implies, *managing* British heritage on behalf of the British requires Japanese *managers* to erase their presence so that British heritage remains, at least in appearance, white and therefore *authentically* British. Mr. and Mrs. Nakajima take pains to ensure that "[n]one of [them] is mentioned in the book" (354), thereby effacing their presence in the narrative world of *Jane Eyre*. Even when she worked as a tour guide before becoming manager of Thornfield Hall, Mrs. Nakajima kept herself and her clients invisible in the narrative: "We touch nothing and never speak to Miss Eyre" (325). Mrs. Nakajima's discreet housekeeping in *The Eyre Affair* is motivated by the need within the diegesis to avoid "disrupting" the narrative of Brontë's novel, but it also raises the question: Do Japanese heritage texts like the Harrods catalog and the *Emma Victorian Guide* play an invisible managerial role in supporting the British heritage industry, and especially its image of whiteness?

    The Harrods catalog is published by a Japanese publishing company, and it appears to have been the initiative of the Japanese publisher rather than a project commissioned by Harrods. The catalog's virtual tour of Harrods in Knightsbridge features the Archive Room, which, the narrator explains, Harrods opened to the editorial team only on special request. The credit page gives thanks to the staff of Harrods in London and Knightsbridge International, presumably for arranging this special access to the Archive Room and other areas in the store. It therefore seems likely that the Japanese publisher approached Harrods to produce this catalog, rather than the other way around. The Japanese publisher, however, downplays its involvement in marketing the Harrods brand. Like Mrs. Nakajima in *The Eyre Affair*, the Japanese publisher plays the role of the unobtrusive tour guide. It actively shapes how the tourist/reader perceives heritage attractions, while seeming to be merely an outsider who is "given special permission to visit" the heritage properties that belong to someone else (*tokubetsu ni ojama dekimashita*) (12). Harrods in fact no longer *belongs* to the British, as it was sold to the Egyptian-born tycoon Mohammed Al Fayed in 1985 and then sold to the Qatari royal family's investment company in 2010. The catalog does not mention these key changes in Harrods's recent history, thereby effacing not only the Japanese managerial presence, but also the Arab ownership of cultural property in the British heritage industry. It instead foregrounds the long and continuous history of Harrods, tracing its origins to the opening of a small tea shop in the East End in 1834, and to the shop's relocation to its current site in Knightsbridge in 1849. Like the American media corporations discussed in the previous chapter, the Japanese publisher of the Harrods catalog collaborates with the British heritage industry for mutual benefit. However, it does not lay claim to the heritage that it looks after, preferring to adopt a subordinate managerial position behind the scenes.

The Harrods catalog thus makes invisible the Japanese publisher's management of the Harrods brand image. In doing so, the catalog reinforces the appearance of whiteness that the British heritage industry projects. Whiteness in the Harrods catalog has two contradictory meanings. On the one hand, the catalog fuels the myth that Victorian Britain and the heritage that it has left behind are exclusively white. The catalog implies that Japanese consumers, regardless of how much cultural knowledge they learn, will never be able to fully incorporate themselves into this white world of aristocratic Englishness. Yet on the other hand, the catalog also sets up whiteness as invisible, as a "transparent . . . signifier" (Kelsky 145) that transcends race to become a universal culture in which the Japanese can participate. As Kelsky has argued, whiteness functions in the discourse on Japanese women's "internationalism" as "a transparent and free-floating signifier of upward mobility and assimilation in 'world culture'; it is the primary sign of the modern, the universal subject, the 'citizen of the world'" (145). Whiteness in the Harrods catalog similarly signifies an apparently universal aristocratic culture of good manners and taste, which originates from Britain but which transcends race and is accessible to all. In the aforementioned article on "English Teatime," the catalog tells the reader that the "culture of English tea" (*kōcha bunka*) first flourished in Britain in the Victorian period and gradually spread from the aristocracy to the industrial middle class to people from all walks of life in Britain, then to people around the world today (24).[11] Tea drinking, like English literature in the *Emma Victorian Guide*, is thus both British heritage and a universal "style" (*ryū*) (24) that anyone outside of Britain can adopt. The catalog teaches the intended Japanese female reader how to adopt this "style" of drinking tea, and it encourages her to put what she has learned into practice by visiting the Harrods Tea Salon in Nihonbashi, where she "can savor the atmosphere of Britain while remaining in Japan" (*Nihon ni inagara ni shite Eikoku kibun o ajiwaemasu*) (35).[12] In representing the aristocratic Englishness that Harrods embodies as a lifestyle that is not racially or geographically delimited, the catalog implies that the young Japanese female consumer can freely assimilate into this British-yet-universal culture.

Yet the racialized whiteness of this apparently universal culture keeps the Japanese female consumer on the margins, where she struggles to catch up with a heritage fantasy of a Victorian past that is projected into her future, while never fully achieving the aristocratic cultural capital that fantasy emblematizes. The reified image of Victorian Harrods that the catalog presents is one of exclusivity. The world of Harrods welcomes those who not only possess the right kind of taste and buying power, but who also belong to a certain race. The catalog creates the illusion that Harrods, and by implication Victorian Britain and British heritage, constitutes a racially exclusive realm of white people. Apart from the Japanese model KIKI-san, the photographs in the virtual tour of Harrods do not feature anyone who is obviously from an ethnic minority. Japanese consumers, like KIKI-san, can only "visit" (*tazuneru*) (4) this white world, not inhabit it. If they wish to become managers of British heritage properties like Mrs. Nakajima, they must render their presence invisible, so as not to disrupt this illusion of homogenous whiteness. The Harrods catalog thus feeds into the popular imagination of Victorian Britain and its heritage as exclusively white, thereby sustaining the racial fantasy that prompts Thursday's surprise in *The Eyre Affair* on finding Japanese people in the "mid-nineteenth-century England" of *Jane Eyre* (325).

This dual treatment of whiteness in the Harrods catalog reveals that the British heritage industry of the twenty-first century thrives on the perception that British high culture is simultaneously universal and particular; a perception that can be traced back to discourses on Greater Britain and Deep England in the long nineteenth century. In the same way that the aristocratic lifestyle depicted in Austen's *Emma* does not deter the implied reader of the *Emma Victorian Guide*, the racialized particularity of Englishness in the Harrods catalog enhances rather than impedes the projected tourist's/shopper's *akogare* or "yearning" for the Harrods brand and its products. Particularity, in this context, provides the British heritage industry with an attractive aura of exclusivity. Like Mrs. Nakajima in *The Eyre Affair*, the Harrods catalog and the *Emma Victorian Guide* discreetly maintain the British heritage economy by marketing British cultural properties (on behalf of their British owners) to Japanese female consumers. In doing so, they (re)produce both the universalism and the particularism of an idealized aristocratic form of Englishness tied to the consumption of heritage. As invisible managers of British heritage, these texts contribute to creating a new British empire in the twenty-first century, as Britain and many other industrialized nation-states focus increasingly on cultural commodity production and other creative-sector industries. However, the Japanese neo-Victorian narratives in the next chapter present a different aspect of Japanese-British interactions in the global creative economy. While articulating the same sense of *akogare* for aristocratic Englishness, *Lady Victorian* and *Kuroshitsuji* contest the elitist particularity of British high culture by proclaiming that contemporary Japanese popular culture is even more universal than the Arnoldian tradition that the former supposedly embodies.

Chapter Four

Empire of Cool

As rival powers in the global creative economy, Britain and Japan not only collaborate for their mutual benefit, but also compete to attract readers, viewers, and visitors in an increasingly transnational consumer culture. As fandoms cross national borders on a larger scale than before, nation-states now feel the need to engage in *nation branding* or risk losing out on international sales, tourism, and global prestige. Koichi Iwabuchi describes this phenomenon as a global trend towards "brand nationalism"; namely, the branding of media culture as *national culture* for the purpose of enhancing national political and economic interests ("Undoing Inter-National Fandom" 90). Brand nationalism, Iwabuchi observes, is characterized by close collaboration between the state and the cultural industries, with the objective of turning culture into a useful resource for the nation-state: "For states to maximize national interests and beat international competition, culture has come to be regarded as important politically and economically: politically to enhance 'soft power' and 'cultural diplomacy,' and economically for attracting multinational capital and developing service sectors in which creative industries or content businesses play a significant role" ("Undoing Inter-National Fandom" 90).

While the Japanese cultural industries actively support the British heritage industry, they simultaneously position Japanese manga, anime, and other cultural commodities as a proudly popular alternative to the British high-cultural empire and its aristocratic forms of cultural capital. Like the Harrods catalog and the *Emma Victorian Guide*, the neo-Victorian manga series *Lady Victorian* [*Redii Vikutorian*] (1999–2007) and *Kuroshitsuji* [*Black Butler*] (2007–present) articulate a sense of *akogare* or "yearning" for elite forms of cultural knowledge that are inscribed as both *aristocratic* and *English*. At the same time, these manga series participate in the discourse surrounding Cool Japan, as they celebrate the apparently hybrid and therefore universal nature of contemporary Japanese popular culture. In 2002, the Koizumi government launched the Intellectual Property Strategic Program—more commonly known as the Cool Japan campaign—to export the products of Japan's creative industries more effectively. Through their reimaginings of Victorian Britain, *Lady Victorian* and *Kuroshitsuji* reveal that this ongoing project to globalize Japanese pop culture strongly resembles imperialist discourses from the late 1930s and early 1940s, which stressed Japan's purportedly unique ability to hybridize different cultures, both within Asia and between Asia and the West. These discourses had in fact emerged in response to late Victorian attitudes towards Japan that lauded but also patronized the country for its beautiful but ultimately useless aesthetics. By championing Japanese pop culture against the backdrop of an ostensibly Victorian and British narrative world, *Lady Victorian* and *Kuroshitsuji* demonstrate how the contested terrain of Japanese aesthetics in the late nineteenth and early twentieth centuries indirectly contributed to Japanese expansionism in the 1930s and 1940s, which in turn continues to inflect the competition between British heritage and Japanese pop culture in the global creative economy today. Like its imperialist precursor, Cool Japan seeks to distinguish Japan's cultural influence from the *civilizing* function of British cultural production, foregrounding instead the supposedly innate ability of the Japanese to hybridize the cultures of the world into a syncretic and democratic popular culture. This hybrid culture, the two manga series assert, stands in contrast to the alleged elitism of English aristocratic cultural capital, thereby making contemporary Japanese pop culture even more universal than British high culture and its ideology of Englishness. *Lady Victorian* and *Kuroshitsuji* in effect present a vision (albeit an overly ambitious one) of a Japanese cultural empire that stakes its claim to global hegemony by subverting the terms of British universalism.

Emporium of Luxury, Empire of Cool

As works of historical fiction set during Queen Victoria's reign, *Lady Victorian* and *Kuroshitsuji* trade in the various stereotypes that make up Victorian Britain in the global collective imagination. The pages of the two manga series abound with references to country houses, lords and ladies, maids and butlers, afternoon tea, and the elaborate fashions of the period. In general, the narrative worlds of *Lady Victorian* and *Kuroshitsuji* are replete with *things*. Like the goods on display in the Harrods catalog, the abundant objects in *Lady Victorian* and *Kuroshitsuji* embody a purportedly English form of aristocratic cultural capital, which the young Japanese female reader apparently lacks and therefore needs to acquire. The very first page of *Lady Victorian*, for instance, assails the reader's gaze with material objects that vie with the characters for the reader's attention. The illustration depicts the protagonist—a young woman named Bell—wearing a frilly floral dress, shimmery fingerless gloves, and an elaborate headdress with a long, flowing veil. Bell leans her elbows on floral cushions. Behind her is a mirror with an intricately carved frame, but instead of reflecting the back of Bell's head, the mirror shows Bell's future husband Noel, holding a top hat in his right hand and a walking stick in his left. Gauzy curtains frame both Bell in the foreground and Noel's image in the mirror. *Kuroshitsuji* is similarly rich in detail and often depicts its characters surrounded by clothes, accessories, furniture, food and drink, carriages, and other objects that make up the paraphernalia of its Victorian narrative world.

Lady Victorian's Bell is actually an impoverished governess, and in subsequent pages of the manga she appears in much plainer outfits. Bell functions as the main point of identification for the manga's projected young female reader. It is through Bell that the manga encourages the young Japanese female reader to acquire the English aristocratic cultural capital that will enable her to consume luxury goods without appearing vulgar or ignorant. Although Bell's friendship with the aristocratic Lady Ethel grants her access to luxury goods, she is extremely clumsy when handling these goods. In the second volume of the manga, Bell's hair gets caught in an elaborately carved candelabra perched precariously on an equally elaborately carved stand. When Bell moves her head, she accidentally pulls the candelabra off the stand, causing both items of furniture to topple onto her. In a later scene, when dancing at a ball Bell trips over the evening dress that Lady Ethel has given her to wear. In contrast, Bell's friend and idol Lady Ethel consumes luxury goods with effortless elegance. Throughout the manga series, the lower middle-class Bell strives to become a "lady" (*redii*) like Lady Ethel (figure 4.1). By contrasting Bell's painfully gauche ineptitude with Lady Ethel's refined tastes and manners, *Lady Victorian* demonstrates that "becoming an English Lady" entails learning how to consume luxury commodities correctly. In this way, *Lady Victorian* echoes the Harrods catalog and the *Emma Victorian Guide* in encouraging the young Japanese female consumer to attain the English aristocratic cultural capital that she apparently lacks.

Figure 4.1. Bell gazes upon Lady Ethel with admiration (2: 22–23). *Source:* Reproduced with permission from Akita Publishing Co., Ltd. Moto, Naoko. *Lady Victorian* [*Redii Vikutorian*]. 20 vols. Akita Shoten, 1999–2007.

Kuroshitsuji similarly translates class differences in cultural capital into an international hierarchy, where middle-class Japan continually lags behind aristocratic Britain in acquiring cultural capital. Many of the characters in *Kuroshitsuji* are national stereotypes, and their interactions with one another allegorize the manga's vision of international relations. When investigating a series of murders involving Anglo-Indian returnees, the aristocratic protagonist Count Ciel Phantomhive encounters a nouveau riche businessman called Harold West. The class-based opposition between the two characters takes on national overtones when Ciel describes Harold as a *burando zuki* ("brand-lover"). The *burando zuki* is a familiar Japanese stereotype, and it refers to a person who obsessively buys products from famous luxury brands, usually with the intention to show off. When the furniture in his house becomes collateral damage in a fight, Harold makes it a point to name the brand of each household item as it is smashed to pieces. By poking fun at Harold for showing off his branded possessions even as they are being destroyed, the manga satirizes those who buy luxury goods purely for the purpose of flaunting their wealth. Despite his name, Harold West represents middle-class Japan and its alleged inability to consume luxury goods in an appropriately tasteful manner. In contrast, Ciel's penchant for English tea and delicate pastries signifies the English aristocratic taste and refinement that Japan lacks. The first episode of the manga opens with a stereotypically English scenario where Ciel begins his day with a cup of tea. Ciel is able to identify the type of tea that his butler Sebastian serves him simply by smelling its fragrance. Sebastian discreetly informs Ciel that the porcelain tea service is from Wedgewood, but Ciel makes no response. Ciel evidently has the specialized knowledge of a connoisseur who prioritizes the aesthetic qualities of the tea and the tea service over their brand names. This contrast between Ciel and Harold West implies that contemporary Japan, like its upstart counterpart in the manga, has only acquired the economic means to purchase luxury goods, while ultimately lacking the crucial cultural knowledge of the *real* West to genuinely appreciate these luxury goods.

Like the Harrods catalog and the *Emma Victorian Guide*, *Kuroshitsuji* and *Lady Victorian* present an idealized image of Britain, then and now, as an emporium of luxury goods that require the young Japanese female consumer to improve her tastes and aesthetic sensibilities, so that she too may consume these goods in the appropriate manner and thereby circulate within the ranks of the cultural nobility (Bourdieu 22). However, *Kuroshitsuji* and *Lady Victorian* counter their own exhortations to "become an English Lady" by asserting that contemporary Japan possesses a different kind of cultural capital, one that would enable the nation to (re)establish its hegemony in Asia and the world in the twenty-first century. The two manga series imply that, while the young Japanese female consumer has to work towards attaining the cultural capital necessary for consuming luxury goods, the Japanese people as a whole already possess the ability to synthesize Western and Asian cultures to produce popular culture commodities that have universal appeal. In this way, *Kuroshitsuji* and *Lady Victorian* articulate a vision of Anglo-Japanese competition, and not simply collaboration, in the global creative economy. Echoing the Cool Japan campaign and its ideological precursors, *Kuroshitsuji* and *Lady Victorian* envision Japanese pop culture challenging the British high-cultural empire in attracting fans and followers in Asia and around the world.

Western discourses on Japan, from *Japonisme* and Aestheticism in the nineteenth century to Roland Barthes in the twentieth, have persistently portrayed Japan as an "Empire of Signs," a land where abstractions and simulacra take the place of a referential reality. *Kuroshitsuji*, however, promotes a vision of Japan as an "Empire of Cool" by juxtaposing the various characters that represent different nations as they seek to outdo one another in a curry-cooking competition. The nouveau riche businessman Harold West turns out to be the mastermind behind a spate of murders involving Anglo-Indians, such as himself, who have returned to Britain to set up curry restaurants. In a bid to win the curry contest and thereby secure the Queen's patronage, Harold resorts to literally killing off the competition. Nevertheless, a handful of contestants remain. Three of the competitors, however, are eliminated for using bland store-bought curry powder. Curry powder, the manga takes pains to explain, is a nineteenth-century Anglo-Indian invention that is not used in "authentic" Indian cuisine. According to Colin Spencer's *British Food: An Extraordinary Thousand Years of History*, imperial Britain created its own version of Indian curry because it "felt itself to be far superior to any other nation in the world, and that like Ancient Rome before it, could steal with impunity any idea or culture it thought desirable" (280–81). The elimination of the three British contestants in *Kuroshitsuji*, however, implies that imperial Britain fails at hybridizing its own culture with Indian culture. On the other hand, Harold's chef, an Indian manservant named Agni, fails to even attempt to hybridize. Agni cooks a delicious and "authentic curry made by a native Indian" (*Indojin no tsukuru honkaku karii*), but he does not win the prize (5: 75). India, the manga implies, is too traditional and therefore incapable of even attempting cultural hybridization, and this is consistent with the manga's Orientalist representation of the Indian characters as backward and superstitious. Only Ciel's "Japanese" butler Sebastian successfully hybridizes Indian and British cultural forms to "invent" what is now known in Japan as the curry bun (*karee pan*) (figure 4.2). As a devil (*akuma*) masquerading as Ciel's butler, Sebastian technically does not have a nationality. However, he is marked as Japanese early in the manga when he helps Ciel organize an impressive Japanese-themed dinner party complete with green tea and *gyūdon* (beef rice bowl). Sebastian's curry bun is another one of his "Japanese" innovations. A bakery in Tokyo called Cattlea claims to have invented the curry bun in 1927 as a type of Japanese-style Western cuisine (*yōshoku*), and the bakery is still selling curry buns today.[1] Sebastian's curry bun wins the competition precisely for not being authentic. When making the curry paste for the bun, Sebastian adds chocolate to the curry mixture. While curry and chocolate may not sound compatible, the manga represents Sebastian's take on Indian curry as a felicitous mixing of British culture and Indian

Figure 4.2. Sebastian "invents" the curry bun or *karee pan*, a kind of doughnut filled with meat, vegetables, and curry paste, rolled in breadcrumbs, and then deep-fried (5: 80–81). *Source:* Reproduced with permission from Square Enix Co., Ltd. Toboso, Yana. *Kuroshitsuji* [*Black Butler*]. 33 vols. Square Enix, 2007–present.

culture. When Agni's former Indian employer Prince Sōma takes a sip of Sebastian's curry, he has an out-of-body experience where he is transported to a European-style ballroom. There, he sees an Indian man in a turban waltzing with a white woman in evening dress. There is also a white man playing a violin, accompanied by an Indian man beating the drums. This metaphor of Britons and Indians overcoming their differences to dance and make music together implies that Sebastian's curry bun successfully blends not only the flavors but also the cultures of Britain and India into a harmonious whole. Only Japan, the manga implies, has this ability to combine different cultures effectively to produce hybrid commodities that can resolve even the most difficult political tensions between colonizer and colonized.

Sebastian's triumph at the curry-cooking competition also implies that the hybrid commodities Japan produces have universal appeal, and thus serve as the source of a new global popular culture. This global popular culture in turn serves as the source of Japan's global economic and cultural power in the twenty-first century. In *Kuroshitsuji*'s worldview, contemporary Japan is exceptionally capable of synthesizing disparate cultures to form popular culture commodities that are not only syncretic but also democratic. Unlike many of the food items featured in *Kuroshitsuji*, Sebastian's curry bun is not a luxury commodity. It does not require the consumer to be wealthy and to have specialized knowledge in order to enjoy it. Queen Victoria awards the prize to Sebastian because his curry bun can be eaten without cutlery, which means that it can be eaten easily by anyone, regardless of age or social status. Rich and poor, young and old—the Queen explains—have "equal access" (*byōdō*) to the curry bun (5: 92). The manga cuts from images of the Queen giving the prize to Sebastian, to images of children in the audience. Some of the children are struggling to eat the complicated curry dish that Agni has cooked, whereas the rest who are eating Sebastian's curry buns have a much easier time eating with their hands. Sebastian's victory thus implies that, although Japan might lack elite forms of cultural capital required to consume luxury goods, it possesses a different kind of cultural knowledge that enables it to produce culturally hybrid commodities that are accessible to everyone, especially children. In his 2005 exhibition *Little Boy: The Arts of Japan's Exploding Subculture*, Japanese pop artist, curator, and cultural commentator Murakami Takashi lamented that the atomic bombings and postwar dependence on the US had made Japan "infantile and impotent," stunted in its growth as a nation and trapped in an endless childhood ("Earth in My Window" 138). "We Japanese," Murakami wrote in the exhibition catalog, "still embody 'Little Boy,' nicknamed, like the atomic bomb itself, after a nasty childhood taunt" ("Earth in My Window" 101). Murakami was ambivalent about this alleged infantilism of the Japanese people, criticizing it on one hand and seeing it as the wellspring of a new *Superflat* Japanese aesthetic on the other.[2] In contrast, *Kuroshitsuji* embraces this charge of infantilism in asserting that contemporary Japanese popular culture is democratic and universal precisely because it is childish. Through Sebastian's victory, the manga reverses the hierarchy implied in the opposition between the "British" Ciel and the "Japanese" Harold West. Japan now becomes the leader in producing hybrid and egalitarian popular culture commodities, with Britain and the rest of Asia falling behind.

Moreover, *Kuroshitsuji* envisions Japan exporting these commodities to the world, thereby achieving global economic and cultural hegemony. The curry-cooking competition is held at the Crystal Palace in conjunction with an imperial exhibition on Indian culture in the British Empire. This fictional exhibition clearly references the Colonial and Indian Exhibition held in South Kensington in 1886.[3] Sebastian's victory in the context of an exhibition celebrating British imperialism suggests that Japan has surpassed Victorian Britain to become the new imperial power of what Queen Victoria in the manga calls the "new century" (*shin seiki*) (5: 92). Sebastian's victory implies that Japan's newfound imperial power is based on the global export of commodities that share the same hybrid and populist sensibility as Sebastian's curry bun. It is not a coincidence that the imperial exhibition at which the curry-cooking competition is held occurs at the same time as an exhibition on world trade at the British Museum. Ciel has received invitations to both events. It is also not a coincidence that, after Sebastian wins the competition, Ciel makes plans to start selling curry buns. Elsewhere in the series, the manga reveals that Ciel owns a toy-making company that produces "Bitter Rabbit" soft toys and anachronistic handheld video game devices. These so-called Victorian toys bear a striking resemblance to the *kawaii* character goods and IT gadgets that Japan produces and exports in the late twentieth and early twenty-first centuries. By associating Sebastian's curry bun with evocations of world trade and contemporary Japanese popular culture products, *Kuroshitsuji* implies that contemporary Japan has supplanted Victorian Britain as the center for producing and disseminating culturally hybrid commodities with global appeal.

Like *Kuroshitsuji*, *Lady Victorian* implies that Japan has a special ability to synthesize different cultures to create pop culture products that speak to a wide audience. *Lady Victorian* ends with Bell and her fiancé Noel building on their successful women's magazine by publishing a groundbreaking new magazine targeted at the *shōjo*, a distinctively Japanese demographic category that encompasses adolescent girls and young unmarried women. This magazine is the symbolic precursor of *shōjo* manga, a genre of comics written predominantly for and by young Japanese women, and of which *Lady Victorian* is itself an example. In invoking the creation of this new magazine, *Lady Victorian* positions Japanese *shōjo* manga as an innovative medium that synthesizes the Victorian periodical with Japanese *shōjo bunka* or girls' culture, thereby mediating between the young Japanese female consumer and the English aristocratic cultural capital that she seeks. Prior to Noel's decision to publish a new magazine for girls, the narrative of *Lady Victorian* had focused on Bell's avid consumption of the *Lady's Magazine*, a fictional nineteenth-century women's magazine published by Noel that features articles about debutante balls, salons, and other aristocratic social practices, as well as serialized romance fiction. As Anna Maria Jones demonstrates in her analysis of *Lady Victorian*, the manga self-reflexively draws parallels between the *Lady's Magazine* and itself, thus making the implied female reader conscious that Bell's reading of the *Lady's Magazine* mirrors her own reading of *shōjo* manga ("Picturing 'Girls Who Read'" 301–03). *Lady Victorian* makes these parallels between Victorian periodicals and *shōjo* manga even more overt at the end of the series, as Noel embarks on his new publishing venture. Noel's decision to move on from publishing a generic women's magazine to a more targeted girls' magazine alludes to the historical development of *shōjo* manga, which evolved in the postwar period partly out of *shōjo* magazines from the early twentieth century that contained serialized fiction and illustrations of adolescent girls, as Deborah Shamoon has shown in her history of the genre. Moreover, the title of Noel's new magazine, the *Girls' Dream*, resembles that of the well-known *shōjo* manga magazine *Hana to yume* [*Flowers and Dreams*].

By drawing these metafictional parallels, *Lady Victorian* implies that *shōjo* manga combines the Victorian practice of serial publication with the needs and desires of adolescent girls and young unmarried women in Japan, who, like Bell, dream of "becoming an English Lady." As Noel puts it, his new magazine will not be a "stuffy" (*katakurushii*) and "boring" (*taikutsu*) etiquette guidebook, but will instead be a magazine that speaks to the "dreams" of its young readers (*yume no aru zasshi*) (19: 103). These dreams include the desire to acquire not only the English aristocratic cultural capital embodied in Bell's idol Lady Ethel, but also, as Jones argues, the "ability to reflect thoughtfully and compassionately on real-life situations" ("Picturing 'Girls Who Read'" 322), an ability that Bell herself develops through the course of the manga's bildungsroman narrative: "Bell, the 'girl reader,' becomes, through her reading—most of all through her ability to be entertained and affected by what (and whom) she reads—the ideal producer of reading material for girls. Girls' reading is reimagined not as a dangerous or frivolous pastime but as cultivating broad-reaching, ethically sound sensibilities" (Jones, "Picturing 'Girls Who Read'" 324). Bell, who will henceforth become a regular contributor to Noel's new *shōjo* magazine, is now in a position to shape the reading practices of other *shōjo*. Contemporary Japanese *shōjo* manga, *Lady Victorian* implies, hybridizes Western culture and Japanese culture to provide girl readers with a popular cultural form that is not only entertaining but also educational. Although the manga does not envisage the *Lady's Magazine* or the *Girls' Dream* circulating outside the national boundaries of their context of production, readers of *Lady Victorian* since the manga's debut in 1999 are likely to know that Japanese *shōjo* manga has a wide following outside of Japan, especially in East and Southeast Asia.

Through their depictions of the curry bun and *shōjo* manga, *Kuroshitsuji* and *Lady Victorian* participate in a particular discourse that became prominent in Japan in the 1990s and 2000s, and that sought to harness globalizing forces for nationalist purposes. Koichi Iwabuchi calls this discourse "trans/nationalist" because it leverages on transnational flows of Japanese popular culture to 1) construct a new national identity for Japan, and 2) enhance the Japanese nation-state's influence over its Asian neighbors (*Recentering Globalization* 52–53). This trans/nationalist discourse first emerged in the context of neo-Asianism in the 1990s, and it later fed into the formulation of Cool Japan in the following decade. According to Iwabuchi, Japanese neo-Asianism saw the spread of Japanese pop culture to other parts of Asia as a sign that global power had shifted from the US to Japan (*Recentering Globalization* 66). Neo-Asianist thinkers argued that, while Japan and its Asian neighbors all had to adapt to Western modernity, Japan had been the most successful at hybridizing Western culture to suit Asian conditions (Iwabuchi, *Recentering Globalization* 67, 69). The Japanese experience of modernization, so the argument went, was thus a model for other Asian countries to emulate (Iwabuchi, *Recentering Globalization* 69). As J-pop music, manga, anime, and video games gained traction in Asia in the 1990s, Japanese neo-Asianists proclaimed that the enthusiasm for Japanese pop culture in the region reflected the "yearning" of other Asian countries for Japan's version of modernity, and that Japan should therefore play a leading role in the region (Iwabuchi, *Recentering Globalization* 66, 69). In the same way that Japan was supposedly yearning to become like Britain, Asia was apparently yearning to become like Japan. These neo-Asianist discourses from the 1990s took on a more global orientation in the early 2000s, with the publication of Douglas McGray's "Japan's Gross National Cool" in *Foreign Policy* in 2002. In this oft-cited article, McGray drew on Joseph Nye's concept of soft power to assert that Japan had emerged from a decade of economic decline as a new cultural superpower (47–48). The Japanese, McGray asserted, possess "the ability to absorb and adapt foreign influences while still retaining an intact cultural core" (52–53). This, for McGray, was the reason why contemporary Japanese pop culture had become so popular not only in Asia, but also in the West. Influenced by such euphoric celebrations of the transnational flow of Japanese pop culture, the Koizumi government launched the Cool Japan campaign in 2002 to give Japan's creative industries an advantage in the global export of cultural commodities. As the name suggests, Cool Japan was also influenced by New Labor's Cool Britannia campaign in the late 1990s, and more generally by the concept of the creative economy that was circulating globally at the time.[4] Since its inauguration in the early 2000s, Cool Japan has become a mainstay of Japanese state policy.

Like McGray and the neo-Asianists, the Cool Japan project promotes what Iwabuchi calls an ideology of "hybridism"; in other words, the pervasive narrative that Japan is innately capable of assimilating foreign (usually Western) influences without changing its national cultural essence (*Recentering Globalization* 53). In principle, anyone can engage in hybridization, but "hybridism," Iwabuchi contends, assumes that the ability to hybridize is an organic and ahistorical aspect of the Japanese national character (*Recentering Globalization* 53–54). While Iwabuchi's critique is directed at the neo-Asianism of the 1990s, the Cool Japan project similarly claims that contemporary Japanese popular culture is the product of the Japanese nation's essentially superior ability to bridge Asian and Western cultures, and that this inherent genius for cultural hybridization justifies Japan's leadership of Asia (Daliot-Bul, "Japan Brand Strategy" 252–53, 259). For instance, in a 2007 promotional video for the *Yōkoso! Japan* tourism campaign, then-Prime Minister Abe Shinzō proudly proclaims that "Japan is ready to become the bridge between Asia and the rest of the world" (qtd. in Daliot-Bul, "Japan Brand Strategy" 259). Like its neo-Asianist precursor, the Cool Japan project makes use of the transnational to rearticulate the national. For Michal Daliot-Bul, Cool Japan is in effect an attempt to construct a new national identity for Japan after more than a decade of economic recession and social malaise ("Japan Brand Strategy" 254, 259–61). While it is designed to help sell the products of Japan's creative industries to overseas markets, Cool Japan ultimately seeks to capitalize on the global export of Japanese pop culture to create a new "cultural image" or "brand" for the nation itself (Daliot-Bul, "Japan Brand Strategy" 249). In championing Japan's success at producing and exporting culturally hybrid commodities, *Kuroshitsuji* and *Lady Victorian* perpetuate Cool Japan's trans/nationalist discourse on Japan's apparently unique aptitude for synthesizing Asian and Western cultures.

Kuroshitsuji in particular reveals that this ideology of hybridism in fact reworks imperialist rhetoric from the early twentieth century on Japan's creation of a cultural and economic empire in Asia. *Kuroshitsuji*'s championing of Japan as the imperial successor of Victorian Britain reveals the hidden connections between Cool Japan, the history of Japanese imperialism, and (as the second section of this chapter will show) the history of Victorian attitudes towards Japanese aesthetics. In his account of Japanese trans/nationalism, Iwabuchi observes that neo-Asianism can be traced back to the first half of the twentieth century, when many Japanese thinkers claimed that Japan was exceptionally adept at assimilating foreign elements, and that this aptitude for assimilation justified Japanese colonial rule in Asia (*Recentering Globalization* 55). These earlier discourses on hybridization, Iwabuchi argues, often emphasized the racially mixed origins of the Japanese people and Japan's long history of importing foreign cultures (*Recentering Globalization* 55). Japanese imperialism, according to these discourses, was therefore not based on racial discrimination, but on the Japanese ability to hybridize different races and their cultures into a harmonious unity (Iwabuchi, *Recentering Globalization* 56). While Iwabuchi is primarily concerned with discourses on the hybrid racial origins of the Japanese and what this meant for Japanese imperialism, contemporary discourses that dealt directly with the Japanese Empire from the late 1930s and early 1940s likewise used the ideology of hybridism to legitimate Japan's expansionist ambitions. The Japanese intellectual and political activist Miki Kiyoshi, and his colleagues in the Kyoto School of Philosophy, were some of the foremost figures in wartime Japan who popularized this vision of Japan as the natural leader of a multiethnic and multicultural empire.

As one of the leading public intellectuals of his time, Miki Kiyoshi (1897–1945) played a central role in promoting the now-familiar narrative of Japan's unique aptitude for cultural hybridization. From around 1932 to 1940, Miki participated actively in a form of quasi-academic journalism, writing numerous articles in various newspapers and journals (Harrington 47–48). In 1938, Miki became the chairperson of the Cultural Problems Research Group in the Shōwa Kenkyūkai [Showa Research Association], a research institute established by Prince (and later three-time prime minister) Konoe Fumimaro to advise him on policymaking (Harrington 52–55). Miki was particularly interested in issues relating to China, especially after the Marco Polo Bridge Incident in 1937, which marked the beginning of Japan's long-drawn-out invasion of China and the start of the Asia-Pacific War (Harrington 48–52). In 1938, Miki delivered a lecture titled "The World-Historical Significance of the China Incident" ["Shina jihen no sekaishiteki igi"], and in the following year, he and his colleagues in the Shōwa Kenkyūkai collectively published what became the manifesto of the research institute: *Principles of Thought for a New Japan* [*Shin Nihon no shisō genri*] (Harrington 55–57). The "world-historical significance of the China Incident," Miki proclaims in this manifesto, "is that it makes the unification of the world possible by actualizing the unification of East Asia" (qtd. in J. Kim 158). Miki goes on to argue that Japan, through its war with

China, has taken on the world-historical mission of unifying East Asia (and later, the world) by disseminating a new universal culture of cooperativism (*kyōdōshugi*) (Harrington 58–60). The result of this unification of East Asia would be the *Tōa Kyōdōtai*, which has been variously translated as "East Asian Cooperative Community" (Harrington 60), "East Asian Cooperative Body" (J. Kim 156), and "East Asian Communal Body" (Harootunian 294). Like many fascist thinkers at the time, Miki envisioned the *Tōa Kyōdōtai* as a regional political and economic bloc that would synthesize, in Hegelian fashion, the divisions between *Gemeinschaft* and *Gesellschaft*, the cultural traditions of the East and the scientific modernity of the West (Harrington 62–63). This amalgamation of old and new, East and West in the *Tōa Kyōdōtai*, was intended to solve all sorts of problems associated with modernity in Japan and Asia, including the instabilities of the capitalist mode of production, the loss of national sovereignty under Western imperialism, and the social alienation caused by Western liberalism, individualism, and rationalism.[5] In Miki's view, Japan is primed to play the leading role in this East Asian Cooperative Body because Japan has historically been successful at synthesizing other cultures:

> . . . what should be observed as Japanese culture's distinctiveness is its inclusiveness. From ancient times Japanese culture has developed by assimilating Chinese and Indian culture, and later Western culture. However, while adopting foreign cultures, it does not impossibly attempt to unify them into set forms. Rather, it was inclusive such that it permitted their coexistence. Belief in both Shinto and Buddhism is for Japanese people not a contradiction, rather they stand side by side. Japanese people do not feel a contradiction in viewing a Japanese painting and a Western painting in one and the same room. In this manner, the breadth and depth of the Japanese mind is located where even things that are objectively incompatible are unified subjectively. It is precisely this mind that is needed in the new Cooperative Body. Among all the nations of East Asia, the distinctiveness of each culture must be brought to life without forcing them into a single form. (qtd. in J. Kim 159)

In contrast to the "blood and soil" nationalism of "Japanism" (*Nipponshugi*), Miki promoted a regionalist conception of Japan's role in world history, thereby aligning himself with the other major strand in wartime Japanese political thought: pan-Asianism. For Miki, the East Asian Cooperative Body is a regional entity that brings together different (ethno-national) cultures to work for the collective good, while maintaining the discreteness of each culture (J. Kim 156–59). This idea that Japan is able to hybridize different cultures without losing its national cultural essence or causing other nations to lose theirs would later become a major refrain in the Japanese state's proclamations of the Greater East Asia Co-Prosperity Sphere from 1940 to the end of the war in 1945.

Although Miki was one of the most vocal intellectuals who championed Japan's leadership in synthesizing the cultures of Asia and the world, he was part of a wider political and philosophical project that sought to define a central role for Japan in world history in terms of the nation's capacity for cultural hybridization. Miki was part of a group of philosophers who had studied under Nishida Kitarō at Kyoto Imperial University, and who would come to be known as the Kyoto School of Philosophy [Kyōto Tetsugakuha]. In November 1941, the Kyoto school organized a symposium called "Japan and the Standpoint of World History" ["Sekaishiteki tachiba to Nihon"] in order to make sense of Japan's involvement in the ongoing Sino-Japanese War. In July the following year, several members of the Kyoto school took part in the "Overcoming the Modern" ["Kindai no chōkoku"] symposium, where they and intellectuals of other affiliations discussed the meaning of modernity in the light of Japan's December 1941 attack on Pearl Harbor (Goto-Jones 118–19). In both of these symposia, the Kyoto school delegates rejected the existing Eurocentric teleological model of world history and argued that each epoch of world history was actually a synthesis of the old international order and the new, rather than a wholesale replacement of the former by the latter (Goto-Jones 112). Because Japanese modernity supposedly mixed Japanese traditions with Western influences, the Kyoto school delegates contended that Japan was therefore at the forefront of creating a new epoch in world history (Goto-Jones 110–23). Although the delegates at the two symposia did not come to a consensus on the meaning of Japan's war with China and the US, the Kyoto school's participation fed the spreading belief that the Asia-Pacific War was Japan's world-historical mission to create the Greater East Asia Co-Prosperity Sphere (Goto-Jones 124), which, by the time of the 1942 "Overcoming the Modern" symposium, had replaced Konoe's "new order" (*shin chitsujo*) and Miki's "East Asian Cooperative Body" (*Tōa Kyōdōtai*) as the preferred catchphrase for Japan's imperial project.[6] While echoing the Cool Japan campaign in celebrating the transnational flow of Japanese pop culture, *Kuroshitsuji*'s portrayal of

Japan as the imperial power of the new century (*shin seiki*) also suggests that these contemporary discourses can be traced back to an earlier history of Japanese imperialism and the ideas that fueled it.

British Perspectives, Japanese Responses

With its neo-Victorian setting, *Kuroshitsuji* goes even further to connect Cool Japan not only to Japanese imperialist discourses from the 1930s and 1940s, but also to the history of Anglo-Japanese cultural exchange from the mid-nineteenth century to the turn of the twentieth. The flow of British culture into Meiji Japan resulted not only in the Japanese striving to adopt British modes of aesthetic taste in a linear model of civilizational progress. Britain's encounter with Japan also resulted in the British seeking to emulate Japanese arts and crafts, which they perceived as being far superior to their own forms of high art and industrial manufacture. Through their detailed depictions of Victorian material culture, *Kuroshitsuji* and *Lady Victorian* provide a pathway into exploring how Anglo-Japanese dialogues on Japanese aesthetics in the late nineteenth and early twentieth centuries contributed in unexpected ways to the rise of Japanese imperialism and, crucially, to the persistence of the ideology of hybridism in the discourses surrounding Cool Japan. By situating their stories within a richly realized Victorian world, *Kuroshitsuji* and *Lady Victorian* implicitly point to the historical development of hybridism in the longue durée, especially through their references to *Japonisme*. In keeping with the spirit of their historical settings, the two manga series occasionally feature Japanese artefacts amongst the many objects that fill the pages of each volume. These Japanese objects function as period detail that marks the European and more specifically, Victorian, fetishization of all things Japanese. In the opening chapter of the first volume of *Kuroshitsuji*, for example, Sebastian organizes a Japanese-themed dinner party for Mr. Klaus, one of Ciel's business associates. On a diegetic level, Sebastian's choice of a Japanese theme is purely strategic, as he has had to make do with whatever remains in Ciel's country house after the bungling domestic staff have ruined the garden, broken the porcelain dinner service, and burned the roast meat. With his characteristic resourcefulness, Sebastian transforms the damaged garden into a Japanese-style stone garden, and salvages portions of the burnt meat to make Japanese-style beef on rice for dinner. Nonetheless, Sebastian's impromptu Japanese-themed party impresses Mr. Klaus, who invokes the Japanese aesthetic concept of *wabi sabi* ("the impermanence of things") when admiring the withered trees and flowers in the stone garden (1: 24). *Lady Victorian* too touches on *Japonisme* as a Western fad that idealized Japanese aesthetics. In a scene from the first volume of the manga, Lady Ethel appears wearing a kimono, accompanied by an authorial aside in tiny script that reads, "It's called *Japonisme*, isn't it?" (*Japonizumu tte yatsu desu ne*) (1: 97). Upon finding Lady Ethel in her bedroom with her kimono falling off her shoulders—regular readers of *shōjo* manga will not be surprised to discover that Lady Ethel is in fact a cross-dressing man—Bell tries to smooth over the awkward situation by complimenting Lady Ethel on her "lovely nightgown" (*suteki na onemaki*) (1: 97). Lady Ethel mentions that her father had bought the kimono for her in Paris, thereby pointing to the wider European obsession with Japanese art objects at the time. Both *Kuroshitsuji* and *Lady Victorian* thus reference *Japonisme* as one of the tropes that make up Victorian Britain in the global collective imagination, while echoing *Japonisme*'s fascination with the decorative forms and surfaces of Japanese art and aesthetics. Aesthetics and politics might seem far removed from one another, but the ideology of hybridism had in fact arisen in response to late Victorian perceptions of Japanese aesthetics, before entering more widely into discourses on Japanese imperialism in the 1930s and 1940s, and then finding its way into the Cool Japan campaign in the early 2000s.

Japanese aesthetics dominated British and European perceptions of Japan in the second half of the nineteenth century, particularly in the context of Aestheticism in late nineteenth-century Britain. As Grace Lavery has observed, Victorian commentators on Japan often described Japanese culture as "quaint," a word that signifies a particular kind of prettified oldness that is aesthetically pleasing but ultimately trivial and irrelevant to major historical developments (xii, 23–24).[7] British Aesthetes such as Oscar Wilde and the painter J. M. Whistler admired Japanese art for its perceived formalism, which seemed (to them) to be the supreme manifestation of the Aestheticist motto of Art for Art's Sake. This celebration of the so-called pure abstraction of Japanese art, however, contributed to the wider impression that Japanese aesthetics (and, by extension, the whole of Japan) had no deeper meaning or historical significance beyond its quaint forms and surfaces (Lavery 59–73). To put it another way, British commentators on Japan in the late nineteenth century often regarded Japan as a curio: a small and peculiar art object from the Far East that is interesting to look at but ultimately not important enough to be preserved as a historical artefact in a major museum. Even Lafcadio Hearn, who lived in Japan from 1890 to

1904 and who became one of the most famous Western interpreters of Japanese culture, often described the country in the well-intentioned but patronizing language of the collector of curios. In *Kwaidan: Stories and Studies of Strange Things*, which Hearn published shortly before his death in 1904, he likens "Old Japan" to the mythical paradise of Hōrai, where everything is "small and quaint and queer" (177). In the opening chapter of *Glimpses of Unfamiliar Japan* (1894), Hearn overflows with enthusiasm for all the tiny and pretty "curiosities" on sale in the Japanese shops of Yokohama:

> It then appears to him [the foreigner in Japan] that everything Japanese is delicate, exquisite, admirable—even a pair of common wooden chopsticks in a paper bag with a little drawing upon it; even a package of toothpicks of cherry-wood, bound with a paper wrapper wonderfully lettered in three different colors; even the little sky-blue towel, with designs of flying sparrows upon it, which the jinrikisha man uses to wipe his face. The bank bills, the commonest copper coins, are things of beauty. Even the piece of plaited colored string used by the shopkeeper in tying up your latest purchase is a pretty curiosity. Curiosities and dainty objects bewilder you by their very multitude: on either side of you, wherever you turn your eyes, are countless wonderful things as yet incomprehensible. (6–7)

Hearn sums up his experience shopping in Yokohama by declaring that "[t]he largest steamer that crosses the Pacific could not contain what you wish to purchase" (7) because:

> . . . what you really want to buy is not the contents of a shop; you want the shop and the shopkeeper, and streets of shops with their draperies and their habitants, the whole city and the bay and the mountains begirdling it, and Fujiyama's white witchery overhanging it in the speckless sky, all Japan, in very truth, with its magical trees and luminous atmosphere, with all its cities and towns and temples, and forty millions [sic] of the most lovable people in the universe. (7)

Hearn's hyperbolic description of shopping in Yokohama evokes a paradoxical sense of vast magnitude and dainty smallness. On one hand, Hearn gestures towards the vastness of Japan and the impossibility of taking possession of it all, both literally and figuratively. On the other hand, Hearn implies that the whole of Japan is like a small and pretty object on display in a shop; in other words, a curio. In the eyes of Wilde, Whistler, Hearn, and their contemporaries, Japan and Japanese aesthetics were objects of beauty that posed a radical challenge to European aesthetic conventions. Yet these same objects of beauty also appeared to be purely decorative and hence meaningless and insignificant in the grand scheme of historical development.

Japanese intellectuals at the turn of the twentieth century took issue with these well-meaning but trivializing and feminizing portrayals of Japanese-ness often found in British discourses on Japan, and especially in the depictions of Japan produced by or associated with the more effeminate strands of Aestheticism. Nitobe Inazō famously wrote *Bushido: The Soul of Japan* (1900) to champion the hyper-masculinity of the samurai code of conduct, which, he proclaimed, "was and still is the animating spirit, the motor force of our country" (170). Nitobe thus posited images of a dynamic, energetic, and productive Japan to counter the languid and indolent passivity characteristic of Whistler's paintings and media portrayals of Wilde and his fellow Aesthetes. While Nitobe was primarily concerned with questions of ethics, other Japanese intellectuals responded more directly to British perceptions of Japanese aesthetics within the field of aesthetics itself. As Michele Marra has observed, Japanese thinkers in the Meiji period became deeply invested in the study of Japanese aesthetics because the discipline of aesthetics was particularly useful in constructing a national identity for the new nation-state (1–2). These Meiji intellectuals drew on Western philosophies of art to produce their own interpretation of Japanese aesthetics, and to thereby "explain Japan" both to the Japanese themselves and to an international audience. The project of explaining Japan had actually begun with an earlier generation of Western Japanologists such as A. B. Mitford, Ernest Satow, B. H. Chamberlain, and Lafcadio Hearn, who had all experienced living in Japan during the second half of the nineteenth century. Japanese Anglophone writers later sought to intervene in this project in order to explain Japan from a Japanese perspective.[8] As Lavery has pointed out, Japanese Anglophone scholars of aesthetics in particular drew connections between Japanese aesthetics, nation-building, and imperial expansion, while responding to British understandings of Japanese aesthetics from the second half of the nineteenth century (15–16). The English-language writings of Okakura Kakuzō (1863–1913), who was the foremost authority on Japanese aesthetics of his time, clearly demonstrate how Japanese intellectuals challenged British perceptions of Japan as quaint and curious by foregrounding what would later become the ideology of hybridism.

It is one of the ironies of history that, while the upper and middle classes in Meiji Japan were trying to acquire British tastes in order to appear civilized, artists in Victorian Britain were trying to emulate the formal challenges that Japanese aesthetics posed to the tired conventions of European art. Okakura developed his aesthetic theories in response to both indiscriminate Westernization in Japan and Western perceptions of Japanese aesthetics. Like Nitobe, Okakura wrote in English for an international audience. He wrote three books in English on Japanese aesthetics: *Ideals of the East* (1903), *The Awakening of Japan* (1904), and *The Book of Tea* (1906). Across these three works, Okakura presents a theory of Japanese aesthetics that recuperates Japanese art from the charge of being beautiful but ultimately empty and insignificant. In *Ideals of the East*, Okakura ascribes a deeper meaning to Japanese aesthetics by arguing that Asian civilization is founded on a shared cultural tradition of spirituality, and that Japanese art uniquely reflects this tradition of spirituality because of Japan's ability to hybridize different cultures. *Ideals of the East* opens with the declaration "Asia is one" (1), followed by Okakura's claim that "Asia" is united by a common "love for the Ultimate and Universal" (1). In contrast, the "peoples of the Mediterranean and the Baltic" [i.e., Europe] are more concerned with "the Particular" and with "the means, not the end, of life" (1). Within Okakura's conceptualization of "Asia" as a unified civilization, Japan occupies a special position. Firstly, Japan is uniquely capable of synthesizing different traditions, especially from China and India, into a cohesive pan-Asian culture. Secondly, Japan is uniquely capable of preserving this pan-Asian culture. Lastly, Japanese art embodies the whole history of intra-Asian intermixing and the pan-Asian culture of spirituality that this intermixing has engendered. The claim that Japan possesses an exceptional capacity for hybridization runs through these three main arguments that Okakura makes in the *Ideals of the East*. In the introduction to the book, Okakura contends that the Japanese race is an "Indo-Tartaric" amalgamation of the Indian and Chinese races, and that this is the reason why the Japanese people have been especially capable of absorbing Indian and Chinese culture since ancient times (2–3). Moreover, Okakura asserts that the Japanese race has the special ability to combine the new with the old, and the foreign with the indigenous. Okakura uses the metaphor of tidal waves shaping the shoreline without overwhelming it: "The history of Japanese art becomes thus the history of Asiatic ideals—the beach where each successive wave of Eastern thought has left its sand-ripple as it beat against the national consciousness." (4) Okakura foregrounds Japanese art because he sees Japanese artworks and historic monuments as embodiments of a hybrid Japanese culture that is coterminous with the values of Asian civilization as a whole. Only the Japanese race, he goes on to argue, has been able to preserve its artworks and monuments due to its long history of isolation as well as the imperial family's unbroken rule over the country. As such, only Japan embodies the whole of Asian spirituality from ancient times through to the present in the form of its artworks and monuments. Okakura uses the motif of the museum to advocate for this apparently unique position of the Japanese people in Asia, describing Japan as "the real repository of the trust of Asian thought and culture" (2) and "a museum of Asiatic civilization" (3). Okakura thus invokes the same discourse of national heritage discussed in chapter one, but in a Japanese and pan-Asian context. By arguing that Japanese art manifests the deep spiritual traditions of Asian civilization, Okakura challenges late Victorian claims that Japanese aesthetics is all form and no content. Far from being trivial and insignificant, Japanese aesthetics embody Japan's supposedly superior ability to hybridize different cultures; an ability that has enabled Japan, in Okakura's account, to become the sole receptacle of Asian spirituality in an increasingly materialistic world.

In seeking to recuperate Japanese aesthetics from dominant British and European perspectives, Okakura also expresses disdain for the particular Japanese art forms that had so enraptured Hearn and the British Aesthetes. In *Ideals of the East*, Okakura positions the Ashikaga period (1400–1600) as the golden age of Japanese art because Ashikaga art, according to Okakura, expresses the ideal of spirit overcoming matter, an ideal that originates in Zen Buddhism and is closely associated with the samurai class (75). In contrast to this deeply spiritual aesthetic tradition, *ukiyo-e* woodblock prints and other art forms from the Edo period (1600–1868) are, in Okakura's view, frivolous and therefore deserving of Western depictions of Japanese aesthetics as purely ornamental, quaint, and curious. The "bourgeois art of Yedo" (87), Okakura explains, was made for commoners and especially for the merchant classes. As a result, it focused on "mundane pleasures, in the theater, or in the gay life of Yoshiwara [the pleasure quarters]" (86). In other words, Edo art foregrounded the delights of urban consumption in early modern Japan. As such, it lacked the aspiration towards spiritual transcendence that had culminated in the samurai art of the Ashikaga shoguns:

> The Popular School [of the Edo period] . . . though it attained skill in color and drawing, lacks that ideality which is the basis of Japanese art. Those charmingly colored woodcuts, full of vigor and versatility, made by Outamaro, Shunman, Kionobu, Harunobu, Kionaga, Toyokuni, and Hokusai, stand apart from the main line of development of Japanese art, whose evolution has been continuous ever since the Nara period. The inros, the netsukis, the sword-guards, and the delightful lacquer-work articles of the period, were playthings, and as such no embodiment of national fervor, in which all true art exists. (86)

Okakura thus echoes William Morris's description of Japanese works of art as "mere wonderful toys, things quite outside the pale of the evolution of art" (qtd. in Lavery 72). However, Okakura agrees with this condescending assessment of Japanese aesthetics only insofar as it applies to the Edo art forms that had captured the attention of Whistler, Wilde, and their fellow Aesthetes. For Okakura, the decorative arts of the Edo era are not representative of "true" Japanese art. He goes on to argue that: "Great art is that before which we long to die. But the art of the late Tokugawa period only allowed a man to dwell in the delights of fancy. It is because the prettiness of the works of this period first came to notice, instead of the grandeur of the masterpieces hidden in the daimyos' collections and the temple treasures, that Japanese art is not yet seriously considered in the West" (87). In subordinating the dainty "prettiness" of Edo popular art to the majestic "grandeur" of samurai art, Okakura implies that Western writers and artists who lauded Japanese aesthetics have not genuinely understood what they purported to admire. Okakura thus presents an alternative conceptualization of Japanese aesthetics, one which celebrates the pan-Asian spirituality of Japanese samurai art.

Okakura rounds off his response to Western discourses on Japanese aesthetics by contending that this pan-Asian spirituality of Japanese aesthetics has granted Japan a special mission in world history, thereby anticipating Miki Kiyoshi and the Kyoto school's invocations of Japan's world-historical significance by several decades. Okakura makes this point most strongly in *The Awakening of Japan* (1904), which he published in the same year as Hearn's *Kwaidan* and in the midst of the 1904–1905 Russo-Japanese War. In the final chapter of the book—rather provocatively entitled "Japan and Peace"—Okakura sets out to justify Japan's war on Russia to an international audience. "We fought," Okakura explains, "not only for our motherland, but for the ideals of the recent reformation [the 1868 Meiji Restoration], for the noble heritage of classic culture, and for *those dreams of peace and harmony in which we saw a glorious rebirth for all Asia*" (218–19; italics mine). In other words, Okakura argues that Japan is fighting Russia for the sake of restoring peace in Asia and reviving the ancient Asian spiritual tradition, which, Okakura asserts, is inherently peaceful. In the final pages of the book, Okakura laments the aggressiveness of Western civilization, and calls upon the West to "learn the blessings of peace" (223) from "the peaceful nations of the far East" (222). In this concluding chapter of *The Awakening of Japan*, Okakura makes explicit the claim that Japan has a world-historical mission to unify and lead Asia towards recovering its ancient culture of spirituality in opposition to Western materialism and expansionism. He had already implied this in *Ideals of the East* when he wrote of Japan's unique position within Asia, but in *The Awakening of Japan* he suggests that Japan might have little choice but to use military force to fulfil its mission. Okakura's claiming of a special mission for Japan as leader of Asia was in fact part of wider discourses on the concept of *civilization* and pan-Asianism in the early twentieth century. As Prasenjit Duara has argued, people in the early twentieth century did not look only to the nation or race as a source of identity. They also looked to older spiritual ideals that were incorporated in a new conception of *civilization* (Duara 99–100). While the Western imperial powers in the latter half of the nineteenth century primarily conceived of civilization as a universal telos in a stadial model of world history (with themselves at the top), the idea that there were multiple, equally valid civilizations began to gain momentum in the late nineteenth century and especially after the First World War (Duara 100–01).[9] In *Ideals of the East*, *The Awakening of Japan*, and his third book *The Book of Tea* (1906), Okakura defines the concept of Asia in overtly civilizational terms as the antithesis of Western materialism, liberal individualism, and imperialism. By claiming a central role for Japan in this clash of civilizations, Okakura not only links Japanese nationalism to civilizational discourse, as Duara has observed (100, 109). In doing so, Okakura also challenges prevailing British and European perceptions of Japan as a quaint object that is, in Lavery's account, ultimately irretrievable by any historical metanarrative (xii). Far from being peripheral to major historical developments, the Japan that emerges out of Okakura's theory of Japanese aesthetics is destined to play a leading part in world history as the synthesizer and preserver of Asian civilization and its culture of spirituality.

Okakura's pan-Asianism in the early 1900s would later contribute to the rise of Japanese fascism and imperialism in the 1930s and early 1940s, although it is unclear whether he would have approved of these developments. As Duara takes pains to point out, pan-Asianist civilizational discourse in the early twentieth century cannot be simply dismissed as Japanese imperialism in disguise, for it was not always neatly aligned with the expansionist aims of the nation-state (111–12).[10] Likewise, Okakura was more than just an apologist for Japanese imperialism in Asia. To be fair, Okakura's English-language writings do not explicitly argue that Japan should colonize other Asian countries. Okakura's writings heavily imply that Japan is responsible for leading Asia and that Japan might have to use military force to fulfil that responsibility, but they do not specify exactly what form Japan's leadership of Asia should take. Okakura was in fact very ambivalent about the use of military force. In *The Awakening of Japan*, he contends that Japan would have remained peaceful if Russia had not compelled it to wage war in order to protect its interests in Korea and Manchuria (209–13, 216–18). Okakura's stance towards the use of military force becomes even more ambiguous in his last English-language work, *The Book of Tea*. Okakura's tone in *The Book of Tea* is more conciliatory, even playful, compared to his earlier works. His critique of Western civilization is gentler, and he speaks of East and West supplementing each other, rather than fighting with each other. Most strikingly, he ironizes the predominant view in the West at the time that Japan's recent military victories over China and Russia signal Japan's entrance into the realm of "civilized" nations. "The average Westerner," Okakura remarks with deadpan humor, "was wont to regard Japan as barbarous while she indulged in the gentle arts of peace: he calls her civilized since she began to commit wholesale slaughter on Manchurian battlefields" (5–7). Despite Okakura's mixed feelings about warfare, his ideas were later appropriated by the militarist state to justify Japan's wars in the Asia-Pacific. Okakura's pan-Asianist ideas were already known in Japan before he wrote the three books in English, as he had discussed these ideas in his lectures on Japanese art history at the Tokyo Fine Arts Academy from 1890 to 1893 (He 102). However, he became widely influential in mainstream Japanese discourse much later in the 1930s and 1940s, when his English-language works were translated into Japanese after his death in 1913 (He 103).[11] The translation of his writings paved the way for Okakura's pan-Asianism to be interpreted in ways that might have been contrary to his intentions (Tankha 94). For example, the Patriotic Association for Japanese Literature [Nihon Bungaku Hōkokukai] appropriated Okakura's famous slogan Asia Is One to commemorate the December 1941 attack on Pearl Harbor (Tankha 96). Nonetheless, regardless of Okakura's intentions, his pan-Asianist ideas fed into the enduring myth that Japan has a superior capacity for cultural hybridization, a myth that continues to make its appearance in the twenty-first century in euphoric celebrations of "Japan's Gross National Cool" and other invocations of Cool Japan.

In the Shadow of Co-Prosperity

Seen in the light of Japan's imperial history, the curry bun and the girls' magazine in *Kuroshitsuji* and *Lady Victorian* take on unsettling overtones. Like McGray's "Japan's Gross National Cool," Anthony Faiola's 2003 article for the *Washington Post* repeats all the familiar tropes of Japanese hybridism. Faiola speaks of "Japan's Empire of Cool," claiming that Japan modifies Western culture to suit Asian audiences, and that the global popularity of contemporary Japanese pop culture is giving Japan "a new kind of influence" in the world. This dream of an Empire of Cool, however, does not quite correspond to reality. While *Kuroshitsuji* and *Lady Victorian* envision Japan as a new cultural superpower, empirical studies of the Cool Japan campaign suggest otherwise. It is open to debate whether the global consumption of Japanese pop culture actually translates into soft power for Japan, despite McGray's optimistic predictions that it would (47–48). Contrary to what one might expect given the history of Japanese colonial rule in Taiwan, Iwabuchi discovered that Taiwanese viewers of Japanese TV dramas in the 1990s did not see Japan as an advanced model of Asian modernity that they should emulate (*Recentering Globalization* 155–57). Instead, the Taiwanese viewers Iwabuchi interviewed saw Taiwan as occupying the same stage as Japan in a teleological process of modernization (*Recentering Globalization* 155–57). While David Leheny is inclined to think that Japan does exercise a degree of soft power by functioning as an exemplary model of Asian modernity, he acknowledges that other Asian nations might not necessarily support Japanese foreign policy goals even if they admire Japan's success in modernization ("Narrow Place" 231–32). Lam Peng Er is even more skeptical of the real extent of Japanese soft power, as he contends that Japan's international influence is limited by its failure to overcome anger in China and South Korea over its imperialist activities in the past (357–58).

The ineffectiveness of using popular culture to achieve foreign policy objectives is not the only problem besetting the Cool Japan project. Cool Japan has also not been as economically successful as expected, especially compared to the global popularity of South Korean popular culture in recent years. Roland Kelts's 2010 article "Japanamerica: Why 'Cool Japan' Is Over" suggests that Cool Japan is floundering not only because of overbearing state intervention in popular culture production—as Daliot-Bul similarly argues in her account of Cool Japan ("Japan Brand Strategy" 262–63)—but also because the Japanese cultural industries are not particularly interested in attracting consumers outside Japan. Kelts criticizes Japanese anime production studios and manga publishing companies for not setting up stalls at anime conventions in the US, and for maintaining only Japanese-language websites or English-language websites that are "amateurish, hard to navigate, and worst of all, dull—just the opposite of their vaunted products." In her 2011 book *Straight from the Heart*, Jennifer Prough similarly observes that, while the Japanese *shōjo* manga industry has slowly begun to take an interest in international audiences, it is still mainly concerned with the domestic market (142). According to Prough, "[m]ost exports have been and are still initiated by outside interest rather than internal motivation; consequently, these publishing houses primarily work through local publishers rather than distributing and translating themselves" (142). Since Prough published her study of the *shōjo* manga industry in 2011, the situation has improved somewhat, although the Japanese cultural industries have not yet achieved the kind of global reach that earlier celebratory discourses on Cool Japan had envisioned.[12] This apparent inertia in exporting Japanese pop culture products is clearly at odds with the globalizing impulse of the Cool Japan campaign and its imperialist precursor, the Greater East Asia Co-Prosperity Sphere.

Like the Cool Japan project, the Greater East Asia Co-Prosperity Sphere or *Dai Tōa Kyōeiken* fell short of its political and economic objectives. In order to serve its wartime economic needs, the Japanese government radically restructured the economies of its Southeast Asian colonies, thereby resulting in extreme inflation, unemployment, and food shortages (W. Beasley 249–50). As a result, the much vaunted "advance into the South" (*nanshin*) ultimately contributed less to Japan's economy than expected (W. Beasley 249–50). In mainland China, Japanese forces continued to face fierce resistance from guerrilla fighters, who were financially supported by the diasporic Chinese in Malaya and Singapore, as we shall see in the next chapter. Nonetheless, despite its failures in practice, the Greater East Asia Co-Prosperity Sphere exercised considerable ideological influence in Japan and its colonies (at least, until the disillusionment with Japanese rule set in). Like Konoe's "new order" and Miki's "East Asian Cooperative Body," the Co-Prosperity Sphere imagined Japan hybridizing the different nations or races of Asia into a regional political and economic system, where each nation or race would perform a specific role determined by its distinctive cultural attributes. The Co-Prosperity Sphere thus interwove the ideology of hybridism with pan-Asianist politics to produce a particular understanding of race that would shape the consumption of Japanese popular culture in Singapore more than half a century later.[13] As Kevin Doak has observed, Japanese pan-Asianism after the First World War and especially from the mid-1930s onward relied heavily on the concept of *minzoku*—the Japanese equivalent of the German Nazi *Volk*—to reconcile the rising nationalism of different Asian countries with the regionalist aims of the Japanese Empire (168–72). While the Japanese term *minzoku* might be more accurately translated as "ethnic nation" rather than "race," discourses on the Co-Prosperity Sphere often adopted a culturalist form of racial thinking, which was just as essentializing as the scientific racism prevalent in Europe in the late nineteenth and early twentieth centuries. While Doak rightly warns against conflating *minzoku* with *jinshu* (the Japanese term for *race*) (168–69), his argument rests on reducing the concept of race to notions of bodies and biology. As such, I have chosen to use the term *race* in this chapter and the next to gesture towards the significant overlap between the concept of ethnicity and the cultural racism of Japanese imperialism in the 1930s and 1940s. Moreover, the concept of *minzoku* was very closely aligned with that of race in colonial Malaya and Singapore, where the coexistence of Malay, Chinese, and Indian populations made it difficult to equate ethnicity with the nation. This culturalist understanding of race continues to inform politics, economics, and social relations in Malaysia and Singapore today. As chapter five demonstrates, this post-imperial legacy of race intersects with that of English literature to present Japanese Lolita fashion as an appealing neo-Victorian cultural practice to a small group of young women in the former British and Japanese colony of Singapore.

Part III

Chapter Five

Becoming "Victorian"

It is October 2015 in Singapore. It is Halloween, and the tropical weather is hot and humid. In the cool air-conditioned comfort of the five-star St. Regis Hotel, Christina, a twenty-nine-year-old Singaporean woman, is having a tea party with a small group of friends (figure 5.1). Christina, better known to her friends as Chris, is wearing a black double-breasted jacket, a waistcoat, and a white cravat with ruffles. Her best friend Lisa, whose hair is dyed a fiery shade of red, is dressed in a red dress with matching deep red lipstick,

Figure 5.1. Chris and her friends celebrating Halloween at the St. Regis Hotel, Singapore. Chris and Lisa are seated on the far left. Even Kenneth, the only man in the group, has briefly put aside his role as photographer to step in front of the camera and join the girls in dressing up for the party. *Source:* Reproduced with permission from Beanie.

black jacket, and a large black floral headpiece pinned to her hair. Chris's and Lisa's friends are similarly decked out in dark-colored outfits that recall the fashions of Victorian Britain, but with a Gothic twist. Although Chris had initially proposed a tea party inspired by the TV drama *Penny Dreadful*, some of her guests have chosen to draw inspiration from the Hollywood period horror film *Crimson Peak*, which they have just seen at the cinema. The majority of the young women, however, have come dressed in Lolita fashion, a Japanese subcultural style modeled on outfits that young girls in Britain wore during the Victorian period. As Masafumi Monden has argued, Lolita fashion is a "trans-periodic" style that takes certain aesthetic elements from historical European dress (especially Rococo and Victorian) and mixes them with more contemporary styles, including the Japanese *kawaii* aesthetic (168–71). In other words, Lolita fashion privileges aesthetics over historical accuracy (Monden 168–71). Monden further argues that globalization has made the "nationality" of Lolita fashion even more ambiguous (176). Since its emergence in the Harajuku district of Tokyo in the late 1990s, Lolita fashion has become a transnational phenomenon, with followers in Europe, the United States, South America, and Asia, as well as in online communities that cut across territorial boundaries (Kawamura 71, 74). Chris, Lisa, and their friends are part of these global flows of Japanese pop culture, but the "neither quite European, nor quite Japanese" quality of the Lolita style takes on added significance in Singapore, a country that has historically experienced both British and Japanese imperialism.

As Chris's Halloween tea party shows, the trans-imperial networks created by the global history of the nineteenth century and the global creative economy today imbricate not only neo-Victorian texts, but also the people who consume these texts and participate in multiple forms of neo-Victorian *play*. In this chapter, I use the term *play* in the dual sense that it has acquired in scholarship on *play* or *asobi* in Japan. Play refers to leisure activities, but it is also "the act of establishing and maintaining an alternative reality," especially one in which players can imaginatively perform alternative identities (Daliot-Bul, *License to Play* xxviii).[1] Chris, Lisa, and their friends are members of a wider community of young women in the small island-state of Singapore who play with neo-Victorian fashion practices at the intersection of the British, American, and Japanese cultural empires. In this final chapter, I turn from neo-Victorian texts to neo-Victorian practices, and from the British, American, and Japanese cultural industries to the fans who consume the commodities that these industries produce. In line with recent scholarship on fandoms and Japanese fashion subcultures, I adopt a qualitative sociological approach that, in the words of fashion studies scholar Megan Catherine Rose, "privileges . . . the participant's perspective, with an emphasis on their emotional experiences of their fashion style" (12).

Chris's and Lisa's neo-Victorian fashion practices point to the presence of a particular group of young women in Singapore who are very keen on nineteenth-century British literature and its historical contexts, especially fashion. However, despite their interest in historical fashion, these young Singaporean women do not take part in the subcultural practice of historical costuming. They do not create and/or wear historically accurate period attire to fan conventions and gatherings. Instead, they prefer to wear Lolita fashion or to *cosplay* (short for *costume play*) characters from Japanese neo-Victorian manga and anime series such as *Kuroshitsuji* (figures 5.2, 5.3, and 5.4). To be sure, many Singaporean female fans of the Lolita subculture see Lolita fashion as distinctively Japanese rather than neo-Victorian, in the same way that steampunk fans often hesitate to use the term neo-Victorian to describe their fan practices.[2] For Chris and Lisa, their interest in the Victorian

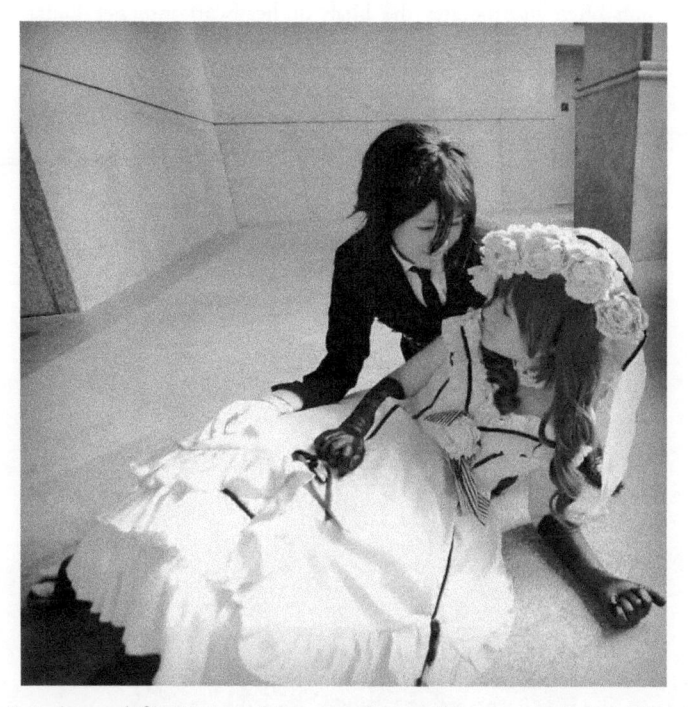

Figure 5.2. (From left) Chris and Lisa cosplaying Sebastian and Ciel (disguised as a girl) from *Kuroshitsuji*. *Source:* Reproduced with permission from Chris and Lisa.

130   Empire of Culture

Figure 5.3. Farah (second from left) and her friends wearing Lolita fashion. The woman on the far left is dressed in the *ōji* ("prince") style. As a Malay-Muslim woman, Farah often incorporates the hijab or headscarf into her Lolita outfits. *Source:* Reproduced with permission from Fuzzylogic Asile.

Figure 5.4. Jennifer wearing Lolita fashion. *Source:* Reproduced with permission from Jennifer.

period converges with their enthusiasm for Japanese popular culture to a much greater degree. My interviews with Chris, Lisa, and other women like them reveal that, while these women seek to adopt certain aspects of British culture for their supposedly universal and timeless qualities, when it comes to performing an idealized Victorian-ness on the surface of their bodies, the perceived whiteness of historical fashion presents an obstacle to these women participating in historical costuming. As a result, these women turn to Japanese forms of neo-Victorian fashion, partly because of the supposed raceless-ness of contemporary Japanese popular culture, but also partly because Lolita fashion and manga/anime cosplay are in fact racialized popular cultural practices. The Lolita subculture in Singapore is dominated by ethnic Chinese, who, consciously or not, perceive Japanese Lolita fashion as a style that is racially proximate to them, and is therefore more accessible than the whiteness of historical costuming.

This continuing preoccupation with race, coupled with the long-standing idealization of British high culture, has deep roots in Singapore's history as a former British and Japanese colony. Singapore was ruled by the British for 144 years, from its "founding" by Sir Stamford Raffles in 1819 to its federation with Malaysia in 1963 (from which it was subsequently expelled in 1965). However, for three years during the Asia-Pacific War (1942–1945), Singapore was occupied by the Japanese. Despite claiming to liberate Asia from Western imperialism, the Japanese military administration kept many of the colonial structures and institutions that had been left behind by the British, not least of which was the artificial construct of race. As a means of categorizing, governing, and *disciplining* the diverse peoples of colonial Singapore, the concept of race increasingly went hand in hand with the *discipline* of English literature, which likewise exerted a regulatory force over the colony's inhabitants. Under British rule, English-medium schools in Singapore began to teach English literature as an academic subject in the late nineteenth and early twentieth centuries, and the subject has since become a mainstay of the local curriculum even after independence. Back then, in order to create a comprador class of English-educated elites, English-medium schools taught English literature to students from the different ethnic groups that made up colonial Singapore's cosmopolitan population. On the other hand, many Malay, Chinese, and Indian students attended vernacular schools that were designed specifically for each "race" (Wong and Gwee 2). The British colonial government actively encouraged this phenomenon as part of its "divide and rule" policy of racial classification and segregation. During the Japanese Occupation, the Japanese military authorities maintained and in fact exacerbated this racial policy of "divide and rule," thereby reinforcing the legitimacy of race as a classificatory concept and a source of identity in Singapore. To this day, all Singaporean citizens are given identity cards that indicate not only their name, sex, and date of birth, but also their race. In other words, race continues to inflect everyday life in Singapore, including the Lolita fashion practices of young Singaporean women such as Chris and Lisa. As they negotiate between the British and Anglo-American cultural industries on the one hand and Cool Japan on the other, these women reaffirm the intertwined legacies of English literature and race, while finding a space within these legacies to perform an imaginary Victorian self that can accommodate their non-white bodies.

In turning to Japanese Lolita fashion and cosplay rather than historical costuming, the young Singaporean women whom I have interviewed perform a kind of Victorian-ness that is, to borrow Homi Bhabha's expression, "not quite/not white" (131). These women's unsettling displays of neo-Victorian fashion might seem like nothing more than a fun and frivolous pastime. However, they illuminate the crucial role that race plays in the logic of cultural imperialism, as trans-imperial interactions in the long nineteenth century give shape to cultural commodity production and consumption in the global creative economy today. The dissemination of English literature from Britain to Singapore in the late nineteenth and early twentieth centuries has contributed not only to the success of the British heritage industry today, but also to the widespread perception that British high culture is an ideal that is both universal and particular. This final chapter builds on the preceding chapters to reveal that this paradoxical combination of universality and particularity is key to the dominance of the British cultural empire in the late twentieth and early twenty-first centuries. If British high culture were to lose its distinctive Englishness and become completely accessible to everyone, the allure of buying items from British heritage brands and visiting heritage attractions in Britain would become much less compelling. This perceived particularity of British high culture is integral to its global appeal. At the same time, this perceived particularity, especially when it takes on a racialized form, carries the risk of undermining its own appeal, as this chapter will show.

On the other hand, the Japanese cultural empire has sought to carve out its own niche in the global creative economy by asserting that its popular culture products are even more universal than those of the British high-cultural empire. Government officials, industry experts, cultural commentators, and even academic scholars have claimed that contemporary Japanese popular culture is essentially democratic and raceless. However, as the fashion practices of my interviewees demonstrate, Japanese pop culture appeals to some people because of its perceived particularity; namely, its racialized Japanese-ness. It remains to be seen whether this racialized quality of Japanese pop culture, like that of British high culture, subverts its own hegemony. The particularity of a cultural form, then, is a double-edged sword in the context of a global creative economy structured on the same ideology of simultaneous universality and particularity that underpinned the global dissemination of British culture in the long nineteenth century. In shifting focus from cultural commodity production to questions of consumption, this final chapter uncovers these contradictions in the logic of cultural imperialism then and now.

Reading English Literature

The arguments that I make in this chapter are based on interviews that I conducted with a small group of Singaporean women in February 2016 and from August to December 2019. I conducted the first round of interviews in 2016 with Chris and Lisa over email. In 2019, I interviewed Chris again and three other young women named Carol, Jennifer, and Farah in a series of face-to-face individual interviews and focus group sessions.[3] At the time of the interviews in 2016, Chris was thirty years old and working in a white-collar civil-service job. Lisa, whom Chris has known for many years, was at the time working as a graphic designer. In 2019, Chris was still working in the civil service. Farah (thirty-six) was the oldest member of the focus group, and at the time of the interviews she had been working as a secondary school teacher for close to a decade. Jennifer (twenty-two) was a third-year student at an art school, working towards a four-year degree in fashion design. Carol (nineteen) was the youngest of the group and had just started undergraduate studies at one of the local universities. Out of these five women, only Chris and Lisa self-identify as fans of both Japanese neo-Victorian manga and anime and English-language period dramas such as *Penny Dreadful*. Nonetheless, all of the women are familiar with Japanese manga and anime, and all of them participate, in varying degrees, in the Lolita fashion subculture in Singapore. Moreover, all of the interviewees enjoy reading English-language fiction, and all but one have studied English literature as an academic subject at tertiary level. This came as a surprise, as I had not included an interest in English literature in my criteria for recruiting interviewees. It is possible that young Singaporean women who are well-versed in English literature are simply more likely to volunteer for interviews. However, when viewed in the context of the country's colonial past, this peculiar correlation between reading English literature and wearing Lolita fashion sheds light on how these women negotiate between the canonicity and the exclusivity of British high culture. To these women, English literature represents a universal ideal of cultural edification, but its association with whiteness poses a problem when attempting to embody this ideal, as the following sections demonstrate.

Despite the general waning of interest in English literature in Singapore over the years, all of the interviewees are familiar with nineteenth-century British literature and its historical contexts. Farah majored in English literature at university, before going on to pursue a master of arts degree in the same subject. Although Chris chose to specialize in a different subject at university, she studied English literature for her *A* level examinations (the equivalent of college entrance examinations in Singapore). Chris obtained an *A* in the subject. Likewise, Jennifer took English literature as an examinable subject in her final year of the international baccalaureate program, before going on to study fashion design at her current college. Like Chris, Jennifer did well, scoring six out of the highest possible score of seven. Carol, the first-year undergraduate, also received an *A* for English literature in her *A* level exams, and at the time of the interviews in 2019, she was taking an introductory course in English literature at her university. The academic success of these young women in the subject of English literature is largely due to the fact that all of them come from middle-class families who are not only English-speaking, but also "English-reading"; in other words, families in which the parents and/or relatives in the extended family actively encourage the children to read English-language fiction from a young age.[4] This childhood habit of reading has clearly contributed not only to Chris, Farah, Jennifer, and Carol doing well in English literature at school, but also to their continuing love for reading English-language fiction, a love that all of the interviewees unanimously profess.

Although these women have diverse tastes in fiction, they are all familiar with nineteenth-century British literature, even if not all of them are particularly passionate about it. These women read some of the nineteenth-century British literary works that they mentioned in the interviews at school, but they also read many of these works at home, especially when they were children. Carol, for example, was introduced to what she calls "Victorian literature" in her fourth year of secondary school, when her English literature class was assigned to read Oscar Wilde's *The Importance of*

Being Earnest. Carol enjoyed Wilde's play so much that she went on to read Wilde's novel *The Picture of Dorian Gray*, as well as Dickens's *Great Expectations* and *A Tale of Two Cities*. At the time of the interview, she was reading Wilkie Collins's *The Woman in White*, which her father had recommended to her twice, once when she was a child, and again when she had become interested in Victorian literature. Jennifer too had studied *The Importance of Being Earnest* at school, but years before that, she had already read *Pride and Prejudice* and had attempted to read *Jane Eyre*. (She gave up when she discovered how long the novel was.) These books, Jennifer informed me, were just some of the many books that she had at home when she was a child. Likewise, because her uncle often left his books lying around the house, Farah was able to read Lewis Carroll's *Alice's Adventures in Wonderland* and less child-friendly works such as R. L. Stevenson's *The Invisible Man*. I should state here that all of the interviewees also read many works of fiction when they were children that were not nineteenth-century British literary works. In fact, they enjoyed, and continue to enjoy, reading twentieth-century and contemporary authors such as Tolkien, Terry Pratchett, and Margaret Atwood. Nevertheless, all of the interviewees claim to have read, or at least to have heard of, many well-known nineteenth-century British literary works, thereby demonstrating their familiarity with the literature of the period, even though some of them prefer to read contemporary fiction, speculative fiction, true crime stories, and other genres by more recent writers. This familiarity, which the interviewees seem to take for granted, implies that nineteenth-century British literature retains a certain level of prestige in Singapore as a form of canonical culture; in other words, as a kind of universal knowledge that everyone is expected to acquire, especially at a young age. According to this mode of thinking, not having read Austen or Dickens (for instance) makes one a lesser person.

Several of the interviewees affirmed the canonical status of nineteenth-century British literature, and that of English literature in general, when they invoked the notion of the *classic* work of English literature during the interviews. Although these young women would not necessarily agree on which literary works count as classics, in invoking the notion of the classic itself, they implicitly uphold the idea that English literature is a canon of universal and timeless masterpieces, rather than simply a corpus of fictional works written in the English language. When Chris and I spoke about her enthusiasm for English-language period dramas, she stated that, as far as she could remember, she read "the more like, classic kind of novels" before watching their screen adaptations. These "classic" novels, as Chris's responses in other parts of the interview reveal, include Austen's works and Emily Brontë's *Wuthering Heights*. Similarly, when Carol was describing the books that she read when she was a child, she mentioned that she read several "classics," such as Austen's *Pride and Prejudice* and Chaucer's *Canterbury Tales*, when she was about eleven years old. Carol had started reading these "classics" (as she called them) so that she could keep up with her friends at school:

> CAROL: I tried getting into the classics when I was eleven because my friends were getting into it, and it was like a cool thing to do in our group. . . .
>
> . . .
>
> . . . So, one of my friends came in[to the classroom] one day, and she was like, "Oh, I'm going to start reading all the classics," and we were like, "Wow! That's pretty cool." And then we started, I started looking into it and you know, just finding out for myself. We didn't really discuss the books. It was more like, "Oh, I read this," and "Did you read this and that?" and the answer was always "No" because we didn't read the same things.

Despite wanting to do this "cool thing" of reading the "classics" of English literature together, Carol and her classmates did not discuss the books they read, nor did they try to read the same books at the same time. Carol explained that she and her classmates did not have the time to coordinate their reading, but the imitative nature of their reading and the cursory manner in which they talked about the books they had read suggest that they were not particularly interested in the contents of each book. For Carol and her classmates, knowing what happens in a book was less important than being able to tell others that they had read this or that "classic" work of fiction. Despite their young age, Carol and her friends saw reading "classic" works of English literature as a means of exhibiting their cultural know-how. In this way, their reading practices reflected, but also reproduced, the perception that English literature is a universal standard of cultural achievement that anyone who wants to be taken seriously should be familiar with, even on the most superficial level.

During the interviews, Carol and the other women repeatedly invoked the notion of the "classic," especially when describing the English-language fiction that they had read when they were children. In doing so, these young women implied that reading well-known works of mainly British and sometimes American literature is a necessary part of a child's education. They further implied that reading English literature as a child, and later studying and doing well in the subject at school, are forms of cultural capital that are valuable to those in their socio-economic group, even as English literature becomes increasingly marginalized in mainstream Singaporean society. These young women's valorization of mainly British literary works as "classics" certainly corroborates Philip Holden's claim that, after so many decades of independence from British rule, Singaporeans still associate English literature with British literature and Englishness, thereby preventing English literature from playing a central role in the postcolonial nation (Holden 31–32). That said, however, these women's fetishization of the "classic" work of English literature also signals that, even as English literature is devalued for its perceived irrelevance to Singapore's needs, these women continue to see it as an important source of cultural capital and social distinction. While the number of students taking English literature as an examinable subject continues to decline, these young women and their middle-class "English-reading" families persist in foregrounding the meaningfulness of English literature, insofar as it functions as a marker of their cultural refinement.[5]

This belief in the canonicity of English literature can be traced back to the institutionalization of English literature as a discipline in colonial Singapore. Carol and the other interviewees regard English literature as a canon of universal and timeless classics partly because the discipline itself has historically encouraged this view in Singapore and elsewhere. Holden sees many parallels between Gauri Viswanathan's account of the rise of English literature in India and the institutionalization of English literature in Singapore, which began in the late nineteenth and early twentieth centuries (35). English literature, Holden argues, was originally introduced as a school subject in Singapore to instill loyalty to the British Empire in local elites, who would then be more willing to work for the British colonizers as a comprador class (31, 35). Over time, the discipline of English literature reified the imperial values that it set out to inculcate into "universal" and "timeless" values that masked the discipline's colonial function (Holden 31). Although historical data is scant, it appears that this discourse on English literature's universality and timelessness has been around in Singapore at least since the 1930s if not earlier, and that it has persisted through Singapore's independence in 1965 to this day. In 1937, the principal of the elite Raffles

Institution, D. W. McLeod, wrote a syllabus outlining how English literature was to be taught at his school. Whereas English classes at the lower levels were meant to teach language skills, at the upper levels where English literature was taught as a subject in its own right, the emphasis was clearly on teaching students to appreciate the author's style and, crucially, the author's insights into the human condition. In his preface to the syllabus, McLeod laments: "Too often, Shakespeare's plays are looked upon as reasons for notes on metre, the sources of the plot, the date of the play, the play, the classical allusions, and archaic words, instead of opportunities for the most interesting study of all—mankind." (29) More than seventy years later, a former student of St. Joseph's Institution said much the same thing about Shakespeare in a coffee table book published in 2009 to commemorate the long history of the school, which was established by Catholic missionaries in colonial Singapore in 1852. Warren Fernandez, the author of the book, fondly remembers studying English literature under the instruction of Brother Henry O'Brien in the early 1980s: "Along the way, [Brother O'Brien] also hoped to teach us to speak and write English properly, and if possible, to absorb a little wisdom from the wonderful works of William Shakespeare." (*Men for Others* 33)

Oral history interviews with former students and teachers reveal similar attitudes towards the study of Shakespeare and English literature. In an interview conducted by the National Archives of Singapore (NAS) in 1995, George Kanagaretnam Paul recalls how he enjoyed studying English literature at Victoria School in 1936 (83–84). When asked how he feels about some schools doing away with English literature as a subject (ostensibly to make space for the study of non-Western cultural forms), Paul asserts that he "feel[s] very strongly" about this new development (86). While Paul sympathizes with the desire to replace Western knowledge with so-called Eastern knowledge from China and India, he feels that English literature is ultimately irreplaceable:

> Have at least one classics [sic], Shakespeare, Longfellow, have a few classics [and] poems. These, they should not be done away with. No, I feel very strongly against this policy of taking, "Oh, that's Western, we are Easterners" and replace by . . . [sic] Of course, there is a lot of good old things that you can borrow from Chinese History . . . Maybe [we] are [onto] something good. But, to me nothing can replace Shakespeare. . . . Lives of great men [such as Shakespeare] all remind us that our lives can be

sublime and departing leave behind us footprints on the sands of time, poems. We should never depart from those [poems]. (86)

Like the young women I interviewed, Paul invokes the notion of the "classic" work of English literature. Moreover, he contends that these classics constitute an intangible cultural heritage—"footprints on the sands of time"—that Singaporeans should continue to preserve for future generations. Paul's remarks on Shakespeare, as well as those of McLeod and Fernandez, reveal that the study of English literature in Singapore was and still is primarily understood as the study of timeless and universal classics that teach the reader essential truths about humanity.

It is important to reiterate here that this aura of canonicity applies to the discipline of English literature as a whole, over and beyond the canonicity of specific works of literature. Although the archival and published materials that I have encountered mention many well-known authors and works such as Shakespeare's *Macbeth*, Dickens's *A Tale of Two Cities*, and Tennyson's "Morte D'Arthur," they also reveal that students of English literature in colonial Singapore studied authors and works that many of us would not be familiar with today. McLeod's syllabus, for instance, mentions Alexander Kinglake's 1844 travelogue *Eothen*, which has all but disappeared from school syllabi in Singapore. Nonetheless, the discourse on English literature's canonicity asserts that, regardless of the specific works that make up the canon at any point in time, the canon as a whole is universal and timeless, yet also quintessentially English. While the (post)colonial subject is highly encouraged to study English literature as a universal hallmark of high culture, s/he is also told that it is impossible for him/her to attain the heights of perfection that English writers of English literature have achieved. In the NAS interview, Paul contends that, if schools in Singapore really want to stop teaching English literature, they should wait till local literature in "Eastern" languages has developed to the same degree (86). However, in insisting that English literature is in the final analysis irreplaceable, Paul implies that local literature will never reach that point where it becomes the equal of English literature. In fact, the possibility that local writers might write in English rather than in their so-called Eastern languages does not appear to have even crossed his mind. Tan Sock Kern, a former principal of the Singapore Chinese Girls' School, is similarly dismissive of local writing in English. When asked to explain her pedagogical methods, she had apparently proclaimed: "History—what do we want with Empire history? So we did the history of China. Books? I said you are teaching them [students]

English, so you buy books from England, stories from England, rather than Singapore written books." (qtd. in Ooi 65) Tan served as principal from 1956 to 1978, when Singapore made the transition from partial self-rule in 1959 to independence from the British in 1963 and then from Malaysia in 1965. As head of a school in a fledgling nation-state, Tan was willing to jettison teaching the history of the British Empire, but she continued to look up to works by English writers as the best means of teaching the English language and literature to Singaporean students. As these examples suggest, many people in Singapore thought, and still think of, English literature as a form of universal culture that is open to all and yet paradoxically remains the exclusive domain of the British.

The syllabi for the Singapore *O* and *A* level English literature examinations reflect, but also reinforce, this long-standing view of English literature.[6] These exams are jointly administered by the Singapore Ministry of Education and Cambridge Assessment, an international exams board affiliated with the University of Cambridge in the UK. Cambridge Assessment is in fact the postcolonial successor of the University of Cambridge Local Examinations Syndicate (UCLES), which was responsible for administering exams in British colonies around the world in the nineteenth and early twentieth centuries. According to the annual reports on education in the Straits Settlements, the Queen's Scholarship Exam in 1890 included English literature as an optional subject for examination, although at the time, the elite Raffles Institution was the only school in Singapore, Penang, and Malacca that provided instruction in English literature ("Annual Education Report, for the Year 1890" 86–87). In the following year, however, with the establishment of UCLES in Singapore, schools in Singapore began offering exams that would culminate in a post-secondary qualification known as the Cambridge Senior Certificate ("Annual Education Report, for the Year 1891" 267). The Cambridge senior exam included English literature as an optional subject. As a result, more English-medium schools in Singapore began teaching English literature on a wider scale ("Annual Education Report, for the Year 1891" 267–68).

As Holden has observed, there is a clear line of inheritance from the colonial Cambridge Senior Certificate to the present-day Singapore-Cambridge GCE *O* and *A* levels (40). Although Singapore literature has been steadily expanding its presence on the *O* level syllabus since Holden published his article in 2000, canonical British literary works from the nineteenth century continue to make up a significant portion of the *A* level syllabus. Between the years 1998–2019, the *A* level English literature syllabus featured well-known British writers including Austen, Wordsworth, Mary Shelley, Dickens, all three Brontë sisters, Elizabeth Gaskell, George Eliot, Thomas Hardy, Tennyson, Wilde, and many others.[7] Nineteenth-century novels in particular remain firm favorites with the examination board, despite the length of the novels and their perceived difficulty. From 1998 to 2019, the syllabus included no fewer than three novels by Austen (*Pride and Prejudice*; *Sense and Sensibility*; *Mansfield Park*), four by Dickens (*Great Expectations*; *Hard Times*; *Little Dorrit*; *Our Mutual Friend*), four by Hardy (*Far from the Madding Crowd*; *Tess of the d'Urbervilles*; *The Mayor of Casterbridge*; *Jude the Obscure*), as well as *Jane Eyre* and *Villette* by Charlotte Brontë, and *Wuthering Heights* by Emily Brontë. Conversely, there were only five Singaporean authors on the syllabus, each represented by only one or two texts. On the one hand, the *O* level syllabus, with its growing emphasis on local literature, appears to have taken to heart Holden's contention that the study of English literature in Singapore should be better attuned to the nation's needs "if [it] is to leave behind the legacies of colonialism and gain a public role in Singapore" (47). On the other hand, the continuing predominance of well-known nineteenth-century British writers (as well as Shakespeare, Milton, and others) in the *A* level syllabus implies that, at the higher levels of study, the discipline of English literature is primarily concerned with conveying knowledge about the canon rather than nation-building. This discrepancy between the *O* and *A* level syllabi makes it evident that, while Singaporean writing in English is accepted and even welcomed as a local addition to English literature, canonical British literary works remain at the center of the discipline and its corpus. Whereas Singapore literature speaks to specific conditions in Singapore, canonical British literary works—the *A* level syllabus implies—transcend such boundaries of space and time. Paradoxically, by privileging the supposed universality of these British literary works, the *A* level syllabus simultaneously reaffirms the myth of English literature's uniquely English character, which apparently no (post)colonial writer can ever emulate.

As avid readers of English-language fiction, the young Singaporean women whom I have interviewed perceive contemporary Britain through the lens of English literature, both as a subject that they studied at school and as a collection of exemplary works that they have been exposed to since childhood. Having internalized the notion that English literature is universal as well as particular, these women seek out the apparently distinctive Englishness of English literature not only in British literary works, but also in British heritage tourist attractions. To put it another way, in the context of heritage tourism, the perceived exclusivity of British literature and history enhances these women's enjoyment of British cultural commodities, in the same way that it does for the Japanese female reader of the Harrods catalog and the *Emma Victorian Guide*. As I will show later in this chapter, this is not the case when the interviewees attempt to perform their admiration for British high culture through practices of bodily adornment and display. Out of the five interviewees, Chris, Lisa, and Farah have visited the UK at least once. The younger members of the group, Jennifer and Carol, have not traveled to the UK before, but they would very much like to if given the opportunity. Regardless of whether they have been to Britain or not, all of the interviewees view the country in terms that are strongly suggestive of the heritage tourism industry. To Farah, contemporary Britain is both a "time capsule" and a "storybook land":

> FARAH: . . . the experience [of visiting Britain] is almost like stepping into a time capsule, except that it's the double experience of stepping into a time capsule *and* stepping into a fantasy world, a fictional world, because the UK is the world that I know from books and stories.

Although Farah has been to the UK only once, her trip left a deep impression on her. From her perspective, it showed her that art does indeed mirror life. Farah's fascination with the fictional-yet-real world of Britain uncannily echoes the description of Britain found in a late nineteenth-century American children's book, which Nicola Watson discusses in her book on literary tourism in Britain (10). Susan Coolidge's 1886 novel *What Katy Did Next* offers its young American female readers an account of how Katy visited "Story-book England" (qtd. in Watson 10). Like many American tourists of the period, Katy sees the real landscape in Britain as an extension of the literary text (Watson 9–10). As Watson wryly observes, the character of Katy, "with her enthusiasm for London as a collection of 'places I know about in books' . . . is still very much alive today" (10). Like the implied nineteenth-century American reader of *What Katy Did Next*, Farah views Britain through her reading of English literature. This is a "structure of feeling" (to borrow Raymond Williams's expression) that the British heritage industry since the nineteenth century has been quick to capitalize on, as earlier chapters have shown. As Farah's mixed metaphor of the "time capsule" and the "storybook land" suggests, the heritage industry actively preserves monuments and landscapes that evoke the historical contexts that have given rise to famous works of literature.

Chris, who has been to the UK on several occasions for work and holidays, similarly visits heritage attractions in order to experience the history that has produced the literary works and the period films and TV dramas that she enjoys. In fact, she once traveled all the way to the historic city of Bath—which she described as having been "stopped in time"—to attend the annual Jane Austen Festival. Even Carol, who has not been to Britain before, makes the same associations between reading English literature and visiting heritage attractions in the UK. During the interview, she expressed disappointment at having missed out on a school trip to London to see Shakespeare's plays at the Globe. Whether directly or implicitly, all of the interviewees reaffirm the principle, heavily marketed by the heritage industry in Britain, that it is important to "stand where history happened" (in the words of the famous slogan from English Heritage). Echoing Neil LaBute's preference for filming *Possession* on location rather than in a studio, Chris signed up for a Jack the Ripper tour when she was in London a few years ago because "there's nothing quite like exploring the actual crime scenes . . . and places associated with the Ripper case, in the dark of night no less." Likewise, Lisa once participated in a walking tour of London inspired by ghost stories. The tour, she claimed, "g[ave] [her] a sense of being transported back in time," as she stepped on "the same cobblestones that Victorian people once walked on." As we can see from these examples, these women's familiarity with English literature preconditions them to engage (or to want to engage) in heritage tourism in Britain, thereby contributing to the success of the British heritage industry. Despite its supposed universality, English literature and its accompanying history remain particularly English. This perceived Englishness in turn motivates these Singaporean women to travel to Britain itself to soak up the atmosphere of its rich literature and history. More than sixty years after Singapore gained independence from the British, English literature's canonicity continues to exert a strong pull on Britain's erstwhile colonial subjects, drawing young Singaporean women to the former imperial metropolis to gaze in awe at "Story-book England" and its heritage attractions.

Performing Victorian-ness

While my interviewees are clearly passionate about reading English literature, what stands out most in their engagements with nineteenth-century British literature and history is their keen interest in the fashions of the period, especially Victorian fashion. Whereas on the one hand they seek to demonstrate their cultural sophistication by talking about the classic works that they have read, on the other hand these women deviate from other women in their socio-economic class in translating their admiration for British heritage and high culture into niche practices of bodily performance that depart from the mainstream. In making this shift from textuality to corporeality, my interviewees' enthusiasm for historical fashion reveals schisms in their consumption of British cultural commodities. For these women, historical fashion provides them with the opportunity to imagine that they inhabit an alternative reality. Within this playful space of the imagination, these young Singaporean women perform a Victorian alter ego that negotiates between the Englishness, and in particular the whiteness, of British high culture and the possibilities offered by Japanese popular culture. All of the interviewees exhibit a deep fascination with historical styles of dress and the subcultural practice of historical costuming; that is, the practice of creating and/or wearing outfits that are strictly appropriate to the historical periods in which they originate. Such historical costumes are usually made according to sewing techniques and with materials that were available in the chosen historical period, and they are worn according to the conventions of the time. When Carol read *The Importance of Being Earnest* for her secondary school literature class, she began to develop an interest not only in Victorian literature, but also in Victorian fashion. At the time, Carol was also studying art, including fashion design. Reading Wilde's play inspired her to research women's fashions in nineteenth-century Britain for her school art project, which has since sparked an abiding interest in fashion styles of the period. Jennifer, who is currently pursuing a degree in fashion design, has an even stronger interest in historical fashion, and also in the practice of historical costuming. In the interview, she explained that she has been attracted to "all the historical fashion," including "the very elegant Victorian-era clothes," since she was a child. Now that she is in her early twenties, Jennifer continues to admire the "fancy" and "frilly" clothing characteristic of the Victorian and Edwardian periods, as well as eighteenth-century French aristocratic styles. Not only does Jennifer like the look of Victorian fashion, but she is also nostalgic for the artisanal workmanship and high-quality materials that went into making Victorian fashion in the nineteenth century, before clothing became mass-produced. As a future fashion designer, Jennifer has great respect for those who make their own period costumes using the correct techniques and materials. During the focus group sessions, Jennifer and Farah, another historical costuming enthusiast, both bemoaned the lack of "Renaissance Faires" (fan conventions where people dress up and interact with others in period costumes) in Singapore.

However, despite their interest in historical fashion and historical costuming, none of the young women I interviewed engage in historical costuming as a hobby. Instead, they prefer to wear Lolita fashion, and especially the Classic Lolita style, as the "closest approximation" to historical costuming, as Jennifer put it during the interview. When Farah was at university, she befriended an exchange student, who taught her and her classmates about historical costuming. Although Farah greatly enjoyed learning how to sew historically accurate costumes, when the exchange student left, she stopped trying to sew her own period costumes. She turned to sewing cosplay costumes instead, while keeping her interest in historical costuming alive by incorporating her knowledge of historical sewing techniques into her cosplay costumes. Whereas Farah considers cosplay to be a closer approximation to historical costuming than Lolita fashion, Carol treats Lolita fashion, and especially its *Classic* variant, as her preferred substitute for the pleasures of historical costuming:

> CAROL: . . . the detail in Lolita is not something you see in modern [contemporary] fashion. . . . the pin-tucks, the ruffles, the scallops, the lace, it's not something you see in modern fashion. And that's a pity. I think we should bring back bustles and bonnets. . . .
>
> INTERVIEWER: Do you think Classic Lolita is more historically accurate?
>
> CAROL: [laughs]. I wouldn't say that any style of Lolita is historically accurate. But I would say, yes, Classic Lolita does borrow more elements from history.

Likewise, although Chris wears historically accurate Regency-style dresses to the Jane Austen Festival in Bath and to the annual dance party organized by the Jane Austen Circle in Singapore, she allows herself a good deal of artistic license in her makeup and accessories. According to Chris, the organizers and the people who attend the Jane Austen dance parties in Singapore have a very relaxed definition of historical costuming. As such, some participants come dressed in Classic Lolita outfits. Chris herself has attended these events with friends who are fans of Lolita fashion. Once she even cross-dressed as a Regency gentleman in the same way that fans of Lolita fashion sometimes dress as *ōji* ("prince"), the male counterpart of the Lolita. Despite being able to sew their own costumes (in the case of

Jennifer and Farah), or at least to buy historically accurate costumes online (in the case of Chris), these young Singaporean women would rather wear Lolita fashion than engage in historical costuming. While their admiration for English literature and history makes them eager to perform an idealized Victorian-ness through fashion and bodily display, these women strangely prefer to adopt a Japanese style of neo-Victorian dress instead of wearing historically accurate Victorian costumes, which would in principle bring them closer to the historical ideal.

When asked why they have chosen to wear Lolita fashion instead of historical costumes, these women cited a number of reasons, ranging from issues of practicality and comfort to the difficulty of obtaining historically accurate costumes. They also evinced the same desire to "become an English Lady" that pervades Japanese neo-Victorian *shōjo* manga (as we have seen in chapters 3 and 4), and that is also present in the Lolita subculture in Singapore. When I spoke with Chris and Lisa in 2016, Lisa explained that wearing Victorian-style outfits, including the Lolita dress that she wore to the Halloween tea party in 2015, makes her feel as if she has been transformed into an aristocratic lady:

> LISA: I feel elegant. I don't want to be a princess. Rather, I want to feel like a refined aristocratic lady. It almost feels like when you put on the whole get-up, you get a different personality. You tend to carry yourself differently as well. I actually feel that's what a lady should feel and look like, although in today's world it probably sounds prudish.

"[D]ressing up for a tea party," according to Lisa, allows her to "relive the past," when having tea with friends was still considered "a fancy event." For Chris and Lisa, dressing *up*, rather than *down*, has distinct class overtones. The two women regard the Victorian period as a time when the upper classes could dress up and enjoy a luxurious aristocratic lifestyle. For Chris and Lisa, wearing Lolita fashion and holding tea parties in five-star hotels are a means of experiencing this bygone aristocratic lifestyle. During the focus group sessions, Farah, Jennifer, and Carol spoke about the gatherings or "tea parties" that the Lolita community in Singapore organizes, often at expensive venues that have an air of luxury mixed in with the Lolita subculture's favored aesthetic of prettiness and cuteness. In fact, at the time of the interviews, one of the Lolitas in the local Lolita Facebook group was organizing an upcoming gathering to be held at a fine-dining restaurant serving a limited-edition afternoon tea menu, which Carol described as "super-pricey." Moreover, the Lolitas themselves are expected to behave in a "ladylike" manner at these events, as Jennifer and Farah testified during the interviews. Judging from their responses in the interviews, it appears that these young Singaporean women prefer to wear Lolita fashion instead of historically accurate period dress partly because the Lolita subculture speaks to their aspirations for a pseudo-aristocratic lifestyle.

There is, however, an unspoken reason for these women's choice of historical-inspired fashion. In contrast to the whiteness of English literature and history, which these women themselves uphold, contemporary Japanese popular culture seems more accessible because of its simultaneously raceless yet racial character. Like amateur reenactments of historical events, the neo-Victorian fashion practices of my interviewees articulate an embodied relationship with the past. As Jerome de Groot describes it, these women locate "the agency of historical investigation":

> . . . in the individual and their experience of the everyday—of cold, hunger, discomfort, difference [or, in the case of my interviewees, of good food, luxury, and opulence]—rather than any grander, totalizing conceptualization of meaning, purpose, or progress. History is consumed by the re-enactor . . . as something which may be put on, worn, a set of tools and behaviors which relate specifically in the first instance to the corporeal body and thence to "culture" or modes of behavior. (105–06)

It is precisely because of this emphasis on the corporeal body that my interviewees are uncomfortable with historical costuming, and that they turn to Japanese Lolita fashion as a viable alternative. Performing Victorian-ness through bodily display (as opposed to reading a Victorian novel or looking at a Victorian monument) makes these women sensitive to the fact that their bodies are not white. With its insistence on historical accuracy, the practice of historical costuming implicitly favors those who look like the *real thing*, or at least, how the mass media and the heritage industry imagine the real thing to look like. This privileging of whiteness in historical costuming puts my interviewees at a distance, thereby pushing them towards Japanese forms of neo-Victorian fashion instead.

Chris's interview responses are particularly instructive. When Chris attended the Jane Austen Festival at Bath, she deliberately wore a historically accurate Regency-style dress that she had bought specifically for the occasion. Although Chris differentiates herself from those who are "really into historical costuming," she put in the effort to wear a historically accurate dress because the festival organizers and the fans at Bath are, in Chris's words, "quite strict about it." Despite Chris's efforts, a woman at one of the festival events drew attention to Chris's painted nails and asked her pointedly, "Is that historically accurate?" Although the woman did not (and perhaps could not) comment on Chris's skin color, Chris is at least subliminally aware that her Chinese ethnicity renders any attempt to dress up as a real-life Elizabeth Bennett historically inaccurate. When asked why she does not engage seriously in historical costuming, she implied that she would not be able to do it well simply because she is not white:

> INTERVIEWER: Would you be interested in wearing historical costumes besides the dresses that you wore to the Austen dance parties?
>
> CHRIS: I am [interested]. It's just that, obtaining it [historical costumes] is difficult. And probably quite expensive because I can't sew. If I had the skills to make my own stuff, or if I had the time to do it, maybe I would.
>
> INTERVIEWER: Okay. But you enjoy looking at other people in period dress?
>
> CHRIS: Yeah, I think it's very pretty. Especially if they can do that whole look, right? Plus the hair and makeup, it's like, wow. Because I think, as an Asian, when I do Regency [costuming], I feel that the look is not the same as when I see a Caucasian lady doing the same thing. I mean, simply because the whole [Regency] era is a Western-centric era, maybe they are better able to carry off that particular look.

From this exchange it is evident that, while Chris is quick to cite practical reasons for not doing historical costuming, her reference to Caucasian women suggests that there are implicit racial motivations behind her preference for Japanese neo-Victorian fashion, and that of the other interviewees as well. In the individual interviews and the focus group sessions, Farah, Jennifer, and Carol all agreed that wearing Lolita fashion is easier than doing historical costuming (no corset, shorter skirts, etc.). Yet they also spoke repeatedly of the difficulties that they face in wearing Lolita fashion in Singapore (too hot, shoes are uncomfortable, outfits take a long time to put on, clothing sizes are too small, too expensive, dress codes are too strict, etc.). If historical costuming is difficult, wearing Lolita fashion is not that much easier. Race, therefore, provides an explanation for why these women have chosen not to engage in historical costuming, despite their interest in it. As non-white women, they are not able, and will never be able, to achieve the ideal of historical accuracy and "do that whole look," as Chris puts it.

Rather than futilely attempting to fit in with the whiteness of historical costuming, these young Singaporean women incline towards Lolita fashion. On the one hand, this Japanese form of neo-Victorian fashion appeals to these women because of its apparently raceless quality. This supposed raceless-ness further contributes to the popular perception, discussed in the previous chapter, that Japanese popular culture is democratic and universal, perhaps even more so than the proclaimed universality of Englishness in British high culture. Farah, who is Malay, explained in the interview that learning about historical costuming during her university days "de-romanticize[d]" her perception of Victorian Britain, which she had earlier acquired from the books that she had read. Thinking about clothes on bodies, Farah clarified, made the Victorian past seem less abstract and more corporeal to her. With this invocation of the corporeal body, however, Farah suddenly shifted the conversation from historical costuming to Lolita fashion, thereby implying that the latter offers certain possibilities of bodily performance, which the former is not able to offer her. Farah sees Lolita fashion as a sartorial style that is neither quite European nor Japanese. It is simply "an aesthetic of pretty [sic], which is achievable by anyone," provided that one has enough money:

> FARAH: You don't have to be born [into] a specific race, or gender, or in a [particular historical] era to be able to access this [Lolita] version of pretty. You just need money.
>
> . . .
>
> But it is liberating in that sense. It's accessible to all . . . who can afford it [laughs]. But regardless of nationality, color, race, gender, that's already a lot. Sexuality [too]. That's already a lot of freedom.

This *freedom* even allows Farah to adapt Lolita fashion for her own purposes, for example, by incorporating the Muslim hijab or headscarf into her outfits. Farah's description of Lolita fashion as raceless echoes the widely held view that contemporary Japanese popular culture is *mukokuseki*. Although *mukokuseki* literally means "without nationality," it often takes on a racial inflexion. In their chapter in Joseph Tobin's *Pikachu's Global Adventure: The Rise and Fall of Pokémon*, Hirofumi Katsuno and Jeremy Maret state that "[i]n anime, characters are often drawn in a *mukokuseki* (no-nationality) style that is intended to be racially ambiguous" (88). Koichi Iwabuchi uses the concept of *mukokuseki* too, both in his chapter in Tobin's book and in his earlier work.[8] Iwabuchi observes that Japanese manga, anime, and video games are popular worldwide because they downplay "Japanese ethnic characteristics" (*Recentering Globalization* 28). The characters and settings in these narratives are drawn in such a fantastical way that they do not look quite human, which means that anyone can identify with them, regardless of the shape of their face or the color of their skin. Likewise, because Lolita fashion is—as Farah described it—"fantasy clothing detached from any real-world [referent]," it allows Malay Singaporean women like her to partake in a form of historical costuming without having to worry about their racial (and religious) identity.

On the other hand, the young Singaporean women I spoke to are also very much drawn to the racialized character of Lolita fashion. When speaking of her reservations about engaging in historical costuming as a non-white woman, Chris explained that she feels the same way about Caucasian people wearing Lolita fashion. From Chris's perspective, "Western" (i.e., Caucasian) men and women who dress up in Lolita outfits do not quite resemble what she expects a Lolita to look like. She stated that Caucasian Lolitas often "try to look Japanese" by adopting "a certain kind of styling," thereby implying that these Caucasian Lolitas ultimately fail to look Japanese. As for Caucasian Lolitas who do not attempt "to follow the whole Japanese aesthetic," they end up "look[ing] very different from what [Chris] see[s] in magazines." In other words, these Caucasian Lolitas do not look like Lolitas at all. Chris made it very clear in the interview that she does not disapprove of non-white people wearing historical costumes and white people wearing Lolita fashion. Nonetheless, in drawing parallels between Asian people wearing Western period dress and Western people wearing Asian Lolita fashion, Chris unconsciously gestures toward the racial connotations of Lolita fashion. In the same way that Chris cannot quite carry off the look of a Jane Austen heroine, Caucasian people are not able to pull off the look of a Japanese Lolita. The "stereotypical image of a Lolita" that Chris sees in her mind's eye is that of a Japanese body, or at least that of an East Asian body, which looks similar to a Japanese body. Despite its *mukokuseki* quality, Lolita fashion is in fact a racialized practice.

In discussing the global appeal of contemporary Japanese popular culture, Iwabuchi introduces the concept of *cultural odor* to describe how certain commodities become inscribed with images (usually stereotypical) of a country and its culture (*Recentering Globalization* 27–32). Iwabuchi argues that many of Japan's exports in earlier decades (such as the Walkman and karaoke) were *mukokuseki* in the sense that they had no cultural odor. On the other hand, manga, anime, and other more recent popular culture commodities are strongly associated in the global imagination with Japan and its apparently distinctive brand of coolness and cuteness (*Recentering Globalization* 27–32). These cultural commodities, Iwabuchi claims, have a cultural odor or indeed a cultural *fragrance* that conjures up positive visions of Japanese-ness (*Recentering Globalization* 27–32). Although he is mainly concerned with abstract connotations of Japanese-ness, Iwabuchi's use of a sensory metaphor draws attention to the bodily nature of the association between the product and its country of origin. Lolita fashion *smells* not only of intangible notions of cool and cute Japanese youth culture, but also of physical Japanese bodies characterized by particular racial features. Although Chris "do[esn't] think it's wrong" for Caucasian people to wear Lolita fashion, the sense of estrangement that she feels reveals that Lolita fashion is coded with a particular racial aura, and that this racial aura constitutes part of its appeal. Chris, like many of the Lolitas in Singapore, is of ethnic Chinese descent. Chris's preference for Lolita fashion over historical costuming suggests that Chinese Singaporean women like her are subliminally attracted to this Japanese subcultural practice because of its perceived racial proximity. It is telling that Farah, whose brown skin puts her at a distance from the ideal Japanese-ness of Lolita fashion, emphasizes the raceless quality of the latter instead. While ethnic Chinese Singaporean Lolitas do not have the ideal Japanese body that accompanies their image of contemporary Japanese popular culture, they are better able to "pass" as Japanese compared to their Caucasian counterparts, and not to mention their Malay, Indian, and Eurasian counterparts in Singapore as well. Despite being Chinese rather than Japanese, Chris is at ease with how she looks in Lolita and especially *ōji* attire. In comparison to the whiteness of historical costuming, Japanese Lolita fashion provides ethnic Chinese women in Singapore with a more accessible means of performing Victorian-ness through its perceived racial proximity. At the same time, its supposed transcendence of race affords Singaporean women of other ethnicities the same opportunity to perform an imaginary Victorian self, one that is capable of accommodating their non-white racial identities.

Race and Empire(s)

This appeal to race in contemporary Japanese pop culture is so compelling in the Singaporean context because racial thinking is deeply entrenched in the country. Race, like English literature, is a product of colonial rule. Providing a comprehensive historical account of the concept of race in Singapore would take up far more space than this chapter would allow, hence I will touch upon only a few key figures and moments in this history. When Sir Thomas Stamford Raffles established a British trading post in Singapore in 1819, he brought with him an emergent colonial discourse on race. As early as his second visit to Singapore in 1819, Raffles mapped out a plan for allocating land on the island along communal lines. This town plan, as the historian C. M. Turnbull describes it, was designed to implement "order and control by grouping the different communities in specified areas under their own headmen" (12). When Raffles returned to Singapore for his third and final visit in 1822, he took issue with the pragmatic manner in which the chief administrator of the trading post had allocated land to different organizations and communities (Turnbull 19). Raffles promptly revised what he saw as the haphazard layout of the town, moving all Chinese settlers to the area west of the Singapore River, allocating adjoining parcels of land in the east to the Malay, Bugis, Javanese, and Arab peoples, and relocating Indian settlers further upriver (Turnbull 21–22). Raffles's policy of segregating the various communities in Singapore thus sowed the seeds for conceptualizing race as a means of classifying people, although it is important to recognize that this segregation came about because the actions of many agents converged with Raffles's vision of urban planning, rather than simply because Raffles had decreed it (Chew 38).[9] Although Raffles's papers indicate that he made distinctions within each community—he set up separate quarters for the different Chinese dialect groups and for the Malays, Bugis, and the Javanese—he also made homogenizing claims about these communities.[10] Raffles was especially keen on setting aside enough land for the expanding number of Chinese immigrants, whom he was pleased to call "that industrious race" (83). This was despite the fact that Chinese traders in the Malay Archipelago had lived amongst the Malays from as early as the fifteenth century and had intermarried with the locals to produce hybrid communities of Peranakans in places such as Malacca and Penang (Koh and Ho 3–4). Raffles's town plan greatly reduced the opportunities for such interethnic mixing. When Raffles left Singapore, he appointed John Crawfurd as the second chief administrator or Resident of Singapore. Crawfurd served in Singapore from 1823 to 1826. Over his long career as a colonial administrator, historian, journalist, and Orientalist scholar, Crawfurd developed a polygenic theory of human creation, arguing that the different races that made up humankind were essentially separate species (Knapman 1, 4–5). Contrary to what one might expect, Crawfurd drew on the concept of race to campaign for equal rights for all races or "species" of human beings, regardless of their status as colonizer or colonized (Knapman 4–5). While Raffles and Crawfurd were not explicitly *racist*, their ideas represent early examples of *racial* thinking in Singapore at the beginning of the nineteenth century, at a time when the meaning of the word *race* was unstable and the concept had not yet entered mainstream discourse in the imperial metropolis.

Over the years of British rule, Raffles's and Crawfurd's early expressions of racial thinking in Singapore became reified into the now-familiar categories of CMIO: Chinese, Malay, Indian, and Other (which usually refers to Eurasians). Edward Beasley observes that, in the case of Britain, it was only in the 1870s that the previously amorphous notion of race became a biological category grounded on apparently fixed, hereditary physical characteristics (especially skin color), and associated with moral attributes and intellectual ability (20). In the second half of the nineteenth century and particularly towards the end of the century, British New Imperialism converged with the rise of racial thinking in Europe. As British intervention in the Malay states intensified from the 1870s onward, colonial administrators took the ideas about race that they had been developing in Singapore into peninsular Malaya, where they transformed these ideas into a fully institutionalized, race-based economic division of labor and political administration.[11] Drawing on their assumptions about each race's capabilities and weaknesses, the British confined the Malays to their "traditional" agrarian and feudal way of life, and actively discouraged them from participating in the capitalist colonial economy. Because the Malays were supposed to be the natives of the land (despite intermixing with immigrants from Java and Sumatra), the British colonial authorities allowed only members of the Malay aristocracy to take on advisory and administrative roles. On the other hand, British colonial policies prevented Chinese and Indian immigrants from engaging in subsistence agriculture and political administration. The British encouraged Chinese immigrants to work as commercial middlemen or as laborers in the tin mines, while importing laborers from India to work on rubber plantations or public building works. In 1907, a tin and gold mine owner in Malaya described the makeup of Malayan society in explicitly racial terms: "From a labor point of view, there are practically three races, the Malays (including Javanese), the Chinese, and the Tamils (who are generally known as Klings). *By nature* the Malay is an idler, the Chinaman is a thief, and the Kling is a drunkard, yet *each in his own class of work* is both cheap and efficient, when properly supervised" (Wanford-Lock, qtd. in Hirschman, "Making of Race" 357; emphasis added). Unlike Malaya, Singapore was a trading port and was governed as part of the Straits Settlements Crown Colony, but it was not impervious to these newer ideas linking race, morality, and occupation. In 1891, the Straits Settlements census adopted the racial categories of Chinese, Malays and Other Natives of the Archipelago, Tamils and Other Natives of India, Eurasians, and Europeans for the first time in the colony's history (Hirschman, "Meaning and Measurement" 562), thereby paving the way for the institutionalization of the CMIO framework in the postcolonial period. It is open to debate whether the British intentionally sought to cultivate intercommunal distrust by practicing "divide and rule."[12] Nevertheless, it is clear that, as British colonialism and racial ideology expanded towards the end of the nineteenth century, Singapore and Malaya became "plural societies" (Furnivall 304) that were structured predominantly along the lines of race, rather than religion, caste, or class.

While many scholars before me have pointed out that racial discourse in contemporary Singapore and Malaysia is a product of British colonial rule, it is crucial to recognize that Japanese colonial rule during the Asia-Pacific War also played a significant role in cementing the concept of race in the two countries. The neo-Victorian fashion practices of my interviewees reveal the trans-imperial intersections between the British and the Japanese empires, not only in cultural commodity production in the twenty-first century, but also in the articulation of racial ideology in the preceding century. Singapore's history as a former British and Japanese colony unsettles the center-periphery model that is prevalent in both postcolonial and Victorian studies, reminding us to shift our gaze towards relations of competition and cooperation between the British and Japanese imperial powers. These two powers were not only wartime enemies fighting over territories in Southeast Asia. They were also, in a sense, collaborators in entrenching racial thinking in Singapore. As recent scholarship on race and Japanese imperialism has shown, Japanese racial discourse during Japan's empire-building years (1895–1945) was highly heterogenous and often inconsistent and contradictory. It was also deeply ambivalent about the concept of race itself. On the one hand, Japanese intellectuals, officials, and commentators were uncomfortable with Western racial theories that claimed that non-white peoples (including the Japanese) were innately inferior. Japanese colonial policies encouraging and later enforcing assimilation implied that racial differences between the Japanese and their colonial subjects could be overcome through acculturation. On the other hand, Japanese colonial discourses and practices reaffirmed the significance of race, not least by perpetuating the British policy of racial segregation in Malaya and Singapore. This was partly a matter of expediency, as the speed and timing of the invasion of Southeast Asia left the Japanese military authorities with little choice but to retain many British colonial institutions and practices, including the race-based policy of "divide and rule." It was also, however, part of an overarching trend in Japanese imperialism in the 1930s and 1940s towards "respecting" the racialized cultural differences of various groups, and incorporating those groups as discrete racialized units within the Japanese Empire. As the following discussion demonstrates, Japanese rule in Malaya and Singapore intersected with its British precursor to produce, or rather to reproduce, the inhabitants of these two territories as racialized subjects; as Chinese, Indian, or Malay. Whereas British colonial rule created "plural societies" in Singapore and Malaya, the Japanese Occupation amplified the existing racial divisions into open conflicts that would have a lasting impact on Singapore and Malaya after the war (Cheah 17–18).[13]

After the British forces surrendered in Singapore on 15 February 1942, the Japanese military administration in Singapore and Malaya set about governing its newfound colonial subjects by ironically adopting and amplifying the race-based policies of the colonial power that it had just ousted. The Japanese continued to treat the Malays favorably, while adopting extremely harsh measures against the Chinese population. While there is little evidence to suggest that the Japanese military administration deliberately promoted animosity between the Malays and the Chinese as a matter of policy, its differential treatment of the two groups created fertile conditions for interracial hostility (Cheah 40–41). Like the British before them, the Japanese employed only Malay civil servants, generally of aristocratic origin (Tarling 199). They allowed the Malay sultans to retain their titles; to receive the same allowances as they had done before the war; and from 1943, to act as official advisors to the Japanese governors who had replaced the British Residents (Tarling 200). On the other hand, the Japanese military administration severely punished the Chinese residents in Singapore and Malaya for supporting anti-Japanese resistance efforts in China. From February to March 1942, the Japanese military police embarked on a campaign called Sook Ching—the term literally means "purification through cleansing"—which quickly turned from a purge of anti-Japanese Chinese into a widespread massacre of entire Chinese communities. As Yoji Akashi notes in his account of the twists and turns in Japanese colonial policy towards the Malayan Chinese, hundreds of people were rounded up for no other reason than being Chinese (68). Akashi argues that the Japanese soldiers stationed in Singapore and Malaya took the Sook Ching campaign to the extreme because they were mostly veterans of the 1937 Sino-Japanese War who had met with fierce Chinese resistance on the mainland, and who consequently harbored a great deal of animosity towards ethnic Chinese in general (63). Akashi puts the reported death toll at five thousand (68), but more recent accounts such as Nicholas Tarling's place the figure much higher at approximately forty to seventy thousand deaths (261).[14] The Japanese military administration also forced Chinese community leaders to raise fifty million Malayan dollars as a "gift" to atone for supporting the ongoing resistance in China (Akashi 70–75).[15] The Japanese military administration later recognized that it was necessary to win the cooperation of the Chinese because of their prominent role in the colonial economy (Tarling 201). It therefore attempted to make amends from late 1943 onward, but ultimately failed to overcome Chinese hostility (Cheah 41). As a result of these vastly differing attitudes towards the Malays and the Chinese, the Japanese authorities inadvertently caused the two groups to split into two camps coterminous with their respective races. The Chinese saw the Malays as pro-Japanese collaborators, while the Malays perceived the Chinese as anti-Japanese guerrillas (Cheah 45). In this way, the Japanese Occupation deepened each community's consciousness of its racial difference, and worsened the latent interracial tensions created by British colonial rule.

Having said all this, the Japanese military authorities' decision to maintain the British colonial policy of racial segregation in Malaya and Singapore was not simply due to the exigencies of war, whether it was the lack of time and resources for replacing British colonial institutions and practices, or the practical and/or psychological need to penalize the diasporic Chinese population for supporting the resistance on the mainland. The continued use of race-based organizations to govern the various communities in Singapore and Malaya was part of a larger trajectory in Japanese imperial discourse, one which Takashi Fujitani describes as a shift from exclusion to inclusion, and from "vulgar" to "polite" racism (21–28). Fujitani contends that, with the onset of "total war" in 1937, Japanese imperialism moved decisively towards a strategy of disavowing racist discrimination and incorporating subordinate populations into a seemingly inclusive multiracial nation-state and empire (7). Because total war required Japan to maximize every available human and material resource within its reach, the Japanese state, Fujitani argues, had to win over its colonized peoples and fashion them as quickly as possible into loyal imperial subjects who would willingly commit themselves to Japan's cause (9–10).[16] At the same time, discussions of race in Japanese imperial discourse took on a more culturalist form, which was as essentializing and deterministic as earlier biological notions of race (Fujitani 9). This culturalist racial ideology, according to Christopher Hanscom and Dennis Washburn, was capable of producing difference and hierarchy, while inculcating acquiescence and allegiance to the Japanese Empire through a politics of inclusiveness (3–4). In other words, while the *kōminka* ("imperialization") program of intensive assimilation (1937–1945) was interpellating the inhabitants of colonial Taiwan and Korea as Japanese, these people were also being interpellated as Koreans, Taiwanese Chinese, Taiwanese aborigines, and so on.[17] Drawing on this logic of *differential inclusion* (Hanscom and Washburn 3), pan-Asianist discourse in the 1930s and early 1940s, together with Japanese colonial policy and practice, asserted that Japan's mission as leader of Asia was not to meld all races and cultures into an undifferentiated whole, but to combine them in such a way that each race and culture performs its destined role within the cooperative system of the Greater East Asia Co-Prosperity Sphere, as discussed in the previous chapter. In Malaya and Singapore, this dual process of assimilation and differentiation formed the ideological context in which the Japanese military administration perpetuated the racial divisions first inscribed by British colonial rule.

It is important to reiterate that, in Fujitani's analysis of Japanese imperial discourse, what the Japanese disavowed was racism and not the concept of race itself. The Japanese colonial regime in Malaya and Singapore governed the different ethnic communities as distinct races, each with its particular cultural attributes that would contribute to the successful operation of the Co-Prosperity Sphere. Like its British precursor, the Japanese military administration made use of ethnic organizations to govern the Chinese, Malay, and Indian communities separately, but it also went much further in reifying these racial categories by removing the linguistic, clan, and regional distinctions that Raffles and his successors had put in place. The Japanese dissolved many existing Chinese organizations, for instance, and instead created the Overseas Chinese Association (OCA) as the principal agency for dealing with a supposedly homogenous Chinese community (Kratoska 100).[18] The Japanese also thought of "Chinese character" in homogenizing terms that reproduced familiar racial stereotypes often found in British colonial discourse, and that had structured the economic division of labor under British rule. Paul Kratoska cites a 1942 speech delivered by a Mr. Mizuno, the industrial administrator for Johore, who exhorted his compatriots in Malaya to "encourage [the overseas Chinese] to utilize their peculiar economic capabilities" in assisting Japan in establishing its new order in Asia (qtd. in Kratoska 93). Other contemporary policy documents advised Japanese officials to secure the cooperation of the Chinese in Malaya and Singapore by playing upon "their greed for profit" and their "speculative spirit" (qtd. in Kratoska 93). Even the hardline army officer whom Akashi claims was chiefly responsible for the military administration's anti-Chinese policy was allegedly "strongly impressed by the diligence of the Chinese, their acute sense of business, cohesiveness, independence, and will to live" (64). Although Akashi argues that this officer's views had been influenced by his experiences in Manchuria and northern China, the officer's impression of "the Chinese" also seems to function within a broader trans-imperial discourse on race, one that makes repeated claims about Chinese business acumen and industriousness. Like the British before them, the Japanese military administration in Malaya and Singapore understood cultural difference in racialized terms, thereby (re)producing the racial categories that continue to inform everyday life in the present.

Moreover, the idea that the ethnic Chinese in Singapore are racially proximate to the Japanese has a similarly trans-imperial provenance. This notion of racial proximity is rooted in British discourses on the *yellow* race in the late nineteenth and early twentieth centuries, as well as Japanese responses to these discourses. With the rise of skin color-based conceptualizations of race in the late nineteenth century, British writers in the early twentieth century began producing a genre of novels depicting Chinese and Japanese immigrants "invading" the imperial center. As Ross Forman notes in *China and the Victorian Imagination*, this genre of "Asiatic invasion novels" glosses over the differences between Chinese and Japanese people and their political leaderships, in order to mold them into a monolithic "East" or "Yellow Peril" that is threatening Britain and the "West" (132). These novels, Forman contends, represent this Sino-Japanese union as "the renewal of 'natural' racial allegiances" between the two countries, notwithstanding their historical differences and more recent hostilities (132). This assumption that Chinese and Japanese people are of essentially the same race continues to this day in Britain and also in the United States, as the instances of anti-Asian racism during the COVID-19 pandemic made all too clear. When COVID-19 broke out in the UK and US, people of East Asian descent reported being attacked simply because they looked Chinese, regardless of their actual ethnicity and/or nationality.[19] Whereas commentaries on the regional popularity of Japanese pop culture today often steer clear of race to emphasize "cultural proximity" and shared experiences of "East Asian modernity," Japanese imperial discourse in the first half of the twentieth century embraced the trope of the Yellow Peril and redeployed it to challenge the Euro-American imperial powers and their ethos of white supremacy.[20] In this way, Japanese imperialism worked in tandem with its British counterpart to produce the notion of racial proximity, despite being on opposite sides of the anti-immigration debate and later, the Asia-Pacific War. From the fin de siècle to the end of the war, Japanese ideologues drew on Western theories of scientific racism and Social Darwinism to argue that the *yellow* race was indeed pitted against the *white* race in an evolutionary struggle for survival (Weiner 224, 226). As "the most powerful *jinshu* (race) amongst the yellow *jinshu* (races)," the Japanese people, these ideologues claimed, would play the leading role in this struggle (Weiner 224, 226). As early as 1898, Prince Konoe Atsumaro—whose son Fumimaro would later become prime minister of wartime Japan—urged the readers of the magazine *Taiyō* [*The Sun*] to recognize the importance of building an alliance (*dōmei*) with the Chinese in the aftermath of the first Sino-Japanese War:

> As I see it, in the future East Asia cannot avoid becoming a stage for a contest between the races (*jinshu kyōsō no butai*). Even if fleeting considerations of foreign policy should produce a different environment [of Sino-Japanese hostility], this will yield no more than a temporary result. The final outcome will be a contest between the yellow and white races (*kōhaku ryō-jinshu no kyōsō*), and in this contest the Chinese people and the Japanese people will be placed in the same position, being both considered as the sworn enemy of the white race (*hakujinshu no kyūteki*). Those who are considering a long-term strategy will do well to consider these facts. (Konoe 89)

Although many of these ideologues also insisted that there were distinct and immutable differences in the civilizational capacities of the Japanese, Chinese, and Koreans (and later, the Manchurians and Mongolians in Manchukuo), their invocations of *yellow* unity against the dominance of the *white* race helped to reinforce existing beliefs that these different groups shared some sort of racial affinity.[21]

These assertions of racial affinity between the Japanese and other *yellow* peoples did not, however, apply to Japanese colonial policy and practice in Malaya and Singapore. The idea of racial proximity lost some of its force when Japan extended its empire into Southeast Asia from 1941 to 1945. Although Japanese intellectuals and ideologues continued to claim that the ancient Japanese race was actually an amalgamation of multiple races from different parts of the Asia-Pacific including the Malay Archipelago, the metropolitan Japanese government called for Japanese and local residents in the Southeast Asian territories to be housed in segregated areas (Koshiro 476). Japanese settlers were also warned to avoid intermarriage with the locals for fear of miscegenation (Koshiro 494). Once again, the Japanese colonial governments in Southeast Asia followed the precedent set by the European imperial powers before them. While this was partly a matter of expediency, it also appears that Japanese anthropologists, government experts, and colonial officials in the early 1940s had read the colonial anthropological studies conducted in Southeast Asia by European scholars and had adopted at least some aspects of the scientific racism that underpinned these studies (Koshiro 495–96). In effect, while segregating the different races in Malaya and Singapore, the Japanese also segregated themselves from these other races. Nonetheless, the idea of racial proximity held strong in Japanese colonies outside of Southeast Asia, especially in Korea. Beginning in the late nineteenth century, even before Korea was formally annexed, scholars and officials repeatedly declared that the Koreans were essentially if not actually the same as the Japanese (Fujitani 22). They spoke of the "common ancestry of the Japanese and Koreans" (*Nissen dōso*) and of the "unity of the mainland [Japan] and Korea" (*Naisen ittai*) (Fujitani 22). In the interwar years in particular, Japanese ideologues frequently claimed that there were blood ties between Korean royalty and the Japanese aristocracy and even the imperial family (Fujitani 22), thus contradicting the equally influential notion of a pure Yamato race descended from the emperor. Colonial intermarriage was tolerated and even officially promoted in Korea, Taiwan, and Manchukuo (Koshiro 495).[22] The latter was in fact envisioned as a model of cooperation amongst the *yellow* peoples of Japan, China, Korea, Manchuria, and Mongolia (with the Japanese in the leading position as usual), coming together to promote *gozoku kyōwa* or "the harmony of the five races"

(Young, "Imagined Empire" 92). Although the Japanese colonial regime in Malaya and Singapore did not encourage the locals to see themselves as racially proximate to the Japanese or vice versa, the fashion practices of my interviewees imply that the idea of racial proximity still persists in the political unconscious, bolstered by the enduring ideological power of race in contemporary Singapore.

Japanese colonial rule thus converged with its British counterpart to give rise to the persistent centrality of race in Singapore's and Malaya's postcolonial articulations of nationhood. Emboldened by Japanese concessions towards the end of the war, Malay nationalists rejected the postwar British proposal to create a trans-communal "Malayan Malaya," calling instead for Malays to be granted special rights in a "Malay Malaya" (Tarling 202–04). Although Singapore left the Federation of Malaysia in 1965 over this issue of Malay special rights, the concept of race remains embedded in the principle of multiculturalism that lies at the heart of Singapore's national identity. As Michael Hill, Lian Kwen Fee, Daniel Goh, Philip Holden, and others have argued, multiculturalism in Singapore is often equated with multiracialism. Since independence in 1965, the Singaporean state has been using the Chinese-Malay-Indian-Other multiracial model as a framework for implementing policies that promote social cohesion, especially in the areas of public housing, education, and political representation (Chan and Siddique 33, 44). As Goh and Holden have observed, state-sponsored multiculturalism in Singapore has institutionalized the racial identities inherited from British (and Japanese) colonial rule to the extent that these identities have become "common sense" to most Singaporeans (2–3). Despite its good intentions, the state's promotion of multiculturalism/multiracialism as the foundation for building a viable postcolonial nation has made thinking beyond the colonial concept of race extremely difficult (Goh and Holden 3, 7). By pointing to the raceless yet racial character of Japanese Lolita fashion, Farah's and Chris's interview responses suggest that neo-Victorian fashion in the Singaporean context is shaped by, but also engages with, the racial legacies of both British and Japanese imperialism in the long nineteenth century.

Chris, Lisa, Farah, Jennifer, and Carol are not passive consumers who are simply duped into consuming the cultural products of the British, Anglo-American, and Japanese cultural industries. They are capable of negotiating between the different images of Victorian Britain that they encounter in books, films, and TV dramas; in anime and manga; at museums and heritage monuments; and in historical costuming and Lolita fashion. The confluence of British and Japanese colonial rule in the nineteenth and early twentieth centuries, together with the more recent importation of British high-cultural and Japanese pop-cultural commodities, has created a *playful* space for young Singaporean female fans of Lolita fashion. Within this space, these young Singaporean women negotiate between their high regard for the apparent universality of Englishness, and their desire for a physical mode of expressing this Englishness that is appropriate to the particularity of their non-white bodies. Although this *playful* space is firmly embedded within the constraints of late capitalist consumerism, it does allow these women some freedom of self-expression. In performing an idealized Victorian self, these women turn to Japanese fashion subcultures that are coded as universal (like Englishness), but also as racially proximate to at least some of their Southeast Asian ethnic identities. By engaging in neo-Victorian fashion practices at the intersection of empires past and present, these women reveal that trans-imperial interactions in the long nineteenth century inform not only cultural commodity production, but also consumption, in the global creative economy today.

Conclusion

Using the neo-Victorian as its lens, this book has explored how the global dissemination of British culture and especially English literature in the long nineteenth century has shaped transnational cultural flows in the global creative economy today. Long after the formal dissolution of the British Empire, the enduring assumption that British culture constitutes a universal touchstone of civilizational progress continues to engender relations of collaboration as well as competition between the British, American, and Japanese cultural industries in the late twentieth and early twenty-first centuries. In the field of consumption too, the post-imperial legacies of race and culture cast their shadow on the present, mediating the ways in which female fans of Lolita fashion in Singapore navigate between their desire for Englishness and their attraction to the supposedly more universal and democratic affordances of contemporary Japanese popular culture.

These transhistorical networks linking Britain, the United States, Japan, and Singapore, however, are only part of an even wider network connecting sites of production and consumption in the global creative economy. Although it is tempting to think of postwar cultural imperialism in terms of *Americanization*, *McDonaldization*, and even *Japanization*, transnational cultural flows are better understood as a polycentric web connecting multiple empires. Likewise, imperialism in the nineteenth and early twentieth centuries did not emanate from a single center towards the rest of the world but arose out of the conflicting and complementary interests and interactions of multiple imperial powers, including the British, the Americans, and the Japanese. By way of conclusion, I would like to briefly discuss South Korean director Park Chan-wook's 2016 film *The Handmaiden* [*Agassi*], which presents Korea as yet another node in the trans-imperial networks that this book has explored. As an adaptation of Sarah Waters's neo-Victorian novel

Fingersmith (2002), *The Handmaiden* also calls into question the category of the *neo-Victorian* and, by extension, the fields of Victorian and neo-Victorian studies in a global context.

Fingersmith follows the lives of two young women separated by the vast socioeconomic inequalities of Victorian Britain, but whose fates become inextricably linked because of a criminal plot. Raised in the back streets of London by a Dickensian family of pickpockets and petty criminals, Sue Trinder is enlisted by a swindler called Gentleman to help him cheat the aristocratic Maud Lilly out of her fortune. Whereas *Fingersmith* is set in mid-nineteenth-century Britain, *The Handmaiden* mainly takes place in Korea in the 1930s, when the country was under Japanese rule. In *The Handmaiden*, Sook-hee—the film's version of Sue—helps a Korean conman who goes by the name of Count Fujiwara to seduce Lady Hideko, a rich Japanese heiress who lives in Korea with her uncle Kōzuki Noriaki. Kōzuki is in fact a Korean man who has made his fortune working for the Japanese, and Hideko is the niece of the aristocratic Japanese woman whom Kōzuki married and whose family name he has adopted. Initially, Sook-hee appears to assist Count Fujiwara in his plan to elope with Hideko, take her inheritance, and then lock her up in a mental asylum in Kobe, Japan. The second act of the film, however, reveals that Hideko has been plotting with the count to put Sook-hee into the madhouse in her place, so that she can escape from her uncle and begin a new life using Sook-hee's identity. This part of the film also reveals that Kōzuki has been training Hideko since she was a child to recite and perform excerpts from his extensive collection of Japanese pornographic books. The final act of the film upturns the viewer's expectations again. It turns out that Hideko and Sook-hee have fallen in love with each other, and that they have been working together to outwit both Kōzuki and the count. In a significant departure from *Fingersmith*, the two women destroy Kōzuki's library of pornographic materials, and they escape from both Korea and Japan by boarding a ship bound for Shanghai.

By changing the setting of the story from Victorian Britain to 1930s Korea, *The Handmaiden* foregrounds colonial relations between Japan and the Korean peninsula in the long nineteenth century. As early as 1868, the new Meiji regime sent a formal letter to the Korean government introducing itself in terms that implicitly put the Japanese emperor on par with the Chinese emperor while relegating the Korean emperor to a lower place, thus signaling the Meiji state's aspirations—right from the outset—to revise Japan's position in the East Asian regional order.[1] In 1875, a clash between Japanese ships and Korean coastal defenses gave Japan the opportunity to send troops to Korea to demand an apology, which resulted in Korea and Japan signing the Treaty of Kanghwa in 1876 (W. Beasley 43–44). In other words, Japan effectively applied the same kind of gunboat diplomacy practiced by the Western imperial powers to open Korea to unequal terms of trade and international relations (Hwang 106). After the Kanghwa Treaty of 1876, Japan proceeded to extend its influence in Korea, first turning Korea into a protectorate in 1905 and eventually annexing the country in 1910. Korea remained under direct Japanese rule until the end of the Asia-Pacific War in 1945.

As a film set in colonial Korea, *The Handmaiden* is particularly concerned with the issue of assimilation. There is nothing more that Kōzuki wants than to become Japanese. Many years ago, Kōzuki divorced his Korean wife in order to marry a Japanese woman whose aristocratic family had fallen on hard times. He then took on his wife's surname (Kōzuki), which enabled him to become a naturalized Japanese citizen. Kōzuki's given name (Noriaki) literally means "teaching" and "light," which echoes the slogan of "civilization and enlightenment" (*bunmei kaika*) that characterized the Meiji modernization reforms discussed in chapter three. Besides adopting a Japanese name, Kōzuki has further erased his Korean ethnic identity by requiring members of his household to take on Japanese names as well, and to speak in Japanese at all times. Hence, Sook-hee is renamed Tamako when she enters Kōzuki's household as Hideko's new lady's maid. Kōzuki's elaborate performance of Japanese-ness prompts the count to ask him, "Why this urge to become Japanese?" Kōzuki replies, "Because Korea is ugly and Japan is beautiful. . . . Beauty is cruel by nature. Korea is soft, slow, dull, and therefore hopeless." Kōzuki's reply alludes to the late Victorian idealization of Japanese aesthetics discussed in chapter four. For Kōzuki, however, Japan is beautiful not because it is quaint, but because it is powerful. Kōzuki thus speaks to late Victorian characterizations of Japanese aesthetics as exquisite—the other aesthetic category in Grace Lavery's book—and to the term's association of beauty with violence. In the colonial context of *The Handmaiden*, the beautiful violence of Japanese aesthetics lies not in its challenge to European realist traditions (as Lavery has argued) but in the exercise of Japan's imperial power. By assimilating into a Japanese identity, Kōzuki manages to participate in the exercise of this imperial power, and to reap some of its privileges within Korean colonial society.

The figure of Kōzuki in *The Handmaiden* thus brings to the fore the history of Japanese colonial assimilation policies in Korea. Although it is not clear precisely which year the film is set in, the story most likely takes place before 1937; in other words, before Japan launched the *kōminka* ("imperialization") program to transform the various peoples of its colonies into dedicated subjects of the Japanese Empire. That said, the film clearly references the radical assimilation policies of the late colonial period (1937–1945). Assimilation policies were an integral part of the *kōminka* program, and these policies facilitated the Japanese state's attempts to mobilize all available resources in the colonies to support the war effort in China. In *Becoming Japanese* and *Race for Empire*, for example, Leo Ching and Takashi Fujitani discuss how the *kōminka* program enabled the Japanese state to recruit Taiwanese and Korean men respectively to serve in the Japanese military. In the case of Korea, the Japanese colonial authorities had promoted assimilation since the territory was annexed in 1910, but in the late 1930s and early 1940s, as Japan increasingly mobilized its colonies for war, the colonial administration in Korea began to implement unprecedented measures to expedite assimilation and coerce Koreans into identifying with the Japanese nation-state (Caprio 141–42).[2] In 1940, the government shut down all the major Korean-language newspapers except for the *Maeil Sinbo*, and it began to phase out Korean-language classes in schools (Caprio 153–56). By 1943, schools no longer taught classes in Korean, and by 1944, Korean-language radio programs had ceased entirely (Caprio 153, 157). The colonial government also ordered all Koreans to officially register their households using Japanese-style surnames (Hwang 160). In the narrative world of *The Handmaiden*, Kōzuki's assimilation into Japanese culture is still voluntary and is enforced only within the boundaries of his own household. Nonetheless, *The Handmaiden* anticipates the most infamous assimilation policies of the *kōminka* program regarding naming and language use.

The Handmaiden critiques this history of colonial assimilation, but its critique is directed at Koreans who, like Kōzuki, actively desired to become Japanese. Rather than adopting a nationalist narrative, the film responds to the history of Korean assimilation by foregrounding the trans-imperial dynamics of Hideko and Sook-hee's homosexual relationship. Firstly, Hideko and Sook-hee communicate predominantly in the Korean language. Early in the film, when Sook-hee asks Hideko why she does not speak in Japanese, Hideko explains that she is "sick of" reading books aloud in Japanese for her uncle. Secondly, Sook-hee's inability to read Japanese protects her from the corrupting contents of Kōzuki's pornographic library, and it eventually allows her to destroy the library in the final act of the film. Sook-hee is initially illiterate. Hideko teaches her how to read and write in Korean, but not in Japanese. Sook-hee only discovers the pornographic nature of the books that

Kōzuki forces Hideko to recite when she flips to a page featuring Hokusai's famous woodblock print *The Dream of the Fisherman's Wife*. Incensed by Kōzuki's exploitation of Hideko, Sook-hee (later joined by Hideko) destroys the books in Kōzuki's library, thereby signaling their repudiation of an entire tradition of Japanese literature and visual art that appropriates the bodies of women for the pleasure of men. Through its repeated references to Hokusai's print, *The Handmaiden* implies that this tradition stretches all the way from *shunga* ("erotic pictures") in the Edo period to the resurgence of erotica in the *eroguro nansensu* ("erotic-grotesque-nonsense") style of the 1920s and 1930s. Lastly, Kōzuki and the count are punished at the end of the film for masquerading as Japanese. Because he knows that he cannot escape from Kōzuki's dungeon, the count poisons himself and Kōzuki with his mercury-laced cigarettes. Moments before he collapses, Kōzuki peers at the blue-tinted cigarette smoke as he muses: "It's odd. Your smoke. It's cold, blue, and [suddenly switching from Korean to Japanese] strangely beautiful" (*myō ni utsukushii yōda*). In the end, Kōzuki is killed by the cruel beauty of Japanese aesthetics that he had admired so much. In contrast to the gruesome deaths of Kōzuki and the count, at the end of the film Hideko and Sook-hee succeed in crossing class, ethnic, and national boundaries to form a loving same-sex relationship in which both parties have equal status. In celebrating the solidarity between a Japanese woman and a Korean woman, *The Handmaiden* critiques the colonial history of Korean assimilation into Japanese culture without being, as Leo Ching would put it, "anti-Japan."[3]

Unlike other contemporary South Korean films set in the colonial period, *The Handmaiden* does not champion a Korean national identity in opposition to the Japanese imperial identity it condemns. *The Handmaiden* departs from recent trends in postmillennial South Korean cinema in refusing to foment feelings of anti-Japanese Korean nationalism. In particular, the film avoids the familiar strategy of juxtaposing evil Japanese against innocent Koreans, and pro-Japanese collaborators against anti-Japanese resistance fighters.[4] Instead, it evokes a vision of worldliness through its emphasis on sea voyages. The film establishes from the start that Sook-hee, despite her low social station, is fascinated by the idea of transnational travel. As she attends to Hideko, Sook-hee brings up the topic of sea travel: "Miss, doesn't it bother you not to know? How many ships sail on the wide sea . . . People leaving, people returning, those saying farewell or welcome back. What's the furthest you've travelled? The hill beyond the manor?" As the narrative progresses, Sook-hee and Hideko travel further and further away from Korea. At the end of part one of the film, Hideko elopes with the count to Japan, bringing Sook-hee with her. In part three, Sook-hee and Hideko escape from the port of Kobe in Japan by disguising themselves and boarding a ship bound for Shanghai. As Sook-hee and Hideko travel from Korea to Japan and then to China, the camera lingers on close-up shots of Hideko's face as she stands on the ship's deck looking out towards the sea (figures C.1 and C.2). As Park, Sanders, and Chung have observed, the film ends on an ambiguous note (182–83). I would like to end this chapter and this book by considering three different but interconnected interpretations of the motif of sea travel in *The Handmaiden*'s final scenes.

Firstly, the motif of sea travel in the film's ending signifies a cosmopolitan identity that is neither Japanese nor Korean. At the end of the

Figure C.1. Hideko looking out towards the sea on the ferry to Shimonoseki, Japan. *Source: The Handmaiden.* Directed by Park Chan-wook, CJ Entertainment, 2016.

Figure C.2. Hideko in male attire looking out towards the sea on the ship to Shanghai, China. *Source: The Handmaiden.* Directed by Park Chan-wook, CJ Entertainment, 2016.

film, Hideko and Sook-hee transcend the dichotomies of mistress/servant and colonizer/colonized to become global subjects. The two women's Western-style outfits, like the idealized portrayals of Englishness in the Harrods catalog and the *Emma Victorian Guide*, position Hideko and Sook-hee as citizens of the world who partake in a supposedly universal culture. As Andrew Kim has argued, the film's celebration of Hideko and Sook-hee's newfound cosmopolitanism is problematic (40–42). Although it is unclear whether Shanghai will be Hideko and Sook-hee's new home or simply the first stop in a longer journey, the film's association of the two women's new Westernized identity with the cosmopolitan city of Shanghai raises doubts about the extent of the women's freedom. Shanghai is, after all, a product of war, informal imperialism, and above all, the ideology of liberalism. As Lisa Lowe has demonstrated in *The Intimacies of Four Continents*, liberalism facilitated the imposition of economic and administrative systems of control in the name of free trade, amongst other things. Moreover, assuming that *The Handmaiden* is set in the early to mid-1930s, Shanghai would soon be occupied by the Japanese with the advent of the Sino-Japanese War in 1937. These historical facts effectively cast a dark shadow over the film's espousal of a liberal cosmopolitan female subjectivity.

A second possible reading of the ending in *The Handmaiden* folds the film's celebration of Hideko and Sook-hee's cosmopolitanism back into a nationalist narrative. In this interpretation of the ending, the motif of sea travel represents a new Korean national identity founded on the global popularity of contemporary Korean popular culture, otherwise known as the Korean Wave. The term *Korean Wave* was first coined by the Chinese media in the late 1990s to describe the sudden craze for South Korean films and TV dramas amongst Chinese youth, but in recent years the term has come to encompass a wide range of South Korean cultural products that have garnered fans not only in East Asia, but also as far as the US, South America, the Middle East, and Europe (Y. Kim, "Introduction" 1). Since the late 1990s, South Korea has emerged as a new center for the production of popular culture commodities in the global creative economy. Although this book has focused on the interactions between the British heritage industry, American media conglomerates, and the Japanese popular culture industries, over the past two decades South Korea's cultural sector has been growing rapidly and exporting not only TV dramas and films, but also K-pop music, online games, fashion, and beauty products. Like the Cool Japan campaign, the Korean Wave is a deliberate creation of state economic and cultural policy. However, successive Korean governments since the 1997 Asian financial crisis have generally been more savvy than their Japanese counterparts in cultivating the popular culture industries as a new source of economic revenue in a post-Fordist economy.[5] According to figures from the Korean Creative Content Agency, the total export value of Korean cultural commodities rose from USD $188.9 million in 1998 to USD $4,679.3 million in 2015 (Dal 50). Given the phenomenal success of the Korean Wave, the vastness of the sea in the closing shots of *The Handmaiden* might be parsed differently. Rather than celebrating cosmopolitanism's *transcendence* of national boundaries, the film seems to be celebrating the *national* achievements of South Korea as a global cultural superpower in the twenty-first century. All of the main roles in *The Handmaiden* are played by Korean actors, including that of Hideko (Kim Min-hee). The actress who played Sook-hee (Kim Tae-ri) later went on to play leading roles in the TV drama *Mr. Sunshine* (2018) and the film *Space Sweepers* (2021), both of which were distributed worldwide by Netflix. In this reading of *The Handmaiden*'s ending, the film foregrounds South Korea's success in producing transnational forms of pop culture as the basis for a new South Korean national identity, thus mirroring what Koichi Iwabuchi has called the "trans/nationalism" of contemporary Japanese discourses on the global appeal of Japanese pop culture.

In my third and final reading of *The Handmaiden*'s ending, the motif of sea travel points to the unmooring of Victorian and neo-Victorian studies. In shifting the story of *Fingersmith* from 1860s Britain to 1930s Korea, *The Handmaiden* compels scholars of neo-Victorian studies to reconsider not only how we define the neo-Victorian, but also what is at stake when we use the category itself. In this book, I have used the term *neo-Victorian* quite broadly to describe fictional narratives from the late twentieth and early twenty-first centuries that are set in Britain during Queen Victoria's reign. I have also used the term to refer to nonfiction texts (such as the Harrods catalog) and to social practices (such as Lolita fashion) that encourage readers and participants to imaginatively recreate certain aspects of nineteenth-century Britain, and crucially, to vicariously experience those aspects. *The Handmaiden*, however, expands this already broad definition of the neo-Victorian to the point where it reveals the limits of the term's usefulness. In the final chapter of *Neo-Victorianism and the Memory of Empire*, Elizabeth Ho examines recent neo-Victorian narratives, such as Amitav Ghosh's *Sea of Poppies* (2008), which use the trope of maritime travel to push against the limitations of neo-Victorian fiction in critiquing forms of power that exceed the geographical and temporal boundaries of Victorian Britain (171–89). Yet, as Ho observes, the further afield these neo-Victorian narratives travel, the harder it becomes to classify them as neo-Victorian (176–77, 188–89). Even if we accept that *The Handmaiden*'s critique of Japanese imperialism requires us to extend the long nineteenth century to 1945 (as this book has done), the film still calls into question our desire to categorize it as a work of neo-Victorian fiction in the first place. What is the heuristic value of classifying texts and practices as neo-Victorian, beyond defining the parameters of the fields of neo-Victorian studies and, by implication, Victorian studies? Should we be wedded to Anglocentric periodizing categories such as the Victorian period when analyzing texts and practices that engage with trans-imperial developments in the long nineteenth century? Perhaps it would be more productive to call texts such as *The Handmaiden* "historical fiction set in the long nineteenth century" rather than neo-Victorian fiction. Being willing to put aside the category of the neo-Victorian would bring to the fore other networks that are not reducible to formal British imperialism, and which involve multiple centers, peripheries, and assorted locations implicated in the various trans-imperial formations of the long nineteenth century.

Having said all this, by performing its critique of Japanese colonial rule via a neo-Victorian source text, *The Handmaiden* suggests possibilities for keeping the category of the neo-Victorian, so that the fields of Victorian and neo-Victorian studies may retain a (necessarily loose) sense of professional identity, while venturing outwards to engage with different spaces and texts. In their recent work on the "wide" nineteenth century, Sukanya Banerjee, Ryan D. Fong, and Helena Michie acknowledge that, while redefining the "Victorian" as "a political, aesthetic, and sociocultural assemblage" helps to expand Victorian studies beyond its conventional focus on Britain, the term *Victorian* nevertheless determines how far this "widening" can go (2). *The Handmaiden* harks back to the Victorian setting of its source text when it implies that, for Korean colonial subjects, becoming Japanese also means becoming English. The presence of Englishness within the predominantly Japanese and Korean world of *The Handmaiden* suggests that neo-Victorian narratives ultimately retain a connection to Britain in the long nineteenth century, although this connection might not be the central focus of the narrative. In *The Handmaiden*, Kōzuki yearns to be seen as Japanese, but the large country house that he lives in is a striking mixture of British and Japanese architectural styles. Half of the mansion is designed by an English architect and resembles an English country manor, whereas the other half is built in the style of a Japanese samurai residence or *yashiki* (figure C.3). The housekeeper proudly informs Sook-hee that the hybrid architecture of

Figure C.3. The main entrance to the English half of Kōzuki's mansion. The Japanese half, which houses Kōzuki's library of pornographic materials, lurks around the corner on the far right of the screen. *Source: The Handmaiden.* Directed by Park Chan-wook, CJ Entertainment, 2016.

Kōzuki's mansion "reflects Master's admiration for Japan and England." The film thus draws upon the icon of the English country house (discussed in chapter two) to symbolize Kōzuki's doubly subordinate status in relation to both the Japanese and the British empires. The hybrid nature of Kōzuki's mansion implies that there is a global hierarchy of civilizational development with Britain at the top, Japan in the middle, and Korea at the bottom. The English-style wing of the house towers over its Japanese counterpart, and it is the first thing that Sook-hee sees when she arrives at Kōzuki's house.

The character of the count further drives home the idea that, in order to become Japanese, the Korean colonial subject must also become English. In fact, what the count really wants to become is an English gentleman, but, like the Singaporean Lolitas discussed in chapter five, his racial identity compels him to take on the role of a Japanese nobleman as the closest approximation. In the third act of the film, the count reveals to Hideko that he is actually "the son of a lowly Korean farmhand and a shaman," and that he was taught how to behave like an English gentleman by several Englishmen who frequented the brothel that he worked in. The count then explains why he had planned to cheat Hideko of her fortune: "Frankly, I'm not that interested in money itself. What I desire is, how shall I put it . . . the manner of ordering wine without looking at the price? Something like that." Like the projected female reader of Japanese neo-Victorian manga and magazines, the count desires to acquire an aristocratic form of cultural capital that is coded as distinctively English. Unfortunately for the count, he can only perform a Japanese version of Englishness. As the count relates his personal history to Hideko at a fancy Western restaurant in Japan, the camera shifts focus from Hideko in the foreground to two well-dressed Japanese men sitting at the table behind them. The juxtaposition of the mise-en-scène with the count's voiceover suggests that, as much as the count wishes to become an English gentleman, he can only aspire to become like the Japanese gentlemen he sees around him in the restaurant. In the case of the count, becoming English means becoming Japanese. *The Handmaiden*'s trans-imperial triangulation of Britain, Japan, and Korea suggests that, even though British imperialism does not take center stage in this narrative, it remains part of the picture, hovering in the background like the English-style wing of Kōzuki's mansion. As such, the category of the neo-Victorian becomes a means of approaching contemporary texts and practices in which the history of British imperialism forms a part, rather than the whole, of a much wider picture. Correspondingly, the field of neo-Victorian studies (and its counterpart, Victorian studies) will be able to continue the work that it has done in critiquing the history of British imperialism, while decentering that history to engage with multiple histories of the long nineteenth century, so that a fuller picture of the past and the present may emerge. This is what this book has sought to do.

Notes

Introduction

1. See Miller and Yúdice; and Lewis and Miller.

2. See, for example, the extensive scholarship on Jean Rhys's *Wide Sargasso Sea* (1966) and Peter Carey's *Jack Maggs* (1997). For more recent examples, see Shachar; and Pascoe on American, French, and Japanese adaptations of *Wuthering Heights*.

3. For surveys of the global turn in Victorian studies, see Agathocleous; Assael; Mukherjee; Pykett; Gagnier; and Agathocleous and Rudy, "Victorian Cosmopolitanisms" and "Circulation." See also the recent special issues on "Undisciplining Victorian Studies" (Chatterjee, Christoff, and Wong) and "Widening the Nineteenth Century" (Banerjee, Fong, and Michie). For works that discuss Britain's relations with East Asia, see Forman; Lowe; and Lavery.

4. Britain and Japan signed a revised treaty in 1894, which came into effect in 1899. All of the other Western powers followed suit, thus marking the end of the treaty port system in Japan after a relatively short period of forty-one years (Hoare xiii).

5. For major works that examine neo-Victorianism from postcolonial and global perspectives, see the epilogue in Joyce; Kaplan; Ho; Llewellyn and Heilmann; and Primorac and Pietrzak-Franger. See Jones, "Transnational Neo-Victorian Studies" for a comprehensive overview of this growing subfield.

6. See also Jones and Mitchell's discussion of the "palimpsest" in Jones and Mitchell 7–8, 20–22.

7. For more information on the objectives of the bicentennial, see Boh; Yuen; and Zaccheus, "Bicentennial Logo Launched" and "Singapore Bicentennial: Why 2019 Is History in the Making."

8. See also Chen Junyi's letter to the *Straits Times*, provocatively entitled "Don't Rob Colonial British of Credit Due Them." At the official launch of the bicentennial on 28 January 2019, Prime Minister Lee Hsien Loong tacitly acknowledged this view in his speech: "We fought for independence from our colonial masters. But we also recognise the decisive and indelible imprint that the British

left on Singapore—the rule of law, our parliamentary system of government, even the language I am speaking today."

9. See Kohlke and Gutleben, *Neo-Victorian Tropes of Trauma* and *Neo-Victorian Gothic*; Arias and Pulham; and Ho.

Chapter One

1. See also Lumley 16–17; and Harrison 6–14.
2. See also Hewison 95–97.
3. For the full financial statements, see the Historic Buildings and Monuments Commission for England's *Annual Report and Accounts* for the financial years 1983–1985 and 1988–1989.
4. The size of the heritage economy in Britain is not easy to determine as one would need to count the people employed by all organizations in the public, private, and nonprofit sectors that have heritage responsibilities (for example, Historic England, the National Trust, local authorities, and amenity societies), as well as the people employed in subsidiary or contracted roles (Cowell 133).
5. For a more detailed discussion of the tensions between the Western Enlightenment concept of property and the notion of patrimony, see Barkan and Bush's introduction to *Claiming the Stones/Naming the Bones*.
6. See also Barkan 21. Although the term *cultural property* was coined in English only in 1954, Barkan traces the provenance of the concept to the Napoleonic Wars and the 1815 Congress of Vienna, which redefined the aristocratic property looted by Napoleon's forces as national cultural property, so as to exclude such objects from being considered as legitimate spoils of war in the future (18).
7. Bailkin, however, begins her account of this "prehistory" in the 1870s with disputes over the ownership of cultural objects and the accompanying crises of liberal politics in Britain at the time.
8. For more information on the practice of country-house visiting in the eighteenth century, see "Prelude: Houses of Taste (to 1815)" in Mandler; chapter four in Tinniswood; and Stobart.
9. For other critical works that examine how literary tourism between Britain and the US helped to construct an Anglo-American literary canon, see Booth; and Watson.

Chapter Two

1. For negative criticism of the film adaptation of *Possession*, see Sorensen; and Grasl.

2. See Tom Lamont's 2012 interview with Moore for the *Observer*.

3. The continental European system of intellectual property rights, on the other hand, protects the author's moral rights even after s/he has sold the rights to his/her work. Authors in Europe are therefore able to actively intervene in the adaptation of their work. For more information on the differences between the Anglo-American and European approaches to intellectual property rights, see Baldwin 8–10.

4. See also Hewison's critique of the "new museums" in Hewison 88–98; and the chapter "Out of the Glass Case" in Dicks 144–69.

5. For more information on the role that period films and TV dramas play in boosting heritage tourism, see Sargeant 308; and Higson 58–59.

6. See also Martin Hipsky's article on "Anglophil(m)ia" or the American fascination with British period films.

7. See also Higson 122–23.

8. See Higson 121; Hilmes 283; Hipsky 102–03, 105–06; West and Laird 322; and Knox 41.

9. See also J. Miller 75.

10. *Masterpiece Theatre*'s programming history from 1971–2006 was originally published on the PBS website, and it is now archived on the *Wayback Machine*.

11. See, for example, Kanesaka; Hu; and Moy.

12. Robert Hall remarks that it has become a critical commonplace to comment on the "timeless" world of Wodehouse's stories (1). See also Voorhees; Mooneyham; Medcalf; and B. Scott 91–115. David Cannadine is the only critic that I have encountered so far who claims that Wodehouse's fiction does engage with historical change beyond the occasional topical reference (485–89).

13. For critical works that describe Wodehouse's fictional world as Edwardian, see Cannadine; Ramsay; Voorhees; and B. Scott 112–13.

14. See also Mandler 4–5.

15. Merchant-Ivory adapted *Howards End* for the cinema in 1992, and ITV-Granada produced a television serial adaptation of *Brideshead Revisited* in 1981. Both adaptations have won numerous awards.

Chapter Three

1. See Harootunian x–xvii for his critique of this stadial model of world history in conventional narratives of Japan's modernization.

2. See chapter one in Checkland, *Japan and Britain*, for a detailed discussion and translation of extracts from *Seiyōishokujū*. See also Karlin on the role that etiquette guidebooks played in constructions of Meiji masculinity.

3. The two most prominent "learning missions" were the 1862 Takenouchi mission and the 1872 Iwakura mission to Britain, Europe, and the US. See

Cobbing 96–97; Hirakawa 460–64; and Checkland, *Britain's Encounter with Meiji Japan* 109–18.

    4. See also Francks 114, 121; Moeran 172–74; and Young, "Marketing the Modern" 56.

    5. See Francks; Moeran; and Young, "Marketing the Modern."

    6. See also Moeran 152–62. I wish to acknowledge here that Japanese department stores also sold high-end Japanese-style goods and promoted Japanese-style painting (*nihonga*). See Francks 113–14; Moeran 162; and Oh 355–56.

    7. In the late 1870s and 1880s, the Meiji state sought to revise the unequal treaties that Japan had signed, by convincing the Euro-American imperial powers that Japan was as "civilized" as they were. Japanese government officials at the time, particularly those who had traveled to the West, recognized that Westerners often judged how "civilized" Japan was based on the behavior of Japanese women at Western-style balls and dinner parties (Hastings 95).

    8. For more information on the "Discover Japan" campaign, see chapter two in Marilyn Ivy's *Discourses of the Vanishing*. For critical works on the *rekijo* phenomenon, see Akiko Sugawa-Shimada's and Philip Seaton's articles in the 2015 special issue of *Japan Forum* on "contents tourism" in Japan. *Contents tourism* is the preferred term in Japan for tourism that is induced by the consumption of media narratives (Seaton and Yamamura 2).

    9. The first newspaper advertisement for "new-style" rental bookshops (*shinshiki kashihon'ya*) appeared in 1886 (Asaoka 15). *Kashihon'ya* in the preceding Tokugawa period were essentially traveling salesmen, but "new-style" *kashihon'ya* in the Meiji period were brick-and-mortar stores (Asaoka 15). See also Kornicki 340–41. There were approximately fifty to sixty thousand students in Tokyo in the 1880s and 1890s, and the majority of *kashihon'ya* were located in the Kanda, Hongō, and Shiba neighborhoods, where most of the residents were students of the nearby schools and universities (Asaoka 42).

    10. The few remaining catalogs from Meiji-era *kashihon'ya* offer a fascinating glimpse into the reading habits of English-literate residents in Tokyo in the late nineteenth century. The 1887 catalog of the Kyōeki Kashihonsha is available online in the National Diet Library Digital Collections. See also the Tokyo Kashihonsha catalog and the 1888 Kyōeki Kashihonsha catalog reprinted in Asaoka and Suzuki's edited collection *Meiji ki "shinshiki kashihon'ya" mokuroku no kenkyū*.

    11. The catalog's account of this history is not entirely accurate. So-called English tea, or *kōcha* in Japanese, is made with black tea leaves. British consumers had actually started out drinking mainly green tea imported from China and later Japan, and had turned increasingly to black tea produced in India and Ceylon only from the 1880s onward. For more information on the tea trade in the nineteenth century, see Rappaport, "Packaging China"; and Hellyer.

    12. The Harrods Tea Salon (also known as the Harrods Tea Room) in Nihonbashi has since ceased operations, as Harrods ended its partnership with the Mitsukoshi department store in Japan in 2022.

Chapter Four

1. See Baseel; Miliaresis; and Washington.
2. See Murakami's essays "Earth in My Window" and "Superflat Trilogy: Greetings, You Are Alive" in the exhibition catalog for *Little Boy*.
3. The 1851 Great Exhibition was held in the Crystal Palace, but it was not an imperial exhibition.
4. See Iwabuchi, "Rethinking 'Japanese' Popular Culture" on the connections between Cool Japan and Cool Britannia.
5. For more information on Miki's conceptualization of the *Tōa Kyōdōtai*, see Harrington 55–63; J. Kim 153–60; Harootunian 41–42; Goto-Jones 104–06; and Fletcher 106–16.
6. Foreign Minister Matsuoka Yōsuke publicly referred to the Japanese Empire as the "Greater East Asia Co-Prosperity Sphere" (*Dai Tōa Kyōeiken*) for the first time in a radio broadcast in August 1940. By July 1941, the Co-Prosperity Sphere had become the central goal of Japan's national policy (Yellen 4).
7. For earlier discussions of the British interest in Japanese art and aesthetics in the nineteenth century (including but not limited to Aestheticism), see Yokoyama; and Checkland, *Japan and Britain after 1859*.
8. The project of "explaining Japan" continues to this day, mainly in the form of Euro-American documentaries and articles seeking to explicate the *weirdness* of Japanese culture, and also in the form of Japanese university programs that claim to teach students English so that they may explain the *uniqueness* of Japanese culture to a foreign audience.
9. Duara cites Oswald Spengler's *Decline of the West* (1918–1922) as one of the foremost examples of this alternative formulation of *civilization* (101–04).
10. See also Hotta 2–3.
11. *The Book of Tea* was translated into Japanese in 1929, followed by *Ideals of the East* in 1938, and *The Awakening of Japan* in 1940 (He 103).
12. In recent years, the manga industry as a whole appears to have taken a more proactive approach to translating and distributing manga to overseas audiences. For example, Shueisha and Shogakukan co-own VIZ Media, which publishes and distributes translated manga and anime for English-speaking audiences in the US. The Kodansha Group now includes overseas branch companies Kodansha USA, Kodansha Europe, and Kodansha (Beijing) Culture Inc.
13. Besides pan-Asianism, the ideological foundations of the Co-Prosperity Sphere included the Confucian concept of *proper place* and the Japanist slogan of *hakkō ichiu* ("eight corners of the world under one roof"). See chapter three in Yellen.

Chapter Five

1. For works that associate *asobi* with leisure (*rejaa*) in Japan, see Linhart and Frühstück; and Leheny, *Rules of Play*.

2. See Elizabeth Ho's discussion of steampunk in chapter 5 of *Neo-Victorianism and the Memory of Empire*.

3. I have changed the names of the interviewees to anonymize their identities.

4. *English-speaking* is a sociological category commonly used in Singapore to distinguish between households that communicate predominantly in English and households that speak in their so-called mother tongues (often Mandarin, Malay, or Tamil). The 2010 census, for instance, includes Language Most Frequently Spoken at Home as one of the key indicators for analyzing the demographics of resident Singaporeans ("Singapore Census" viv).

5. In his 2000 article "On the Nation's Margins: The Social Place of Literature in Singapore," Holden cites a 1995 article in the *Straits Times* pointing to a decline in literature enrolment for *O* level studies in Singapore (30). In 2013, the *Straits Times* again reported a "big drop" in the number of students taking literature as a subject at *O* level (Chia). Literature again made the headlines in 2015, when the number of students who sat for the *O* level literature exams further decreased from about 6,000 in 2012 to about 5,500 in 2014 (P. Lee).

6. Most students in Singapore take the *O* level exams at the end of four years of secondary school education. Those who wish to pursue university studies go on to take the *A* level exams at the end of two years of tertiary education.

7. I have derived this information from a list of prescribed exam texts (1998–2019) kindly provided to me by the Singapore Examinations and Assessment Board (SEAB).

8. See Iwabuchi, "Marketing 'Japan' "; and "How 'Japanese' Is Pokémon?"

9. See Goh and Holden 4–5; and Clammer 132, for similar interpretations of Raffles's town plan as an early example of racial thinking in colonial Singapore.

10. Some of Raffles's papers regarding his town plan are reprinted in Charles Burton Buckley's 1902 compilation of historical documents, *An Anecdotal History of Old Times in Singapore, 1819–1867*. See Buckley 79–87.

11. See, for example, Abraham; Clammer; Hirschman; chapter one in Cheah; and Goh and Holden.

12. In her 2018 book *Inglorious Empire*, Shashi Tharoor argues that the policy of "divide and rule," at least in the context of British India, was consciously designed to foment intercaste and interreligious hostility, so as to prevent Indians from working together to challenge British rule (101–02). However, in Donald Horowitz's much earlier work on interethnic conflict, he contends that European colonialism on the whole did not deliberately foster such conflicts. Horowitz foregrounds the multidirectional nature of colonial rule, arguing that while colonizers sometimes treated various ethnic groups differently, colonial subjects also responded differently to the economic opportunities that were available in the colonies. These interactions between colonizer and colonized gave rise to group inequalities, which in turn engendered interethnic conflict (156, 160).

13. See also Tarling 197–204.

14. For detailed discussions of Sook Ching, see Akashi 67–68; Cheah 21–23; Kratoska 95–100; and Tarling 200–01, 260–61.

15. See also Cheah 24–25; and Kratoska 102–03.

16. Gerald Horne makes a similar argument in *Race War*, in which he posits that Japan sought to win the support of black and Asian people in the US by claiming to be the "champion of the colored races" (vii–viii).

17. For recent scholarship on Japanese imperialism and the Foucauldian production of colonized peoples as "subjects," see Ching, *Becoming "Japanese"* (Taiwan); Fujitani (Korea); Barclay (Taiwanese aborigines); and Hanscom and Washburn.

18. See also Akashi 89.

19. See Telling; Campbell; and Parry.

20. Examples of scholarly works that foreground "cultural proximity" and "East Asian modernity" include Iwabuchi, *Recentering Globalization*; Chua; and Wee.

21. For scholarship on Japanese conceptualizations of racial difference within its own empire, see Weiner 226; and Young, "Rethinking Race for Manchukuo."

22. See also Fujitani 17.

Conclusion

1. For more information about this letter, see W. Beasley 41–43.

2. See also Hwang 159–60.

3. In his 2019 book *Anti-Japan*, Ching examines strong feelings of "anti-Japanism" in postwar East Asia as an expression of the unresolved historical traumas of Japanese imperialism, as well as a response to more recent changes in geopolitical conditions due to global capitalism and the rise of China. In chapter three of his book, Ching discusses the "comfort women" protests in South Korea as a key example of "anti-Japanism."

4. For recent scholarship on how contemporary South Korean films often fall back onto familiar metanarratives of anti-Japanese Korean nationalism, see the coda in An; Shin; and Bae.

5. See, for example, Y. Kim, "Introduction" 3–4; Lee, "Cultural Policy"; Walsh; and Dal.

Works Cited

Abraham, Collin E. R. "Racial and Ethnic Manipulation in Colonial Malaya." *Ethnic and Racial Studies*, vol. 6, no. 1, 1983, pp. 18–32.
Agathocleous, Tanya. "Imperial, Anglophone, Geopolitical, Worldly: Evaluating the 'Global' in Victorian Studies." *Victorian Literature and Culture*, vol. 43, 2015, pp. 651–58.
Agathocleous, Tanya, and Jason R. Rudy. "Circulation." *Keywords*, special issue of *Victorian Literature and Culture*, vol. 46, no. 3–4, 2018, pp. 621–25.
———. "Victorian Cosmopolitanisms: Introduction." *Victorian Cosmopolitanisms*, special issue of *Victorian Literature and Culture*, vol. 38, 2010, pp. 389–97.
Ainsworth, William Harrison. *The Tower of London*. 1840. *The Works of William Harrison Ainsworth*, vol. 3–4, New York, Nottingham Society, circa 1900. *Internet Archive*, U of California Libraries, 15 Feb. 2008, archive.org/details/worksofwilliamha05ains/page/n7. Accessed 7 Aug. 2018.
Akashi, Yoji. "Japanese Policy towards the Malayan Chinese, 1941–1945." *Journal of Southeast Asian Studies*, vol. 1, no. 2, 1970, pp. 61–89.
An, Jinsoo. *Parameters of Disavowal: Colonial Representation in South Korean Cinema*. U of California P, 2018.
Arias, Rosario, and Patricia Pulham, editors. *Haunting and Spectrality in Neo-Victorian Fiction: Possessing the Past*. Palgrave Macmillan, 2009.
Arnold, Matthew. "Preface to *Culture and Anarchy* (1869)." *Culture and Anarchy and Other Writings*, edited by Stefan Collini, Cambridge UP, 1993, pp. 188–211.
Asaoka, Kunio. "Meiji ki 'shinshiki kashihon'ya' to dokusha tachi: Kyōeki Kashihonsha o chūshin ni." *Meiji ki "shinshiki kashihon'ya" mokuroku no kenkyū*, edited by Asaoka Kunio and Suzuki Sadami, Kokusai Nihon bunka kenkyū sentaa, 2010, pp. 12–53.
Asaoka, Kunio, and Suzuki Sadami, editors. *Meiji ki "shinshiki kashihon'ya" mokuroku no kenkyū*. Kokusai Nihon bunka kenkyū sentaa, 2010.
Assael, Brenda. "Beyond Empire: Globalizing the Victorians." *Victorian Literature and Culture*, vol. 43, 2015, pp. 643–50.

Bae, Keungyoon. "Admitting an Attraction: Colonial Villainy, Visuality, and *The Handmaiden* as Critique." *International Journal of Korean History*, vol. 25, no. 2, 2020, pp. 175–87.

Bailkin, Jordanna. *The Culture of Property: The Crisis of Liberalism in Modern Britain*. Chicago UP, 2004.

Baldwin, Peter. *The Copyright Wars: Three Centuries of Trans-Atlantic Battle*. Princeton UP, 2014.

Banerjee, Sukanya. "Trans-imperial." *Keywords*, special issue of *Victorian Literature and Culture*, vol. 46, no. 3–4, 2018, pp. 925–28.

Banerjee, Sukanya, Ryan D. Fong, and Helena Michie, editors. *Widening the Nineteenth Century*, special issue of *Victorian Literature and Culture*, vol. 49, no. 1, 2021.

Barclay, Paul D. *Outcasts of Empire: Japan's Rule on Taiwan's "Savage Border," 1874–1945*. U of California P, 2018. *UC Press Luminos*, doi.org/10.1525/luminos41.

Bardsley, Jan. "The Oyaji Gets a Makeover: Guides for Japanese Salarymen in the New Millennium." *Manners and Mischief: Gender, Power and Etiquette in Japan*, edited by Jan Bardsley and Laura Miller, U of California P, 2011, pp. 114–35.

Barkan, Elazar. "Amending Historical Injustices: The Restitution of Cultural Property—An Overview." *Claiming the Stones/Naming the Bones: Cultural Property and the Negotiation of National and Ethnic Identity*, edited by Elazar Barkan and Ronald Bush, Getty Research Institute, 2002, pp. 16–46.

Barkan, Elazar, and Ronald Bush. "Introduction." *Claiming the Stones/Naming the Bones: Cultural Property and the Negotiation of National and Ethnic Identity*, edited by Elazar Barkan and Ronald Bush, Getty Research Institute, 2002, pp. 1–15.

Barringer, Tim. "Victorian Culture and the Museum: Before and after the White Cube." *Journal of Victorian Culture*, vol. 11, no. 1, 2006, pp. 133–45.

Baseel, Casey. "This Is Japan's Oldest Curry Bread Bakery, and It's Awesome." *Sora News 24*, 3 Dec. 2019, soranews24.com/2019/12/03/this-is-japans-oldest-curry-bread-bakery-and-its-awesome%E3%80%90taste-test%E3%80%91/. Accessed 22 Oct. 2021.

Baucom, Ian. *Out of Place: Englishness, Empire, and the Locations of Identity*. Princeton UP, 1999.

Beasley, Edward. *The Victorian Reinvention of Race: New Racisms and the Problem of Grouping in the Human Sciences*. Routledge, 2010.

Beasley, W. G. *Japanese Imperialism, 1894–1945*. Oxford UP, 1987.

Bhabha, Homi K. *The Location of Culture*. 1994. Routledge Classics, 2004.

Boehm-Schnitker, Nadine, and Susanne Gruss. "Introduction: Fashioning the Neo-Victorian—Neo-Victorian Fashions." *Neo-Victorian Literature and Culture: Immersions and Revisitations*, edited by Nadine Boehm-Schnitker and Susanne Gruss, Routledge, 2014, pp. 1–17.

Boh, Samantha. "Raffles Who? 200 Years since the British Colonialist, Singapore Would Rather He Disappear." *South China Morning Post*, 27 Jan. 2019, www.

scmp.com/week-asia/society/article/2183714/raffles-who-200-years-british-colonialist-singapore-would-rather. Accessed 22 Mar. 2019.
Booth, Alison. *Homes and Haunts: Touring Writers' Shrines and Countries*. Oxford UP, 2016. *Oxford Scholarship Online*, doi:10.1093/acprof:oso/97801987590 96.001.0001.
Bourdieu, Pierre. *Distinction: A Social Critique of the Judgement of Taste*. 1979. Translated by Richard Nice, Routledge, 1984.
Brouillette, Sarah. *Literature and the Creative Economy*. Stanford UP, 2014.
Buckley, Charles Burton. *An Anecdotal History of Old Times in Singapore, 1819–1867*. 1902. U of Malaya P, 1965.
Burton, Anthony. *Vision and Accident: The Story of the Victoria and Albert Museum*. V&A Publications, 1999.
Burton, Antoinette. *Empire in Question: Reading, Writing, and Teaching British Imperialism*. Duke UP, 2011.
Butt, Richard. "The Classic Novel on British Television." *A Companion to Literature, Film, and Adaptation*, edited by Deborah Cartmell, Wiley-Blackwell, 2012, pp. 159–75.
Buzard, James. *The Beaten Track: European Tourism, Literature, and the Ways to Culture, 1800–1918*. Clarendon, 1993.
Byatt, A. S. *Possession: A Romance*. 1990. Vintage, 1991.
Campbell, Lucy. "Chinese in UK Report 'Shocking' Levels of Racism after Coronavirus Outbreak." *Guardian*, 9 Feb. 2020, www.theguardian.com/uk-news/2020/feb/09/chinese-in-uk-report-shocking-levels-of-racism-after-coronavirus-outbreak. Accessed 11 June 2023.
Cannadine, David. "Another 'Last Victorian': P. G. Wodehouse and His World." *South Atlantic Quarterly*, vol. 77, 1978, pp. 470–91.
Caprio, Mark E. *Japanese Assimilation Policies in Colonial Korea, 1910–1945*. U of Washington P, 2009.
Carey, A. E. "Tattershall Castle." *The Academy and Literature*, vol. 2057, 7 Oct. 1911, pp. 449–50. *ProQuest British Periodicals*, search.proquest.com/britishperiodicals/docview/6826044/abstract/49E7DC7168A049F0PQ/1?accountid=14888. Accessed on 16 Aug. 2018.
Chan, Heng Chee, and Sharon Siddique. *Singapore's Multiculturalism: Evolving Diversity*. Routledge, 2019.
Chatterjee, Ronjaunee, Alicia Mireles Christoff, and Amy R. Wong, editors. *Undisciplining Victorian Studies*, special issue of *Victorian Studies*, vol. 62, no. 3, 2020.
Cheah, Boon Kheng. *Red Star over Malaya: Resistance and Social Conflict during and after the Japanese Occupation, 1941–1946*. 1983. 3rd ed., Singapore UP, 2003.
Checkland, Olive. *Britain's Encounter with Meiji Japan, 1868–1912*. Macmillan, 1989.
———. *Japan and Britain after 1859: Creating Cultural Bridges*. RoutledgeCurzon, 2003.

Chen, Junyi. "Don't Rob Colonial British of Credit Due Them." *Straits Times*, 11 Jan. 2019, www.straitstimes.com/forum/letters-in-print/dont-rob-colonial-british-of-credit-due-them. Accessed 22 Mar. 2019.

Chew, Ernest C. T. "The Foundation of a British Settlement." *A History of Singapore*, edited by Ernest C. T. Chew and Edwin Lee, Oxford UP, 1991, pp. 36–40.

Chia, Stacey. "Big Drop in Number of Students Taking Literature." *Straits Times*, 25 Feb. 2013, www.straitstimes.com/singapore/big-drop-in-number-of-students-taking-literature.

Ching, Leo T. S. *Anti-Japan: The Politics of Sentiment in Postcolonial East Asia*. Duke UP, 2019.

———. *Becoming "Japanese": Colonial Taiwan and the Politics of Identity Formation*. U of California P, 2001.

Chua, Beng Huat. "Conceptualizing an East Asian Popular Culture." *Inter-Asia Cultural Studies*, vol. 5, no. 2, 2004, pp. 200–21.

Clammer, John. "The Institutionalization of Ethnicity: The Culture of Ethnicity in Singapore." *Ethnic and Racial Studies*, vol. 5, no. 2, 1982, pp. 127–39.

Cobbing, Andrew. *The Japanese Discovery of Victorian Britain: Early Travel Encounters in the Far West*. Japan Library, 1998.

Cohen, Deborah. *Household Gods: The British and their Possessions*. Yale UP, 2006.

Cohen, Debra Rae. "The Place of the Pig: Blandings, Barsetshire, and Britain." *Middlebrow Wodehouse: P. G. Wodehouse's Work in Context*, edited by Ann Rea, Ashgate, 2016, pp. 105–21.

"Commons Sitting of 2 April 1869." *Hansard*, 3rd series, vol. 195, pp. 26–130. *ProQuest UK Parliamentary Papers*, parlipapers.proquest.com/parlipapers/docview/t71.d76.cds3v0195p0-0002?accountid=14888. Accessed 15 Aug. 2018.

Cowell, Ben. *The Heritage Obsession: The Battle for England's Past*. Tempus, 2008.

Creighton, Millie R. "The *Depaato*: Merchandising the West While Selling Japaneseness." *Re-made in Japan: Everyday Life and Consumer Taste in a Changing Society*, edited by Joseph J. Tobin, Yale UP, 1992, pp. 42–57.

Curzon, George Nathaniel, and Blanche Gordon-Lennox. "Legislation for Antiquities." *British Architect*, 9 Aug. 1912, pp. 105–06. *ProQuest British Periodicals*, search.proquest.com/britishperiodicals/docview/7217499/citation/F4EBCBBC-9CCC442BPQ/1?accountid=14888. Accessed 16 Aug. 2018.

Dal, Yong Jin. "A Critical Interpretation of the Cultural Industries in the Era of New Korean Wave." *The Korean Wave: Evolution, Fandom, and Transnationality*, edited by Tae-Jin Yoon and Dal Yong Jin, Lexington, 2017, pp. 43–64.

Daliot-Bul, Michal. "Japan Brand Strategy: The Taming of 'Cool Japan' and the Challenges of Cultural Planning in a Postmodern Age." *Social Science Japan*, vol. 12, no. 2, 2009, pp. 247–66.

———. *License to Play: The Ludic in Japanese Culture*. U of Hawaii P, 2014.

Damrosch, David. *What Is World Literature?* Princeton UP, 2003.

De Groot, Jerome. *Consuming History: Historians and Heritage in Contemporary Popular Culture*. Routledge, 2009.

Works Cited

Department of Statistics, Singapore. "Singapore Census of Population 2010: Statistical Release 1: Demographic Characteristics, Education, Language, and Religion." *SingStat*, www.singstat.gov.sg/publications/cop2010/census10_stat_release1. Accessed 31 Aug. 2020.

Dicks, Bella. *Culture on Display: The Production of Contemporary Visitability*. Open UP, 2003.

Dilke, Charles Wentworth. *Greater Britain*. 1868. Cambridge UP, 2009. 2 vols. *Cambridge Core*, doi.10.1017/CBO9780511702563.

Doak, Kevin M. "The Concept of Ethnic Nationality and Its Role in Pan-Asianism in Imperial Japan." *Pan-Asianism in Modern Japanese History: Colonialism, Regionalism, and Borders*, edited by Sven Saaler and Victor Koschmann, Routledge, 2007, pp. 168–81.

Donaldson, Frances. *P. G. Wodehouse: A Biography*. Weidenfeld and Nicolson, 1982.

Doyle, Laura. "Inter-Imperiality." *Interventions*, vol. 16, no. 2, 2014, pp. 159–96.

Duara, Prasenjit. "The Discourse of Civilization and Pan-Asianism." *Journal of World History*, vol. 12, no. 1, 2001, pp. 99–130.

English Heritage Home Page. English Heritage, www.english-heritage.org.uk/. Accessed 8 June 2015.

Esty, Jed. *A Shrinking Island: Modernism and National Culture in England*. Princeton UP, 2004.

Faiola, Anthony. "Japan's Empire of Cool: Country's Culture Becomes Its Biggest Export." *Washington Post*, 27 Dec. 2003, www.washingtonpost.com/archive/politics/2003/12/27/japans-empire-of-cool/ab1ae69f-756a-487c-8b34-2823072f342a/. Accessed 14 Dec. 2021.

Fanon, Frantz. *Black Skin, White Masks*. 1952. Translated by Charles Lam Markmann, Pluto, 1986.

Fernandez, Warren. "Instead of Angst over the Bicentennial, Draw Lessons from the Past." *Straits Times*, 27 Jan. 2019, www.straitstimes.com/singapore/looking-back-to-chart-way-forward. Accessed 18 Mar. 2019.

———. *Men for Others: A Portrait of the Josephian over the Years*. Straits Times Press, 2009.

Fforde, Jasper. *The Eyre Affair*. Hodder, 2001.

"The Fireplaces at Tattershall Castle." *Times*, 13 Sept. 1911, p. 5. *The Times Digital Archive*, tinyurl.galegroup.com/tinyurl/9c3bL5. Accessed 16 Aug. 2018.

Fletcher, William Miles III. *The Search for a New Order: Intellectuals and Fascism in Prewar Japan*. U of North Carolina P, 1982.

Florida, Richard. *The Rise of the Creative Class and How It's Transforming Work, Leisure, Community, and Everyday Life*. Basic, 2002.

Forman, Ross G. *China and the Victorian Imagination: Empires Entwined*. Cambridge UP, 2013.

Forster, E. M. *Howards End*. 1910. Edited by Oliver Stallybrass, Penguin, 2000.

Francks, Penelope. *The Japanese Consumer: An Alternative Economic History of Modern Japan*. Cambridge UP, 2009.

Fujitani, Takashi. *Race for Empire: Koreans as Japanese and Japanese as Americans during World War Two*. U of California P, 2011.
Furnivall, John Sydenham. *Colonial Policy and Practice: A Comparative Study of Burma and Netherlands India*. 1948. Cambridge UP, 2014. *Cambridge Core*, doi.10.1017/CBO9781107051140.
Gagnier, Regenia. "Global Circulation." *Keywords*, special issue of *Victorian Literature and Culture*, vol. 46, no. 3–4, 2018, pp. 719–23.
Ganguly, Debjani. "Polysystems Redux: The Unfinished Business of World Literature." *Cambridge Journal of Postcolonial Literary Inquiry*, vol. 2, no. 2, 2015, pp. 272–81.
Gardiner, Michael. *The Return of England in English Literature*. Palgrave Macmillan, 2012.
Gikandi, Simon. *Maps of Englishness: Writing Identity in the Culture of Colonialism*. Columbia UP, 1996.
Goh, Daniel P. S., and Philip Holden. "Introduction: Postcoloniality, Race, and Multiculturalism." *Race and Multiculturalism in Malaysia and Singapore*, edited by Daniel P. S. Goh, Matilda Gabrielpillai, Philip Holden, and Gaik Cheng Khoo, Routledge, 2009, pp. 1–16.
Goldhill, Simon. *Freud's Couch, Scott's Buttocks, Brontë's Grave*. U of Chicago P, 2011.
Goto-Jones, Christopher. *Political Philosophy in Japan: Nishida, the Kyoto School and Co-Prosperity*. Routledge, 2005.
Grasl, Caterina. "Voyeuristic Revisionism? (Re-)Viewing the Politics of Neo-Victorian Adaptations." *The Politics of Adaptation: Media Convergence and Ideology*, edited by Dan Hassler-Forest and Pascal Nicklas, Palgrave Macmillan, 2015, pp. 21–34.
Great Britain, Historic Buildings and Monuments Commission for England. *Annual Report and Accounts 1988/1989*. Historic Buildings and Monuments Commission for England, 1989.
———. *Heritage Counts 2010: Economic Impact of the Historic Environment*. Historic Buildings and Monuments Commission for England, 2010. *Heritage Counts*, Historic England, historicengland.org.uk/research/heritage-counts/2010-economic-impact/. Accessed 8 June 2015.
———. *Heritage Counts 2014: The Value and Impact of Heritage*. Historic Buildings and Monuments Commission for England, 2014. *Heritage Counts*, Historic England, historicengland.org.uk/research/heritage-counts/2014-the-value-and-impact-of-heritage/. Accessed 8 June 2015.
———. *Report and Accounts 1983–1985*. Historic Buildings and Monuments Commission for England, 1985.
Hadley, Louisa. *Neo-Victorian Fiction and Historical Narrative: The Victorians and Us*. Palgrave, 2010.
Hall, Robert A., Jr. "Timelessness and Contemporaneity in P. G. Wodehouse." *Plum Lines Supplement*, vol. 3, no. 5, 1982, pp. 1–4.

The Handmaiden. Directed by Park Chan-wook, CJ Entertainment, 2016.
Hanscom, Christopher P., and Dennis Washburn. "Introduction." *The Affect of Difference: Representations of Race in East Asian Empire*, edited by Christopher P. Hanscom and Dennis Washburn, U of Hawaii P, 2016, pp. 1–18.
Harootunian, Harry. *Overcome by Modernity: History, Culture, and Community in Interwar Japan.* Princeton UP, 2000.
Harozzu to Eikoku ryū jōshitsu sutairu [*Harrods and Fine English Style*]. Takarajimasha, 2010.
Harrington, Lewis E. "Miki Kiyoshi and the Shōwa Kenkyūkai: The Failure of World History." *positions*, vol. 17, no. 1, 2009, pp. 43–72.
Harrison, Rodney. *Heritage: Critical Approaches.* Routledge, 2013.
Hastings, Sally A. "A Dinner Party Is Not a Revolution: Space, Gender, and Hierarchy in Meiji Japan." *Manners and Mischief: Gender, Power and Etiquette in Japan*, edited by Jan Bardsley and Laura Miller, U of California P, 2011, pp. 95–113.
He, Jing. "Okakura Tenshin and Pan-Asianism, 1903–1906." *Pan-Asianism: A Documentary History*, edited by Sven Saaler and Christopher W. A. Szpilman, vol. 1, Rowman and Littlefield, 2011, pp. 101–11.
Hearn, Lafcadio. *Glimpses of Unfamiliar Japan.* Tuttle, 2009.
———. *Kwaidan: Stories and Studies of Strange Things.* Tuttle, 1971.
Hellyer, Robert. "1874: Tea and Japan's New Trading Regime." *Asia Inside Out: Changing Times*, edited by Eric Tagliacozzo, Helen F. Siu, and Peter C. Perdue, Harvard UP, 2015, pp. 186–206.
Hewison, Robert. *The Heritage Industry: Britain in a Climate of Decline.* Methuen, 1987.
Higson, Andrew. *English Heritage, English Cinema: Costume Drama since 1980.* Oxford UP, 2003.
Hill, Michael, and Lian Kwen Fee. *The Politics of Nation Building and Citizenship in Singapore.* Routledge, 1995.
Hilmes, Michele. *Network Nations: A Transnational History of British and American Broadcasting.* Routledge, 2012.
Hipsky, Martin A. "Anglophil(m)ia: Why Does America Watch Merchant-Ivory Movies?" *Journal of Popular Film and Television*, vol. 22, no. 3, 1994, pp. 98–107.
Hirakawa, Sukehiro. "Japan's Turn to the West." Translated by Bob Tadashi Wakabayashi, *Cambridge History of Japan*, edited by Marius B. Jansen, vol. 5, Cambridge UP, 1989, pp. 432–98.
Hirschman, Charles. "The Making of Race in Colonial Malaya: Political Economy and Racial Ideology." *Sociological Forum*, vol. 1, no. 2, 1986, pp. 330–61.
———. "The Meaning and Measurement of Ethnicity in Malaysia: An Analysis of Census Classifications." *Journal of Asian Studies*, vol. 46, no. 3, 1987, pp. 555–82.
Ho, Elizabeth. *Neo-Victorianism and the Memory of Empire.* Continuum, 2012.

Hoare, J. E. *Japan's Treaty Ports and Foreign Settlements: The Uninvited Guests 1858–1899*. Japan Library, 1994.
Holden, Philip. "On the Nation's Margins: The Social Place of Literature in Singapore." *Journal of Social Issues in Southeast Asia*, vol. 15, no. 1, 2000, pp. 30–51.
Horne, Gerald. *Race War: White Supremacy and the Japanese Attack on the British Empire*. New York UP, 2004.
Horowitz, Donald L. *Ethnic Groups in Conflict*. 1985. 2nd ed., U of California P, 2000.
Horsman, Reginald. *Race and Manifest Destiny: The Origins of American Racial Anglo-Saxonism*. Harvard UP, 1981.
Hotta, Eri. *Pan-Asianism and Japan's War, 1931–1945*. Palgrave Macmillan, 2007.
Howard, Peter. *Heritage: Management, Interpretation, Identity*. Continuum, 2003.
Howkins, John. *The Creative Economy: How People Make Money from Ideas*. 2001. 2nd ed., Penguin, 2007.
Hu, Jane. "Orientalism, Redux." *Undisciplining Victorian Studies*, special issue of *Victorian Studies*, vol. 62, no. 3, 2020, pp. 460–73.
Hussain, Zakir. "Looking Back 700 Years in Singapore's History to Glean Lessons for the Future." *Straits Times*, 13 Jan. 2019, www.straitstimes.com/opinion/looking-back-700-years-to-glean-lessons-for-the-future. Accessed 18 Mar. 2019.
Hutcheon, Linda. *A Theory of Adaptation*. Routledge, 2006.
Hwang, Kyung Moon. *A History of Korea: An Episodic Narrative*. 2010. 2nd ed., Palgrave, 2017.
"Interview with PAUL, George Kanagaretnam." *Education in Singapore (Part 1: English)*, Accession Number 001713. National Archives of Singapore, Singapore. Transcript.
Ivy, Marilyn. *Discourses of the Vanishing: Modernity, Phantasm, Japan*. U of Chicago P, 1995.
Iwabuchi, Koichi. "How 'Japanese' Is Pokémon?" *Pikachu's Global Adventure: The Rise and Fall of Pokémon*, edited by Joseph Tobin, Duke UP, 2004, pp. 53–79.
———. "Marketing 'Japan': Japanese Cultural Presence under a Global Gaze." *Japanese Studies*, vol. 18, no. 2, 1998, pp. 165–80.
———. *Recentering Globalization: Popular Culture and Japanese Transnationalism*. Duke UP, 2002.
———. "Rethinking 'Japanese' Popular Culture." Japan Foundation Public Seminar, 13 Apr. 2015, The Swedenborg Society, London. Lecture.
———. "Undoing Inter-National Fandom in the Age of Brand Nationalism." *Mechademia*, vol. 5, 2010, pp. 87–96.
Iwabuchi, Koichi, Stephen Muecke, and Mandy Thomas, editors. *Rogue Flows: Trans-Asian Cultural Traffic*. Hong Kong UP, 2004.
James, Henry. "Abbeys and Castles." *Collected Travel Writings: Great Britain and America*, edited by Richard Howard, The Library of America, 1993, pp. 183–96.
———. *The American*. Edited by William Spengemann, Penguin Books, 1981.

———. "In Warwickshire." *Collected Travel Writings: Great Britain and America*, edited by Richard Howard, The Library of America, 1993, pp. 164–82.

———. "A Passionate Pilgrim." *A Passionate Pilgrim and Other Tales*, Boston, James R. Osgood and Company, 1875.

Jeffers, Jennifer M. *Britain Colonized: Hollywood's Appropriation of British Literature*. Palgrave Macmillan, 2006.

Jones, Anna Maria. "'Palimpsestuous' Attachments: Framing a Manga Theory of the Global Neo-Victorian." *Neo-Victorianism and Globalization: Transnational Dissemination of Nineteenth-Century Cultural Texts*, special issue of *Neo-Victorian Studies*, vol. 8, no. 1, 2015, pp. 17–47, www.neovictorianstudies.com.

———. "Picturing 'Girls Who Read': Victorian Governesses and Neo-Victorian Shōjo Manga." *Drawing on the Victorians: The Palimpsest of Victorian and Neo-Victorian Graphic Texts*, edited by Anna Maria Jones and Rebecca N. Mitchell, Ohio UP, 2017, pp. 300–30.

———. "Transnational Neo-Victorian Studies: Notes on the Possibilities and Limitations of a Discipline." *Literature Compass*, vol. 15, no. 7, 2018, pp. 1–18.

Jones, Anna Maria, and Rebecca N. Mitchell. "Introduction: Reading the Victorian and Neo-Victorian Graphic Palimpsest." *Drawing on the Victorians: The Palimpsest of Victorian and Neo-Victorian Graphic Texts*, edited by Anna Maria Jones and Rebecca N. Mitchell, Ohio UP, 2017, pp. 1–36.

Joyce, Simon. *The Victorians in the Rearview Mirror*. Ohio UP, 2007.

Kanesaka, Erica. "Part-Victorian Imagination: On Being a Victorianist of Color." *V21 Blog*, 5 June 2018, v21collective.org/part-victorian-imagination-victorianist-color/. Accessed 16 Dec. 2023.

Kaplan, Cora. *Victoriana: Histories, Fictions, Criticism*. Edinburgh UP, 2007.

Karle, Deepika. "A Reader's Guide to P. G. Wodehouse's America." *Studies in American Humor*, New Series 2, vol. 7, 1989, pp. 32–44.

Karlin, Jason G. "The Gender of Nationalism: Competing Masculinities in Meiji Japan." *Journal of Japanese Studies*, vol. 28, no. 1, 2002, pp. 41–77.

Katsuno, Hirofumi, and Jeffrey Maret. "Localizing the Pokémon TV Series for the American Market." *Pikachu's Global Adventure: The Rise and Fall of Pokémon*, edited by Joseph Tobin, Duke UP, 2004, pp. 80–107.

Kawabata, A. *A Hermit Turned Loose: An Interesting Account of European Travels*. 2nd ed., Tokyo, 1915.

Kawamura, Yuniya. *Fashioning Japanese Subcultures*. Bloomsbury, 2013.

Keen, Suzanne. *Romances of the Archive in Contemporary British Fiction*. U of Toronto P, 2001.

Kelsky, Karen. *Women on the Verge: Japanese Women, Western Dreams*. Duke UP, 2001.

Kelts, Roland. "Japanamerica: Why 'Cool Japan' Is Over." *3:AM Magazine*, 17 May 2010, www.3ammagazine.com/3am/japanamerica-why-cool-japan-is-over/. Accessed 14 Dec. 2021.

Kim, Andrew. "Looking Back on Colonial Korea: Nostalgia and Anti-Nostalgia in Park Chang-wook's *The Handmaiden*." *Journal of Commonwealth and Postcolonial Studies*, vol. 7, no. 2, 2019, pp. 32–47.

Kim, John Namjun. "The Temporality of Empire: The Imperial Cosmopolitanism of Miki Kiyoshi and Tanabe Hajime." *Pan-Asianism in Modern Japanese History: Colonialism, Regionalism, and Borders*, edited by Sven Saaler and Victor Koschmann, Routledge, 2007, pp. 151–67.

Kim, Youna. "Introduction: Korean Media in a Digital Cosmopolitan World." *The Korean Wave: Korean Media Go Global*, edited by Youna Kim, Routledge, 2013, pp. 1–27.

———, editor. *The Korean Wave: Korean Media Go Global*. Routledge, 2013.

Kirshenblatt-Gimblett, Barbara. *Destination Culture: Tourism, Museums, and Heritage*. U of California P, 1998.

"Kioyekikashihonsha's Catalogue of English Books." *Kyōeki Kashihonsha shoseki bunrui mokuroku: Wakansho, yakusho, eisho no bu*, Kyōeki Kashihonsha, 1887. National Diet Library Digital Collections, dl.ndl.go.jp/info:ndljp/pid/897177.

Knapman, Gareth. *Race and British Colonialism in Southeast Asia, 1770–1870: John Crawfurd and the Politics of Equality*. Routledge, 2017.

Knox, Simone. "*Masterpiece Theatre* and British Drama Imports on US Television: Discourses of Tension." *Critical Studies in Television*, vol. 7, no. 1, 2012, pp. 29–48.

Koh, Jaime, and Stephanie Ho. *Culture and Customs of Singapore and Malaysia*. Greenwood Press, 2009.

Kohlke, Marie-Luise, and Christian Gutleben, editors. *Neo-Victorian Gothic: Horror, Violence, and Degeneration in the Re-imagined Nineteenth Century*. Rodopi, 2012.

———. *Neo-Victorian Tropes of Trauma: The Politics of Bearing After-Witness to Nineteenth-Century Suffering*. Rodopi, 2010.

Konoe, Atsumaro. "Dōjinshu dōmei, tsuketari Shina mondai kenkyū no hitsuyō." ["An Alliance of the Same Race and the Necessity of Studying the Chinese Question."] *Taiyō* [*The Sun*], vol. 24, no. 1, 1898. Translated by Urs Matthias Zachmann. *Pan-Asianism: A Documentary History, vol. 1: 1850–1920*, edited by Sven Saaler and Christopher W. A. Szpilman, Rowman and Littlefield, 2011, pp. 85–92.

Kornicki, P. F. "The Publisher's Go-Between: *Kashihon'ya* in the Meiji Period." *Modern Asian Studies*, vol. 14, no. 2, 1980, pp. 331–44.

Koshiro, Yukiko. "East Asia's 'Melting Pot': Re-Evaluating Race Relations in Japan's Colonial Empire." *Race and Racism in Modern East Asia: Western and Eastern Constructions*, edited by Rotem Kowner and Walter Demel, Brill, 2014, pp. 475–98.

Kratoska, Paul H. *The Japanese Occupation of Malaya, 1941–1945: A Social and Economic History*. U of Hawaii P, 1997.

Kuwahara, Yasue, editor. *The Korean Wave: Korean Popular Culture in Global Context*. Palgrave Macmillan, 2014.

Lam, Peng Er. "Japan's Quest for 'Soft Power': Attraction and Limitation." *East Asia*, vol. 24, 2007, pp. 349–63.
Lamont, Tom. "Alan Moore: Why I Turned My Back on Hollywood." *Observer*, 15 Dec. 2012, n. p. *The Guardian*, www.theguardian.com/books/2012/dec/15/alan-moore-why-i-rejected-hollywood-interview. Accessed 31 Jan. 2016.
Lavery, Grace E. *Quaint, Exquisite: Victorian Aesthetics and the Idea of Japan*. Princeton UP, 2019.
Lee, Hsien Loong. "Speech by PM Lee Hsien Loong at the Launch of the Singapore Bicentennial on 28 January 2019." Launch of the Singapore Bicentennial, 28 Jan. 2019, Boat Quay, Singapore. Speech. *Prime Minister's Office, Singapore*, www.pmo.gov.sg/Newsroom/PM-Lee-Hsien-Loong-at-the-launch-of-the-Singapore-Bicentennial-Jan-2019. Accessed 18 Mar. 2019.
Lee, Hye-Kyung. "Cultural Policy and the Korean Wave: From National Culture to Transnational Consumerism." *The Korean Wave: Korean Media Go Global*, edited by Youna Kim, Routledge, 2013, pp. 185–98.
Lee, Pearl. "Fewer Lit Students a Worrying Trend." *Straits Times*, 24 Aug. 2015, www.straitstimes.com/singapore/education/fewer-lit-students-a-worrying-trend.
Le Fanu, Sheridan. "Green Tea." *In a Glass Darkly*, edited by Robert Tracy, Oxford UP, 1993, pp. 5–40.
Leheny, David. "A Narrow Place to Cross Swords: Soft Power and the Politics of Japanese Popular Culture in East Asia." *Beyond Japan: The Dynamics of East Asian Regionalism*, edited by Peter J. Katzenstein and Takashi Shiraishi, Cornell UP, 2006, pp. 211–33.
———. *The Rules of Play: National Identity and the Shaping of Japanese Leisure*. Cornell UP, 2003.
Leighton Hall: The Historic Seat of the Gillow Family. Leighton Hall, 2020, www.leightonhall.co.uk/. Accessed 16 Aug. 2023.
Leitch, Thomas. *Film Adaptation and Its Discontents: From* Gone with the Wind *to* The Passion of the Christ. Johns Hopkins UP, 2007.
Levine, Caroline. "From Nation to Network." *Victorian Studies*, vol. 55, no. 4, 2013, pp. 647–66.
Lewis, Justin, and Toby Miller, editors. *Critical Cultural Policy Studies: A Reader*. Blackwell, 2003.
Linhart, Sepp, and Sabine Frühstück, editors. *The Culture of Japan as Seen Through Its Leisure*. State U of New York P, 1998.
Llewellyn, Mark, and Ann Heilmann. "The Victorians Now: Global Reflections on Neo-Victorianism." *Critical Quarterly*, vol. 55, no. 1, 2013, pp. 24–42.
"Lords Sitting of 30 April 1912." *Hansard*, 5th series, vol. 11, pp. 859–96. *ProQuest UK Parliamentary Papers*, parlipapers.proquest.com/parlipapers/docview/t71.d76.lds5lv0011p0-0032?accountid=14888. Accessed 15 Aug. 2018.
Lowe, Lisa. *The Intimacies of Four Continents*. Duke UP, 2015.
Lowenthal, David. *The Past Is a Foreign Country*. Cambridge UP, 1985.

Lumley, Robert. "The Debate on Heritage Reviewed." *Heritage, Museums and Galleries: An Introductory Reader*, edited by Gerald Corsane, Routledge, 2005, pp. 15–25.

Macaulay, Thomas Babington. "Minute on Education in India." 1835. *Selections from Educational Records, Part I (1781–1839)*, edited by H. Sharp, National Archives of India, 1965, pp. 107–17. *South Asian Literature: Some Primary Sources*, www.columbia.edu/itc/mealac/pritchett/00generallinks/macaulay/txt_minute_education_1835.html. Accessed 13 Mar. 2019.

Mandler, Peter. *The Fall and Rise of the Stately Home*. Yale UP, 1997.

Marra, Michele. *Modern Japanese Aesthetics: A Reader*. U of Hawaii P, 1999.

"The *Masterpiece* Archive: Program History." *Wayback Machine*, 18 Dec. 2016, web.archive.org/web/20161218000729/http://www.pbs.org/wgbh/masterpiece/archive/programs.html. Accessed 17 Sep. 2019.

McDonnell, Schomberg. "The Protection of Ancient Buildings and Monuments." Society of Antiquaries of London, 7 Dec. 1911, Burlington House, Piccadilly, London. Speech. *Proceedings of the Society of Antiquaries*, 2nd series, vol. 24, n. d., pp. 15–32.

McGray, Douglas. "Japan's Gross National Cool." *Foreign Policy*, vol. 130, 2002, pp. 44–54.

Mckercher, Bob, and Hilary du Cros. *Cultural Tourism: The Partnership between Tourism and Cultural Heritage Management*. Routledge, 2002.

McLeod, D. W. "Syllabus of Instruction: English." *Syllabus of Instruction*, by D. W. McLeod, Raffles Institution, 1937. Raffles Institution Archives and Museum, Singapore.

Medcalf, Stephen. "The Innocence of P. G. Wodehouse." *The Modern English Novel: The Reader, the Writer and the Work*, edited by Gabriel Josipovici, Barnes and Noble, 1976, pp. 186–205.

Miliaresis, Grigoris. "Cattlea Karepan: Where It All Started." *Tokyo Cheapo*, 23 Sep. 2015, tokyocheapo.com/food-and-drink/karepan-started/. Accessed 22 Oct. 2021.

Miller, Andrew H. *Novels behind Glass: Commodity Culture and Victorian Narrative*. Cambridge UP, 1995.

Miller, Jeffrey S. *Something Completely Different: British Television and American Culture*. U of Minnesota P, 2000.

Miller, Toby, and George Yúdice. *Cultural Policy*. SAGE, 2002.

Mitchell, Kate. *History and Cultural Memory in Neo-Victorian Fiction: Victorian Afterimages*. Palgrave, 2010.

Moeran, Brian. "The Birth of the Japanese Department Store." *Asian Department Stores*, edited by Kerrie L. MacPherson, Curzon, 1998, pp. 141–76.

Monden, Masafumi. "The 'Nationality' of *Lolita* Fashion." *Asia through Art and Anthropology: Cultural Translation across Borders*, edited by Fuyubi Nakamura, Morgan Perkins, and Oliver Krischer, Bloomsbury Academic, 2013, pp. 165–78.

Monk, Claire. "The British Heritage-Film Debate Revisited." *British Historical Cinema: The History, Heritage and Costume Film*, edited by Claire Monk and Amy Sargeant, Routledge, 2002, pp. 176–98.

Mooneyham, Laura. "Comedy among the Modernists: P. G. Wodehouse and the Anachronism of Comic Form." *Twentieth Century Literature*, vol. 40, no. 1, 1994, pp. 114–38.

Moretti, Franco. "Conjectures on World Literature." *New Left Review*, vol. 1, 2000, pp. 54–68. *Distant Reading*, Verso, 2013, pp. 43–62.

Mori, Kaoru, and Rico Murakami. *Emma Victorian Guide [Ema Vikutorian gaido]*. Entaaburein [Enterbrain], 2003.

Moto, Naoko. *Lady Victorian [Redii Vikutorian]*. 20 vols. Akita Shoten, 1999–2007.

Moy, Olivia Loksing. "Reading in the Aftermath: An Asian American Jane Eyre." *Undisciplining Victorian Studies*, special issue of *Victorian Studies*, vol. 62, no. 3, 2020, pp. 406–20.

Mukherjee, Pablo. "Introduction: Victorian World Literatures." *Victorian World Literatures*, special issue of *Yearbook of English Studies*, vol. 41, no. 2, 2011, pp. 1–19.

Murakami, Takashi. "Earth in My Window." *Little Boy: The Arts of Japan's Exploding Subculture*, edited by Murakami Takashi, Yale UP, 2005, pp. 99–149.

———. "Superflat Trilogy: Greetings, You Are Alive." *Little Boy: The Arts of Japan's Exploding Subculture*, edited by Murakami Takashi, Yale UP, 2005, pp. 151–61.

Nitobe, Inazō. *Bushido: The Soul of Japan*. 1900. Republished as *Bushido: The Samurai Code of Japan*, edited by Alexander Bennett, Tuttle, 2019.

Nunokawa, Jeff. *The Afterlife of Property: Domestic Security and the Victorian Novel*. Princeton UP, 1994.

O'Connor, Justin. *The Cultural and Creative Industries: A Literature Review*. 2nd ed., Creativity, Culture and Education, 2010.

Oh, Younjung. "Shopping for Art: The New Middle Class' Art Consumption in Modern Japanese Department Stores." *Journal of Design History*, vol. 27, no. 4, 2014, pp. 351–69.

Okakura, Kakuzo. *The Awakening of Japan*. 1904. New York: The Century Co., 1905.

———. *The Book of Tea*. 1906. Macmillan Collector's Library, 2020.

———. *Ideals of the East: The Spirit of Japanese Art*. 1903. Dover Publications, 2005.

Ooi, Yu-lin. *Pieces of Jade and Gold: An Anecdotal History of the Singapore Chinese Girls' School, 1899–1999*. Singapore Chinese Girls' School, 1999.

Osterhammel, Jürgen. *The Transformation of the World: A Global History of the Nineteenth Century*. 2009. Translated by Patrick Camiller, Princeton UP, 2014.

Park, Heebon, Julie Sanders, and Chung Moonyoung. "Secondary Pleasures, Spatial Occupations and Postcolonial Departures: Park Chan-wook's *Agassi/The*

Handmaiden and Sarah Waters's *Fingersmith*." *Neo-Victorian Studies*, vol. 11, no. 2, 2019, pp. 177–205.

Parry, Simon. "How East Asians in the UK Are Fighting Back against a Rising Tide of Racism." *South China Morning Post*, 31 May 2020, www.scmp.com/magazines/post-magazine/long-reads/article/3086438/how-east-asians-uk-are-fighting-back-against. Accessed 11 June 2023.

Pascoe, Judith. *On the Bullet Train with Emily Brontë:* Wuthering Heights *in Japan.* U of Michigan P, 2017.

Plotz, John. *Portable Property: Victorian Culture on the Move.* Princeton UP, 2008.

Possession. Directed by Neil LaBute, Warner Bros., 2002.

Primorac, Antonija, and Monika Pietrzak-Franger. "Introduction: What Is Global Neo-Victorianism?" *Neo-Victorianism and Globalization: Transnational Dissemination of Nineteenth-Century Cultural Texts*, special issue of *Neo-Victorian Studies*, vol. 8, no. 1, 2015, pp. 1–16, www.neovictorianstudies.com.

Prough, Jennifer S. *Straight from the Heart: Gender, Intimacy, and the Cultural Production of* Shōjo Manga. U of Hawai'i P, 2011.

Pykett, Lyn. "The Changing Faces and Spaces of Victorian Studies." *The State, or Statelessness of Victorian Studies*, special issue of *Critical Quarterly*, vol. 55, no. 1, 2013, pp. 9–23.

Raffles, Sir Thomas Stamford. "Letter to Captain C. E. Davis." *An Anecdotal History of Old Times in Singapore, 1819–1867*, compiled by Charles Burton Buckley, 1902, U of Malaya P, 1965, pp. 81–86.

Ramsay, Allan. "The Green Baize Door: Social Identity in Wodehouse Part Two." *Contemporary Review*, vol. 286, no. 1668, 2005, pp. 39–46.

Rappaport, Erika Diane. "Packaging China: Foreign Articles and Dangerous Tastes in the Mid-Victorian Tea Party." *The Making of the Consumer: Knowledge, Power and Identity in the Modern World*, edited by Frank Trentmann, Berg, 2006, pp. 125–46.

———. *Shopping for Pleasure: Women in the Making of London's West End.* Princeton UP, 2000.

Rose, Megan Catherine. "'My Heart Fluttered': Affect and Emotion in Kawaii Fashion Communities." *TAASA Review*, vol. 27, no. 1, 2018, pp. 12–14.

Sadoff, Dianne F., and John Kucich. "Introduction: Histories of the Present." *Victorian Afterlife: Postmodern Culture Rewrites the Nineteenth Century*, edited by John Kucich and Dianne F. Sadoff, U of Minnesota P, 2000, pp. ix–xxx.

Sargeant, Amy. "Making and Selling Heritage Culture: Style and Authenticity in Historical Fictions on Film and Television." *British Cinema: Past and Present*, edited by Justine Ashby and Andrew Higson, Routledge, 2000, pp. 301–15.

Schiller, Herbert. *Mass Communications and American Empire.* Westview Press, 1992.

Scott, Bede. *On Lightness in World Literature.* Palgrave Macmillan, 2013.

Scott, Walter. *Kenilworth.* Edited by Andrew Lang, London, Macmillan and Co., 1901.

Seaton, Philip. "Taiga Dramas and Tourism: Historical Contents as Sustainable Tourist Resources." *Japanese Popular Culture and Contents Tourism*, special issue of *Japan Forum*, vol. 27, no. 1, 2015, pp. 82–103.

Seaton, Philip, and Takayoshi Yamamura. "Japanese Popular Culture and Contents Tourism—Introduction." *Japanese Popular Culture and Contents Tourism*, special issue of *Japan Forum*, vol. 27, no. 1, 2015, pp. 1–11.

Shachar, Hila. *Cultural Afterlives and Screen Adaptations of Classic Literature*. Palgrave Macmillan, 2012.

Shamoon, Deborah. *Passionate Friendship: The Aesthetics of Girl Culture in Japan*. U of Hawai'i P, 2012.

Shin, Jeeyoung. "Screening Colonial Modernity: Cinematic Re-Imaginations of Colonial Korea in the 2000s." *Quarterly Review of Film and Video*, vol. 36, no. 8, pp. 690–720.

Skrydstrup, Martin. "Cultural Property." *A Companion to Folklore*, edited by Regina F. Bendix and Galit Hasan-Rokem, Blackwell, 2012, pp. 520–36.

Smith, Chris. *Creative Britain*. Faber, 1998.

Smith, Helena. "Labour to Keep Elgin Marbles." *Guardian*, 5 May 1997, p. 7. *ProQuest Historical Newspapers: The Guardian (1821–2003) and The Observer (1791–2003)*, search.proquest.com/hnpguardianobserver/docview/187986654/B411D530D58B4B6DPQ/1?accountid=14888. Accessed 8 June 2015.

Sorensen, Sue. "Taking *Possession*: Neil LaBute Adapts a Postmodern Romance." *Literature/Film Quarterly*, vol. 32, no. 1, 2004, pp. 71–77.

Spencer, Colin. *British Food: An Extraordinary Thousand Years of History*. Columbia UP, 2002.

Stobart, Jon, editor. *Travel and the British Country House: Cultures, Critiques, and Consumption in the Long Eighteenth Century*. Manchester UP, 2017.

Storey, John. *An Introductory Guide to Cultural Theory and Popular Culture*. Harvester Wheatsheaf, 1993.

Straits Settlements and Federated Malay States, Education Department. "Annual Education Report, for the Year 1890." *Annual Reports on Education in the Straits Settlements* (1874, 1884, 1886–1907, 1909–1933). Lee Kong Chian Reference Library, National Library, Singapore. Microfilm.

———. "Annual Education Report, for the Year 1891." *Annual Reports on Education in the Straits Settlements* (1874, 1884, 1886–1907, 1909–1933). Lee Kong Chian Reference Library, National Library, Singapore. Microfilm.

Su, John. "Fantasies of (Re)collection: Collecting and Imagination in A. S. Byatt's *Possession: A Romance*." *Contemporary Literature*, vol. 45, no. 4, 2004, pp. 684–712.

Sugawa-Shimada, Akiko. "*Rekijo*, Pilgrimage, and 'Pop-Spiritualism': Pop-Culture-Induced Heritage Tourism of/for Young Women." *Japanese Popular Culture and Contents Tourism*, special issue of *Japan Forum*, vol. 27, no. 1, 2015, pp. 37–58.

Surman, Bronwen. "The Search for the Real Thing: Japanese Tourism to Britain." *Japanese Tourism and Travel Culture*, edited by Sylvie Guichard-Anguis and Okpyo Moon, Routledge, 2009, pp. 193–202.

Tankha, Brij. "Okakura Tenshin: 'Asia Is One,' 1903." *Pan-Asianism: A Documentary History*, edited by Sven Saaler and Christopher W. A. Szpilman, vol. 1, Rowman and Littlefield, 2011, pp. 93–99.

Tarling, Nicholas. *A Sudden Rampage: The Japanese Occupation of Southeast Asia, 1941–1945*. Hurst and Company, 2001.

"Tattershall Castle: Protests against the Reported Sale." *Times*, 22 Sept. 1911, p. 6. *The Times Digital Archive*, tinyurl.galegroup.com/tinyurl/9c5TH9. Accessed 16 Aug. 2018.

"The Tattershall Mantelpieces." *Times*, 21 May 1912, p. 9. *The Times Digital Archive*, tinyurl.galegroup.com/tinyurl/9c5XD4. Accessed 16 Aug. 2018.

Tay, Tiffany Fumiko. "Farquhar, Not Raffles, the Real Hero of Early Modern Singapore, Says New Bicentennial Book." *Straits Times*, 29 Jan. 2019, www.straitstimes.com/singapore/farquhar-not-raffles-the-real-hero-of-early-modern-singapore-says-new-bicentennial-book. Accessed 18 Mar. 2019.

Tee, Zhuo. "Singapore's Bicentennial: Our Colonial Conundrum." *Straits Times*, 13 Jan. 2019, www.straitstimes.com/opinion/singapores-bicentennial-our-colonial-conundrum. Accessed 18 Mar. 2019.

Telling, Oliver. "Hate Crime against 'Oriental' People in London Soars." *Financial Times*, 15 May 2020, www.ft.com/content/52e7062b-0cb2-448a-b944-05b3025d4542. Accessed 11 June 2023.

Tharoor, Shashi. *Inglorious Empire: What the British Did to India*. Penguin, 2018.

Thatcher, Margaret. *The Downing Street Years*. HarperCollins, 1993.

Thomas, Julia. *Shakespeare's Shrine: The Bard's Birthplace and the Invention of Stratford-upon-Avon*. U of Pennsylvania P, 2012.

Thurley, Simon. *Men from the Ministry: How Britain Saved Its Heritage*. Yale UP, 2013.

Tinniswood, Adrian. *The Polite Tourist: Four Centuries of Country House Visiting*. National Trust Enterprises Ltd., 1998.

Tobin, Joseph, editor. *Pikachu's Global Adventure: The Rise and Fall of Pokémon*. Duke UP, 2004.

Toboso, Yana. *Kuroshitsuji* [*Black Butler*]. 33 vols. Square Enix, 2007–present.

Turnbull, C. M. *A History of Singapore, 1819–1975*. Oxford UP, 1977.

United Kingdom Tourism Report: Q4 2014. Business Monitor International, 2014.

"V for Vendetta (2005)." *IMDb*, www.imdb.com/title/tt0434409/. Accessed 17 Sep. 2019.

Viceroy's House. Directed by Gurinder Chadha, Pathé, Reliance Entertainment, BBC Films, Ingenious Media, and British Film Institute, 2017.

Viswanathan, Gauri. *Masks of Conquest: Literary Study and British Rule in India*. Columbia UP, 1989.

Voorhees, Richard J. "The Jolly Old World of P. G. Wodehouse." *South Atlantic Quarterly*, vol. 61, 1962, pp. 213–22.

Walsh, John. "Hallyu as a Government Construct: The Korean Wave in the Context of Economic and Social Development." *The Korean Wave: Korean Popular Culture in Global Context*, edited by Yasue Kuwahara, Palgrave Macmillan, 2014, pp. 13–31.

Washington, Bryan. "Japanese Curry Bread, A Food Fit for Quarantine." *New Yorker*, 15 Apr. 2020, www.newyorker.com/culture/kitchen-notes/japanese-curry-bread-a-food-fit-for-quarantine. Accessed 22 Oct. 2021.

Waters, Sarah. *Fingersmith*. Virago, 2002.

Waterson, Merlin. *The National Trust: The First Hundred Years*. 1994. 2nd ed., National Trust, 1997.

Watson, Nicola J. *The Literary Tourist: Readers and Places in Romantic and Victorian Britain*. Palgrave Macmillan, 2006.

Watts, Janet. "The Word Made Fresh: Novelists and Film-Makers Usually Trade Insults over Film Adaptations. So How Come These Two Get On So Well? Janet Watts Reports." *Guardian*, 8 Dec. 1995, p. T.008. *ProQuest Historical Newspapers:* The Guardian *(1821–2003) and* The Observer *(1791–2003)*, webcat.warwick.ac.uk/record=e1001083~S1. Accessed 17 Sep. 2019.

Waugh, Evelyn. *Brideshead Revisited*. 1944. Little Brown, 1945.

Wee, C. J. W.-L. "Imagining the Fractured East Asian Modern: Commonality and Difference in Mass Cultural Production." *Criticism: A Quarterly for Literature and the Arts*, vol. 54, no. 2, 2012, pp. 197–225.

Weiner, Michael. "Discourses of Race, Nation, and Empire in Pre-1945 Japan." *Race, Ethnicity, and Migration in Modern Japan*, edited by Michael Weiner, vol. 1, Routledge, 2004, pp. 217–39.

West, Nancy, and Karen E. Laird. "Prequels, Sequels, and Pop Stars: *Masterpiece* and the New Culture of Classic Adaptation." *Literature/Film Quarterly*, vol. 39, no. 4, 2011, pp. 306–26.

Westover, Paul. "How America 'Inherited' Literary Tourism." *Literary Tourism and Nineteenth-Century Culture*, edited by Nicola J. Watson, Palgrave Macmillan, 2009, pp. 184–95.

Williams, Raymond. *Culture and Society: Coleridge to Orwell*. 1958. Hogarth, 1990.

———. *Keywords*. Fontana, 1983.

Wodehouse, P. G. "The Custody of the Pumpkin." 1935. *The World of Blandings*, Arrow Books, 2008, pp. 263–89.

———. *Full Moon*. 1947. Overlook, 2006.

———. "The Go-Getter." 1935. *Blandings Castle and Elsewhere*, Penguin Books, 1954, pp. 94–114.

———. *Leave It to Psmith*. 1924. Vintage Books, 2005.

———. "Lord Emsworth Acts for the Best." 1935. *The World of Blandings*, Arrow Books, 2008, pp. 289–311.

———. "Pig-Hoo-o-o-o-ey!" 1935. *The World of Blandings*, Arrow Books, 2008, pp. 312–37.

———. *Something Fresh*. 1915. *The World of Blandings*, Arrow Books, 2008, pp. 11–262.

———. *Summer Lightning*. 1929. *The World of Blandings*, Arrow Books, 2008, pp. 338–641.

Wong, Francis H. K., and Gwee Yee Hean, editors. *Official Reports on Education: Straits Settlements and the Federated Malay States, 1870–1939*. Pan Pacific Book Distributors, 1980.

Woodson-Boulton, Amy. "Victorian Museums and Victorian Society." *History Compass*, vol. 6, no. 1, 2008, pp. 109–46.

Wright, Patrick. *On Living in an Old Country: The National Past in Contemporary Britain*. Verso, 1985.

Yellen, Jeremy A. *The Greater East Asia Co-Prosperity Sphere: When Total Empire Met Total War*. Cornell UP, 2019.

Yokoyama, Toshio. *Japan in the Victorian Mind: A Study of Stereotyped Images of a Nation, 1850–1880*. Macmillan, 1987.

Yoon, Tae-Jin, and Dal Yong Jin, editors. *The Korean Wave: Evolution, Fandom, and Transnationality*. Lexington, 2017.

Young, Louise. "Imagined Empire: The Cultural Construction of Manchukuo." *The Japanese Wartime Empire, 1931–1945*, edited by Peter Duus, Ramon H. Myers, and Mark R. Peattie, Princeton UP, 1996, pp. 71–96.

———. "Marketing the Modern: Department Stores, Consumer Culture, and the New Middle Class in Interwar Japan." *International Labor and Working-Class History*, vol. 55, 1999, pp. 52–70.

———. "Rethinking Race for Manchukuo: Self and Other in the Colonial Context." *Race, Ethnicity, and Migration in Modern Japan*, edited by Michael Weiner, vol. 3, Routledge, 2004, pp. 280–95.

Yuen, Sin. "Singapore to Mark 200th Anniversary of Raffles' Arrival." *Straits Times*, 1 Jan. 2018, www.straitstimes.com/singapore/singapore-to-mark-200th-anniversary-of-raffles-arrival. Accessed 18 Mar. 2019.

Zaccheus, Melody. "Bicentennial Logo Launched, Design Reflects 700 Years of History." *Straits Times*, 3 Dec. 2018, www.straitstimes.com/singapore/bicentennial-logo-launched-design-reflects-700-years-of-history. Accessed 18 Mar. 2019.

———. "Singapore Bicentennial: Why 2019 Is History in the Making." *Straits Times*, 27 Jan. 2019, www.straitstimes.com/opinion/why-2019-is-history-in-the-making. Accessed 18 Mar. 2019.

Index

Abe, Shinzō, 108
Aestheticism, 113–15, 117–18
aesthetics: aesthetic taste, 37–38, 80–81, 86, 101; Japanese aesthetics, 112–21, 165, 167. *See also* Okakura, Kakuzō
Asianism: neo-Asianism, 107–109; pan-Asianism, 110–11, 116–21, 122–23, 157. *See also* Okakura, Kakuzō
Austen, Jane, 90–91; events related to, 143, 145, 147–48; mentioned, 89, 135, 136, 141
Asia-Pacific War (1937–1945), 14, 109–11, 120, 122–23, 131, 154–61, 165
assimilation, colonial, 155, 157, 165–67, 171–73

Brontë, Charlotte, 75–76, 90, 92; mentioned, 89, 135, 141
Brontë, Emily, 60–61; mentioned, 76, 89, 136, 141
Brontë Parsonage Museum (Haworth), 76–77
Byatt, A. S. See *Possession* (novel)

Chinese, ethnic in Malaya and Singapore, 122, 131, 148, 151–52, 152–54, 155–56, 157–58

civilization, theories of, 116–20, 172. *See* Asianism
civilization and enlightenment, 83, 165. *See also* Meiji modernization
civilizing mission, ideology of the, 47, 98
Cole, Henry, 37–38
Colonial and Indian Exhibition (1886), 104–05
colonial rule, British: in India, 1–3, 137; in Singapore, 17–19, 137–39, 152–54, 161
colonial rule, Japanese: in Korea, 13–14, 157, 160, 164–67, 171–73; in Singapore, 154–58, 160–61
Cool Japan, 98, 107–08, 121–22, 169–70
cooperativism, 109–11, 157, 160–61. *See also* Greater East Asia Co-Prosperity Sphere
cosmopolitanism, 88, 89, 168–70
cosplay, 129, 145
country house. *See* heritage
Crawfurd, John, 153

culture: British high culture, 5–6, 37–38, 59, 77–78, 80–81, 84–85, 89–90, 98, 132, 143–44; cultural capital, 59, 78–106 passim, 136–37, 172–73; cultural imperialism, 8–9,

culture *(continued)*
163; cultural property, 24, 29–31, 32–36, 38–39, 51–52, 92–93, 176n6, 177n3; definitions of, 5–6, 36–37; Japanese popular culture, 16–17, 97–98, 101–08, 121–22, 128, 129–31, 132–33, 145–52, 159
curio, 113–15, 118

Deep England, 62, 64–67, 70–71, 91, 94
Dickens, Charles: mentioned, 89, 90, 135, 139, 141
Dilke, Charles Wentworth, 62, 67, 69–70
divide and rule, 131, 154, 155, 180n12

Emma Victorian Guide, 78, 80, 86–87, 89–91
Englishness: admiration for, 79–88, 97–98, 98–101, 135–37, 141–43, 144, 171–73; aristocratic, 16, 77–78, 80–81, 86–88, 93–94, 98–101, 105, 172–73; definition of, 9, 64; globalization of, 9–10, 11, 62, 68–71. *See also* Deep England *and* Greater Britain
English literature: canon of, 2–3, 7, 9–10, 43–44, 59–60, 89–91, 135–40, 140–41; discipline of, 9–10, 90, 131, 133–35, 137–41; film and TV adaptations, 50–61, 67, 135; nineteenth-century British literature, 7, 89–91, 134–36, 140–41, 143–44; as post-imperial inheritance, 2–3, 19, 43–46, 49, 59–61, 89–90, 131, 137–41; relation to heritage tourism, 43–46, 75–77, 141–43; relation to whiteness, 46–47, 132, 147–48; Singapore literature, 140–41
Eyre Affair, The, 75–76, 91–92, 94

fashion, 77, 127–34, 143–52, 161–62. *See also* Lolita subculture
Fforde, Jasper. See *Eyre Affair, The*
Fingersmith, 163–64
First World War (1914–1918): mentioned, 119, 123
Forster, E. M., 65–67

globalization: of British culture, 3–11 passim, 43–44, 90, 131, 132, 137–40; of Japanese culture, 98, 104–05, 107–08, 121–22, 128, 132–33, 151
Greater Britain, 62, 67–71, 91, 94
Greater East Asia Co-Prosperity Sphere, 110–12, 122–23, 157, 179n6, 179n13
gunboat diplomacy, 78–79, 164–65. *See also* treaty port system

Handmaiden, The, 163–73
Harrods, 78, 80–81, 85–89, 92–95, 178n12
Hearn, Lafcadio, 90, 113–15; mentioned, 118
heritage: Anglo-Saxon, 43, 45, 46–47, 60, 69; British heritage industry, 4–6, 23, 25–31, 32, 48, 50, 53–59, 67, 70, 71, 78–79, 91–93, 176n4; conflicts over ownership of, 23–24, 26, 28, 29–30, 33, 38–48, 51; conservation of, 33, 66, 142; country house, 46, 62–70, 76, 171–72; definition of, 24; English Heritage, 23, 26–28, 28–29, 54, 143; films and TV series, 50–51, 53–61, 67, 77–78, 133, 135; museum, 25, 28, 29–30, 37–38, 38–39; national, 30, 32–36, 38–43, 66; tourism, 31–46 passim, 53–8, 75–78, 80–81, 84–85, 88–89, 141–43
hybridism, 98, 101–12, 115–21

James, Henry, 41–42, 44–46
Japonisme, 112–115. *See also* aesthetics and Okakura, Kakuzō

Kanghwa Treaty (1876), 13, 164–65
Konoe, Atsumaro, 159
Konoe, Fumimaro, 109
Korean Wave, 169–70
Kuroshitsuji, 16, 97–99, 100–05, 108, 112–13
Kyoto School of Philosophy, 111

LaBute, Neil. See *Possession* (film)
Lady Victorian, 97–99, 105–06, 112–13
liberalism, 69, 169
Lolita subculture, 127–32, 133–34, 143–52, 161–62
long nineteenth century (concept), 14–15, 171

Macaulay, Thomas Babington, 3
Marco Polo Bridge Incident (1937): mentioned, 109
McGray, Douglas, 107, 121
Meiji modernization, 79, 83–86, 88, 90, 115–16, 164–65, 177n3, 178n7
Masterpiece Theatre, 59–61
Miki, Kiyoshi, 109–11
Morris, William, 118
Moto, Naoko. See *Lady Victorian*
mukokuseki. *See under* race
multiracialism, 156–57, 161
museum. *See* heritage
Murakami, Takashi, 104

nation branding, 6, 97, 108
national heritage. *See* heritage
National Trust, 28–29, 35–36, 66
neo-Victorian (concept), 7–8, 14–15, 170–73
New Labor, 10–11

Nitobe, Inazō, 115

Okakura, Kakuzō, 115–21, 179n11

pan-Asianism. *See* Asianism
Park, Chan-wook. See *Handmaiden, The*
particularity: elitism, challenges to, 98, 101–06; English, 2–3, 11, 33–36, 62, 64–67, 70–71, 139–43; racial, 93–95, 133, 147–49, 150–52, 155–57, 172–73
Pearl Harbor attack (1941): mentioned, 111, 120
play, 128, 144, 161–62
Possession (film), 50–52, 53–58
Possession (novel), 23–24, 25–26, 28, 30, 31–32, 38–39, 47, 49, 52

quaint, 113–15, 118

race: Anglo-Saxon racial ideology, 46–47, 69; Japanese imperial discourse, 156–61, 181n16; race and Japanese popular culture, 149–52; race in Singapore, 152–58, 160–61; racial proximity, 158–61, 172–73; whiteness, 46–47, 60–61, 91–94, 147–49, 172–73. *See also* divide and rule
Raffles, Sir Thomas Stamford, 17–19, 152–53; mentioned, 131, 157
Ruskin, John, 37–38; mentioned, 65
Russo-Japanese War (1904–1905): 118–19, 120; mentioned, 13

Scott, Walter, 34–35
sea travel, 82–84, 167–71
Shakespeare, William: birthplace, 39; mentioned, 45–46, 90, 138–39, 141, 143
shōjo manga, 78, 105–06, 122

Shōwa Kenkyūkai [Showa Research Association], 109–11
Sino-Japanese War (1894–1895): mentioned, 13, 120, 159
Sino-Japanese War (1937–1945): mentioned, 111, 122, 156, 169
Smith, Chris, 11, 29–30
social distinction, 6, 88–89, 136–37. *See* culture
soft power, 6, 97, 107, 121

Thatcher, Margaret, 5, 10, 23, 26–28
Toboso, Yana. See *Kuroshitsuji*
total war, 157, 166
trans/nationalism, 107–08, 169–70
trans-imperiality (concept), 12–14, 154, 170, 173
treaty port system, 8, 13, 78–79, 83, 164–65, 169, 175n4

universality, claims to: British, 4–5, 7, 9–10, 11, 62, 69–70, 79, 90–91, 93–95, 132–33, 135–41, 168–69; Japanese, 7, 98, 101, 103–04, 132–33, 149–50

Viceroy's House, 1–3, 11

Waters, Sarah. See *Fingersmith*
Waugh, Evelyn, 66–67
whiteness. *See* race
Wilde, Oscar: mentioned, 113, 134–35, 141, 144
Wodehouse, P. G., 61–68, 70–71
world history, conceptions of, 78–79, 109–12, 118–19
world literature, 12, 68

Yellow Peril, 158–61
young women: Japanese, 77–81, 87–89, 93–94, 99, 101, 105–06; Singaporean, 127–37, 141–52, 161–62